THIS is a book about ex-Nazis who have been allowed to live out their lives, in quiet ease, as respected and even honored Americans. When investigations are started, they are blocked by the U.S. Immigration and Naturalization Service and by the Justice Department. This suspense-filled account of disappearing files, intimidated witnesses, quashed inquiries, conspiracy, and treachery is fully documented. It suggests the looming presence of ODESSA, a Nazi-protection organization, which has infiltrated the very fabric of America.

―――――――――――――――――――――――

"THIS IS THE KIND OF REPORTING FOR WHICH NEWSPAPERS WIN PULITZERS."
—Harrison E. Salisbury

"READS LIKE DOCUMENTED DETECTIVE STORIES, EACH POWERED WITH SUSPENSE AND INTRIGUE."
—*Boston Globe*

"A STUNNINGLY EFFECTIVE EXPOSÉ . . . BLUM HAS DONE A MAGNIFICENT JOB IN STIRRING THE AMERICAN CONSCIENCE."
—*Minneapolis Tribune*

"A CHILLING, TIGHTLY RESEARCHED AC-COUNT . . . GRIPPING TESTIMONY."

WANTED!

The Search for Nazis in America

Howard Blum

A FAWCETT CREST BOOK

Fawcett Books, Greenwich, Connecticut

WANTED!: THE SEARCH FOR NAZIS IN AMERICA

THIS BOOK CONTAINS THE COMPLETE TEXT OF THE ORIGINAL HARDCOVER EDITION.

Published by Fawcett Crest Books, CBS Publications, CBS Consumer Publishing, a Division of CBS Inc., by arrangement with Quadrangle/The New York Times Book Company, Inc.

ISBN: 0-449-23409-6

Portions of this book appeared previously in *Esquire* magazine in slightly altered form.

Alternate Selection of the Literary Guild, February 1977
Alternate Selection of the Jewish Book Club, March 1977
Selection of the Playboy Book Club, March 1977

Printed in the United States of America

10   9   8   7   6   5   4   3   2   1

A Note to the Reader

This is a true story. The names, dates, and events are authentic, as documented by my own observations, personal interviews, and official records. In the interest of privacy, however, there have been two slight changes made: Harold Goldberg and Kurt Wassermann are pseudonyms. Nothing in their stories—or elsewhere in this book—is fictitious.

Howard Blum
New York City
July 1976

"True wars, wars between races, are merciless and fought to the last man, until one side or the other is eliminated without trace."

—HEINRICH HIMMLER

"The past is never dead; it is not even past."

—WILLIAM FAULKNER

This book is for my parents
and to the memory of Anna Gross.

WANTED!

Part I

THE LIST

DURING the day he read. At night, while his wife and daughter slept, he wrote.

He wrote hunched over a desk in the living room. The desk was very small—actually a child's desk—so that while he worked he unavoidably hovered as though protecting his papers. It was as if he were crouching to whisper secrets. And, he did know secrets: secrets of names uncovered, secrets of identities once more covered up.

The only light in the room shone from the lamp on his desk, an insufficient, pale yellow glow. Lately, even during the day, he had been drawing the green drapes tight, keeping the small room very dark: tense shadows and cigarette smoke. The room was not helped by its "wood" paneling, the paneling really just a thin piece of plastic veneer roughly the diluted color of stale chocolate. A pair of antlers hung from this paneled wall, his wife's touch, a bit of Bavaria. Across from the desk stood a wooden bookcase stretching almost to the ceiling. It was filled with books, books disorderly wedged and angled into any free space as if arranged in a panic. Many of the books were dog-eared and carefully underlined in black ink. The books all concerned the same broad topic: Nazis. There were books about Nazi spies, Nazi generals, Nazi victories, Nazi defeats, Nazi atrocities. He spent the day reading these books. He considered himself an expert and enjoyed demonstrating his knowledge of the Third Reich, carefully pronouncing any untranslatable German with an arrogant precision and deliberateness.

Throughout the night he would write, drink black

coffee, and smoke. He smoked Raleighs like an addict and after twenty years he had paid the price. His small, ill-formed teeth were stained a pasty, nicotine yellow so that when he smiled he suddenly looked old and even decrepit. His fingertips, too, were colored this same ghostly, sick yellow. It was almost as if a singeing plague were rushing through his body, marking and coloring his skin.

He sat at his desk in his brown slippers. He had not bothered to shave for the past few days and his round face was covered with a white-gray stubble. His hair, though, was neatly combed, brushed straight back and kept a shiny gunmetal gray. As he wrote, he held a ciga-rette with the very tips of his short fingers. It was an incongruously elegant gesture.

In the morning, he knew his wife would complain. For weeks she had been complaining about the plants. Three or four green spider plants hung from a gold-colored rod angled between two of the living room's box-like windows. The plants were choking on the smoke.

His wife complained about the plants, but that was only an excuse, only the latest excuse. She simply was not happy to have him around all day. It was not so much that he got in her way—it wasn't that; he was quiet and un-demanding—but it just didn't seem proper that he was no longer working. She felt he was trapped in their house on Long Island. Sometimes she would tell him that he should not have retired. Sometimes she would say she wished he had never gotten involved, that she wished the trial had never taken place, that she wished he had never received the list with 59 names. But, mostly she com-plained about the plants.

He was not sorry he had retired. There had been, he remained convinced, no choice. And, his writing went well. He worked rapidly. In the morning, after filling pages, he would tell his wife, "It comes so easy. It's like there's a fire burning within me and I've got to let it out."

He had quickly become accustomed to his new life simply because he realized things could never return to the way they once were. Not after what he now knew.

All the time Tony DeVito wrote, though, he knew his attempts at vengeance would be futile. He realized all his efforts would fail. Too many of the 59 men, he was certain, had purchased influential protection. Too many people had chosen or been paid to forget.

Yet despite the knowledge that his work was doomed, he could not stop. He was determined to continue, goaded by this internal hell of unsatisfied emotion, until 59 Nazi war criminals living in America were forced to confront justice.

PRIVATE Anthony DeVito spent a good part of the war dressed in a sergeant's uniform getting drunk. That was his job. Five months after Pearl Harbor, Tony DeVito found himself stuck in Egypt as part of the Ninth Air Force Weather Squad. As a child growing up in Hell's Kitchen, New York, he boasted he had learned all he would ever know about the weather: "When it rained, you got wet." He was glad, then, when a lieutenant asked for Italian-speaking volunteers for an assignment in Tripoli. In Tripoli, DeVito was made a Criminal Investigation Department (CID) agent. He spent the Italian campaign and the rest of the war policing petty intrigues and passions, opportunistic footnotes to the main drama: black markets trafficking in stolen Army property, whores rushing to provide a warm welcome for the conquering heroes, and taverns eagerly representing anything that could be swallowed as liquor. Most of DeVito's assignments began the same way: He would sit in a cafe for hours dressed in a sergeant's uniform, drinking in quick gulps until he felt his stomach was about to explode. After that, anything might happen. A drunk U.S. Army sergeant was everyone's favorite pigeon.

It was a matter of chance, then, that Tony DeVito en-

tered Dachau concentration camp only hours after it was
liberated by the Seventh Army. He had been jeeping
through the area interrogating witnesses in a rape case
when he stopped at a Seventh Army encampment in Augs-
burg for some hot chow. The lunch-time talk was not about
the war, or rape. Curious and unbelieving, DeVito drove
the short distance to Dachau to see for himself.

What he saw that afternoon is remembered as a frantic
and hideous jumble of images and noise: first the high
barbed wire fence and then the railroad tracks, tracks
winding to a dense, gray concrete structure with a tall,
red-brick chimney—a bit of color—on its roof; inside a
pile of clothes, gray-and-white striped pants and shirts—
like awnings, he thought—carefully folded and piled quite
high; beyond the uniforms stood two brick kilns, not kilns
he immediately realized, but ovens, and a man, a U.S.
Army captain, pushing a tarnished steel conveyor back
and forth, back and forth into the oven, the captain re-
peating the gesture as if hypnotized and the tight, me-
chanical click each time the conveyor was pulled into the
oven and the click again as it was pulled out; and outside,
awful, noxious air: it was thick with typhus; while wild
men in their awning outfits, vague faces, ran or shouted;
yes, the shouting, so many languages—French, Polish,
Russian, German—a Babel of confusion.

But beyond the jumble, two images remain clear, fierce
and indelible experiences: A steel door adjacent to the
crematorium was open just a crack, so he pushed it and
inside, reaching to the roof, were bodies packed like logs:
skulls piled on top of skulls, feet piled on top of feet; and
then outside a circle of men in the gray-striped pants and
shirts kicking up the brown dust with rocks and sticks, so
he walked closer and inside the circle, on his hands and
knees, crawled a solitary man in the same awning outfit
trying unsuccessfully to dodge the rocks and the blows: a
collaborator now the victim, vengeance now the weapon.
These two sights would stay with DeVito forever, haunt-
ing and, in time, haunted.

TONY DeVito might have remained hating Germans, all Germans, if he had not gone weeks later to look for a tailor in the hospital town of Erlangen. The narrow, medieval streets twisted and turned following an irrational, baroque will and DeVito, searching on foot for the tailor that a friend in his company had recommended, was quickly very lost. He soon resigned himself to spending the rest of the war in uncomfortably large pants and concentrated on the more immediate problem of finding his way back to his jeep parked outside the Old City. Stranded in this fourteenth-century maze, DeVito stopped a girl pedaling by on her bicycle. She was obviously very frightened of the GI in uniform; the girl tightly gripped the handlebars and avoided looking the soldier in the face. But DeVito could not help noticing she was very beautiful, a girl of not more than twenty with long, soft brown hair and bright blue eyes. Hesitant and in an awkward mixture of German and English, she directed him out of the Old City. She was about to pedal off when DeVito, eager to make conversation with the blue-eyed *fraulein,* asked if she knew a nearby tailor. Still reluctant and cautious, she led the GI to a small shop only a block away. And then she quickly pedaled off. Resigned, DeVito gave up on the girl and instead settled for having his pants altered. He had been in the tailor shop for nearly an hour when the blue-eyed *fraulein* entered, kissed the tailor, and then disappeared into the back room. The tailor explained to the curious GI that the girl was his daughter.

Over the next two months DeVito went through his entire kit bag searching for clothing to take to the tailor in Erlangen. When he ran out of uniforms, he borrowed from his buddies. Gradually the blue-eyed *fraulein* became less shy, greeting the GI and often staying to talk.

A valued and comfortable routine emerged. He gave her father pieces of his clothing. And she gave the GI pieces of her life. She told how her husband of just a few months had been killed in the war, how her younger brother, a glider pilot, was also killed, and how her family was now ruined, penniless. She said they were poor working people, they had never wanted to fight. DeVito listened and learned (or, surely sincerely tried) to think about the war in a different way. By the time DeVito was the most meticulously tailored private in Europe, he had decided to marry the blue-eyed *fraulein.*

The Allied invasion of Europe, DeVito sourly remarked, was probably less complicated than arranging his marriage to Frieda. The tailor was not happy about a marriage between his daughter and any representative of the army that had killed both his son and son-in-law. For a while, he forbade his daughter to see the GI with so many uniforms. The Erlangen tailor's antagonism toward Americans was perhaps only exceeded by a Hell's Kitchen longshoreman's antagonism toward Germans. DeVito remembers that he "caught hell in the mail." His mother wrote long and pleading letters begging Tony to reconsider. Worse, his father, the longshoreman, would not even write. But DeVito's mind was set. That was his way. When he decided he must do something—whether it was to hang out in a cafe drinking until an interesting offer was proposed or whether it was to marry—DeVito could not be deterred. He was a short, stiff man, certainly not an obvious fighter, but when he made up his mind, he liked to say he would "grit my teeth and no one could move me." When the Catholic Army chaplain refused to perform the marriage because Frieda's husband was not "officially" dead, DeVito considered for only a moment before shouting, "O.K., Padre, you're now looking at a Protestant." That was the last time in his life Tony DeVito ever stepped into a Catholic church.

The newlyweds stayed in Germany for two years after the war. DeVito worked as a civilian investigator for the Army, once more policing the black markets. It was, though, a period of rootless exile for DeVito, a time when he deliberately cut himself off from his country and parents. He would tell friends, "What's there to return to in Hell's Kitchen?" But DeVito stayed out of infuriated principle: He was determined that his parents accept his marriage and welcome his wife. If he had to remain abroad to accomplish that, he would because he knew he was right. That was simply his way. From his solitariness, he would draw strength and resolve.

When the time was right, he and his pregnant wife came to America. They went, said DeVito, because of all the opportunities; there was nothing more for him to do in Germany. The couple moved in with his parents in Hell's Kitchen. He went to college, the New School, during the day under the GI Bill. At night he worked in a post office to support his wife and newborn son. They were on a waiting list for an apartment in one of the projects. But the opportunity DeVito was seeking appeared one afternoon on television. He watched a broadcast of the Kefauver Committee investigating organized crime. It was an exciting experience. Here was a job, no, a cause that DeVito swiftly understood: good triumphantly ferreting out evil. He was energized by all the possibilities. That week he took a government service test for the Treasury Bureau. When he learned he had passed and received an appointment in the Immigration and Naturalization Service (INS), the family celebrated: This was not only a job, but also a future—a career with a pension. DeVito also was elated. He, however, saw the opportunity differently. Here was a mission for a firm, dedicated man. He slipped into a satisfied smile whenever he bragged he had been appointed "not as a dumb-cluck border patrolman, but as a GS-7."

A GS-7 is a federal investigator.

IT was a sticky, hot night in Spanish Harlem and the dark, narrow tenement hallway seemed to radiate heat, so it was only natural that DeVito loosened his tie and flung his suit jacket over his shoulder. It was only natural, but it was a mistake. DeVito went first, confident as if he had been there before, leading his partner up six flights of winding stairs. At every landing there was a sly, quick squeak as a door opened—furtive eyes checking out the two intruders—and then immediately slammed shut. And at every landing someone noticed the exposed .38 revolver strapped to DeVito's waist. The shiny gun was a signal, a warning, and the alarm went out.

The arrest was simple. As soon as they knocked on the door, Marcello Bermudez knew he was caught. He had been in the U.S. for nearly two months raising money and arranging arms shipments for the anti-Trujillo Dominicans, before the FBI caught on to him. And then for another month he had been on the run until Tony DeVito knocked on the door of his room in Spanish Harlem.

DeVito cuffed Bermudez and led him down the stairs. In the sixth floor hall, DeVito thought he heard a strange murmuring. As they descended, the murmuring grew louder, clearer, the sound gaining a wicked momentum until, by the time the men had reached the ground floor, the noise had erupted into a loud, belligerent chant. The two Immigration agents led their prisoner to the front steps of the building and stared into a crowd that did not want Bermudez to be taken anywhere. It was just the kind of situation DeVito had always wanted: There was something romantic, even heroic in its elements as if it had been contrived in Hollywood. It was a showdown, a situation scripted for grand gestures.

DeVito knew his part and played it dashingly well. "This is my prisoner. I'm taking him in and nobody is going to stop me," he shouted. Gun drawn, he took Bermudez in. And nobody stopped him.

Yet while the Bermudez incident was the glamorous highpoint of DeVito's eighteen years as an Immigration investigator, he took little satisfaction in the arrest. He had a certain pride, that was deserved, he felt, because he had acted like a man. However, there was something hollow and even petty about the incident, as there was, DeVito realized, to his whole career with Immigration. He personally did not care about Bermudez. It was his job to arrest him, so he did. But DeVito pointedly told his friends as though intent on shrugging off unwanted compliments, "You can't blame Bermudez. Trujillo is a villain and he deserves to die." What once had seemed to DeVito clearly impossible, now seemed only unnatural and depressing: Tony DeVito on the side of "the villains." His work at Immigration seemed pointless and daily insinuations of despair spread like nasty rumors through his self-respect.

DeVito felt he had been fooled by the Immigration Service. A proud veteran of a "just" war in Europe, he had once again eagerly enlisted in what he had thought would be another just fight. But life in this Service, DeVito found, was one of special deals and favors, money and influence, the unmentioned rewards of a circumspect Justice that could blink its eyes at the right moment. His bosses were political appointees, the bureaucratic favorite sons of clubhouse tyrants who would, in return, request discreet favors: a file overlooked, a naturalization act quickly passed. He felt dirty and cheap working in the same office with men who abused its power with a benign disinterest, little men who were not even consciously ashamed of their treachery. "I was one of the few men who worked for Immigration who never took a dime, who never tried to fix a case," says DeVito. "And because I was on the up and up they treated me like an outsider."

He was proud of his role as an outsider, an honest stranger in a corrupt government. Yet he had a quick temper and he became mean with accusations because he was ashamed. "This place is corrupt," he yelled. "I don't know whether I'm working in a brothel or for the United States government. It's all so hypocritical."

DeVito found escape from his work in his family. They were the one piece of his American Dream that had managed to remain unfrayed in his confrontation with reality. In 1956, he took a mortgage and gave his family trees and suburban Long Island air. The house, like all the others on the surrounding blocks, was a tract house, but DeVito worked on it during weekends for three years. It became, by default, the focus of all his ambition and energy. When he was done, he had added another story; a home fit for raising his three children.

But after all the years, two of his children had gone off and married, his youngest daughter was in high school, and the house was suddenly too big, too big for Frieda and him.

All that remained from the old days was the mortgage, a symbol of the hope he had once had of creating a better life, a symbol of commitment to his job and the Service. Now the mortgage was only a burden, an exasperating monthly reminder that he was bound to the Service simply because there were debts to pay. But the debts DeVito desperately wanted to cancel were larger and grander: He still expected the mission, the cause he could enlist in and pursue with pride and enthusiasm. That was why he had joined the Service and, after eighteen years of melancholic despair—melancholy for what should have been—there was a bruised hope that still remained.

WHILE DeVito was finishing his twentieth year with the Immigration and Naturalization Service, still anxiously waiting for his cause, the Service was doing all it could to avoid the one case that might have interested him.

In July 1964, *The New York Times*—reporting information provided by Simon Wiesenthal, the Austrian self-proclaimed "Nazi hunter"—revealed that a Queens housewife, Mrs. Hermine Braunsteiner Ryan, had been a guard and supervisor at Ravensbruck and Majdanek concentration camps. After the war she had immigrated to Canada and in 1958 she married an American citizen, Russell Ryan. The newlyweds moved to Queens, New York, where Mrs. Ryan, who had become a naturalized

U.S. citizen in 1963, pretended she was just another housewife. Then, in 1964, Hermine Braunsteiner Ryan's secrets became headlines.

It was the INS's jurisdictional responsibility to follow this discovery with action. The West German government, which has jurisdiction over war crimes committed in countries Germany had occupied, quickly agreed to prosecute Mrs. Ryan; however, deporting her from the United States was a complicated legal problem. Since she had been naturalized, it was first necessary for the INS to institute denaturalization hearings. While, surprisingly, there is no statute prohibiting the admittance of a war criminal, all immigrants upon entrance to America must sign a statement declaring that they did not participate in the persecution of a minority because of race, creed, or national origin. If it could be proven that Mrs. Ryan had falsely signed this statement, then she could be denaturalized and a case for extradition to West Germany could be investigated and presented.

Establishing a successful case for extradition, however, would also be an intricate bureaucratic procedure. There is no mention in the extradition statutes of war crimes. And the Supreme Court's requirement that evidence be "clear, unequivocal and convincing" would be complicated by a grim reality: Nearly all the eyewitnesses were dead, victims of the crime. So, the INS, if not willing to forgive, was prepared to forget. It hoped the Ryan case, today a headline, would quickly become old news. For years the Service conscientiously tried to forget about the housewife in Queens who had once commanded a death camp filled with 11,000 women prisoners. But the newspapers and the Jewish organizations would not allow the past to remain past. They could not or would not forget, so they forced the Immigration Service to remember.

In 1971—a full seven years after the *Times* report— Assistant Commissioner for Investigations Carl Burrows tried to put a neat, bureaucratic finish to the Ryan affair. In a memo to the regional commissioner in charge of the New York area, he wrote:

"In all probability, there is insufficient evidence of a

clear, unequivocal and convincing nature upon which we could initiate deportation proceedings. . . . However, in view of the periodic and highly vocal interest in this case, it is requested that the New York office review the evidence at hand and furnish a memorandum through your office setting forth what evidence is available to support any deportation charge and the manner in which such evidence might be used if deportation proceedings were authorized."

But in a conversation with INS chief trial lawyer Vincent Schiano, Burrows said, "Why punish her twice," explaining that Mrs. Ryan had been tried and convicted in Austria in 1949 for war crimes. He had now decided on a legalistic solution to the entire episode that would make the problem of "clear and unequivocal" evidence superfluous. "I want you to draft a memo showing that the law forbids the United States from prosecuting because of the Woody rule." Schiano was ordered by Burrows to give a few legal twists and turns to a statute designed to protect aliens who had once been convicted of minor crimes and had subsequently married American citizens. The Woody rule, the assistant commissioner for investigations instructed, should be tailored to apply to Mrs. Ryan.

Only, Schiano refused. "Go pound rocks," he told Burrows.

Schiano had a career of confrontations with the Service and he was not reluctant to fight another battle. In fact, there would be a certain satisfaction. There was a tousled casualness in his manner, the independent way of a man who feels constricted by suits and ties. And rules. An order would come from Washington and Schiano would rush to fight it, shaking his fists and talking out of the side of his mouth like a street fighter. For years he had battled Washington and for years he had lost. He anticipated this new opportunity as a chance to get even: The last time he had fought with the bosses they had exiled him to the Service's office in Alaska.

Schiano replied to Burrows with a terse memo insisting, "We must reject the suggestion of 'further punishment' by deportation. Aliens become deportable by reason of certain criminal convictions." And that memo became just the start for Schiano. He began to gather information on Mrs. Ryan, contacting the Austrian and Israeli governments for background and witnesses. He was determined that a case for deportation be presented against Hermine Braunsteiner Ryan.

In April 1972, he wrote still another memo, this time to Sol Marks, INS New York district director. This memo would help to tighten the noose of evidence circling around Mrs. Ryan. And this memo, unknowingly, would culminate in another startling discovery: a trail that would lead like bloody footprints through the incredible bureaucratic snow, a trail exposing other secret lives and secret fears, a trail leading to other Nazi war criminals in America. The memo said: ". . . I urge that an investigator be assigned to this case to work under my direction and make proper requests of the various government agencies and control of overseas leads. . . . I have been conducting the investigation including research, interviews, documentation, etc., without the benefit and the valuable help which can be given by the assignment of an investigator."

Marks agreed an investigator was necessary. He chose a man with twenty years' experience, a member of the elite subversive section, a man he knew had learned German from his wife, a man he knew had entered Dachau only hours after the liberation and still talked about what he had seen.

Tony DeVito was appointed chief investigator of the case against Hermine Braunsteiner Ryan.

THE chief trial attorney's office is on the fourteenth floor of the Immigration headquarters in downtown New York. It is not an impressive place, merely functional: two steel desks, typewriters, and a long row of file cabinets, each four drawers high; a room of gray metal and institutional green paint. It was here that Vincent Schiano and Tony DeVito built the case against Mrs. Ryan.

The room, though, suited DeVito. He spent long hours in this tight, almost airless office chasing every lead, every new clue. He didn't mind the hours; rather, the work had become invigorating, every detail pursued with an intense, even moral commitment. The investigation immediately became a relentless occupation. On weekends he spent his time reading any book he could find about Nazis, adding to his armory of knowledge for the battle he was certain lay ahead. When he sat in the small office questioning survivors of Ravensbruck or Majdanek, writing neat, definite notes as those interviewed tried not to crumble under the weight of impossible memories, his thoughts invariably returned to Dachau and the man in the circle of prisoners being beaten and stoned. DeVito made that journey in his mind so often until he realized—it seemed certainly logical—that he now was the legal instrument of this vengeance: He now would make certain those who packed rooms with corpses would finally be punished. This was not only his job. It was also a unique opportunity. And, it was his mission.

Yet into this excited mood of commitment, certain doubts and certain mysteries began to intrude, strange and unnatural events that filled DeVito with fear and terrible suspicions. The first mystery occurred only two months after DeVito was assigned to the Ryan case.

It had been an unusually long day for DeVito, but he had succeeded in questioning twelve witnesses, all survivors of Majdanek. Before he left for the night, DeVito completed his summaries of these interviews. On the top of each 8 × 11 sheet he wrote the witness's name, address, and phone number. Since these were the only records of a witness's identity, it was official policy that the summaries be carefully guarded. DeVito placed the twelve folders in the bottom drawer of one of the chief trial attorney's filing cabinets. He then secured the file with a combination lock; only Schiano, DeVito, Schiano's chief clerk, and the security officer on the floor knew the combination. The next morning, seven of the twelve files were missing.

DeVito reported the theft to Sol Marks, district director. Later, he told Schiano, "I told Marks but he didn't seem shocked or anything. He didn't flinch a muscle. I finally had to scream, 'You're a Jew, don't you care?' "

An investigation was started and quickly ended: Nothing was discovered, the mystery remained. From that day on, DeVito carried the essential files with him wherever he went; the manila folders in his briefcase becoming tangible reminders of his doubts and suspicions.

As the case went to trial, DeVito had other suspicions, little anxieties he wanted to dismiss until the frequency of these unexplainable acts convinced him that something was wrong and irregular. He became certain Schiano and he were up against something more imposing than a Queens housewife.

His mind filled with questions. How did Mrs. Ryan, who according to his investigation had trouble making ends meet on the modest salary of her husband, an electrical construction worker, raise sufficient funds to hire the Barry firm, one of the most experienced and expensive law firms specializing in immigration work? And who had financed Barry's two research trips to Austria? The money had to be coming from somewhere other than the Ryans. These mysteries funneled down to the bottom-line questions: Who, then, was paying the bills? And why?

New doubts resurrected old ones. DeVito remembered the Service had never been too intent upon prosecuting Mrs. Ryan. Why? Didn't the INS want to pursue Nazis? And then during the extradition trial other unexpected events forced him to think about the Service in a way that even he, the outsider, had not thought about it before.

Tony DeVito sat nearly every day in the first row of the Brooklyn courtroom of Judge Jacob Mishler. He sat intently taking notes; each mark on his pad, another witness's memory of Majdanek, became an infuriating and painful reminder of his present suspicions. The daily testi-

mony seemed to him to be further justification for his
doubts.

He was in the courtroom when one woman described
how Mrs. Ryan, unprovoked, whipped an inmate to death.
And he was sitting in the first row when a Polish survivor
remembered the hanging. Mrs. Ryan had ordered the
prisoners assembled to watch the hanging of a fourteen-
year-old girl who had tried to pretend she was a Gentile
to escape the gas chambers. The girl was only a small
child so Mrs. Ryan ordered an SS man named Ender to
bring a stool. Mrs. Ryan wanted the girl to step up into
the noose.

DeVito stopped taking notes as the witness continued
in controlled, deliberate sentences: "On the way to the
gallows I had to translate Ender's questions as to whether
she was aware she was to be hanged. She answered that
she was aware of it.

"Then Ender pushed away the stool and hanged the
girl. Before she was put to death, the girl said in Polish,
'Remember me.' There was a great silence. The Germans
went away. Somebody threw some flowers on the body,
and it was taken away. . . . All of us went quietly to our
barracks, and in my barracks people were praying."

That night DeVito went home and found it difficult to
sleep. He promised himself that the girl's death would be
avenged. He would remember her.

It was in this mood, against a background of such testimony, that DeVito sat in the courtroom, challenged by a
series of new, uneasy concerns. Not long after the account of the hanging, Mrs. Ryan's lawyer, John J. Barry,
happened to mention that INS Investigator Anthony De-
Vito had employed the CIA to obtain a certified copy
of the Austrian court record against Hermine Braunsteiner. DeVito was certain that someone in the INS
central office had leaked this confidential information to
Barry.

Once more, DeVito was filled with questions. He wrote
an angry memo to Marks who considered it just a minute
before responding, "Don't expect an answer." The memo

was then passed up the departmental ladder to Carl Burrows, the man who originally wanted Schiano to put a quick end to the investigation. There never was an answer.

The INS's treatment of government witnesses erupted into another struggle between DeVito and the bosses. Two female witnesses, one from France, the other from Poland, were asked to testify against Mrs. Ryan. They were told they would receive $37 a day from the government for expenses, barely the cost of a New York hotel room. Still, they came to America. And then, even this money was withheld.

The two witnesses arrived and DeVito learned from Marks that the government funds had not yet cleared. There was some sort of bureaucratic foul-up, Marks explained. They would just have to wait. The witnesses had arrived in New York on September 19, 1972. They were finally called to testify in early November. Oddly, the government expense money managed not to clear until November 9. The witnesses left this country on the next day. If it had not been for Tony DeVito, his rage against what he was certain was something more than the machinations of a disinterested bureaucracy, the witnesses could never have remained in America. Each day he passed a hat around the fourteenth floor of the INS building, collecting over the weeks a total of $604. The passing of the hat became a ritual, another infuriating reminder to DeVito that he was fighting not just Mrs. Ryan, but also the Service. And, perhaps, unknown others.

DeVito also worried about the calls. In his mind, they were all actions in a coordinated plot; his suspicions had already progressed this far. The day after Mary Finkelstein, a survivor of the Majdanek concentration camp, testified against Mrs. Ryan she received a call at her Brooklyn home. The caller warned that "all Jews will someday be killed." The day after Nuna Wiezbicka, another survivor who had immigrated to America, testified, there was a knock at her door. She looked through the peephole and saw a man in a ski mask. He continued knocking on the door and hissing, "Witness . . . witness

. . . witness." The next day, she, too, began to receive phone calls. The phone calls also reached Eva Konikowski, after she testified in open court about her life in Majdanek. And, she received neatly typed post cards, post cards promising that "dirty Jewish witnesses will be killed."

But what disturbed DeVito most was a call his wife received. The caller spoke in a calm, almost soothing voice. The language was German. The caller wanted to know why Frieda was allowing her husband to pursue Nazis. After all, hadn't she been born a German? Didn't she know her husband's work could be dangerous? Frieda, crying hysterically, immediately called Tony. He told her to relax, there was nothing to worry about. It was, he was certain, just another crank call. But he didn't tell Frieda what he really was thinking: Only someone in the Service would both know that his wife was German and have access to his unlisted phone number.

As the trial progressed, DeVito's doubts and fears grew, the pressure of events finally forcing a theory. It remained for months an almost unthinkable explanation, a logic he tried to avoid. But there were too many clues, clues and signs DeVito saw both in his work and also in his reading. It all seemed to fit. For months he had been staying up late after work reading about the aftermath of the Third Reich, reading in books of fact and fiction how the Nazis escaped to the corners of the globe, fortified with stolen Jewish wealth and directed by a secret organization, a network called Odessa (Organisation der ehemaligen SS-Angehorigen) dedicated to the protection of any Nazi forced to stand trial. The similarities between the unexplainable events that occurred each day throughout the Ryan case and the speculation of the books he read each night became gradually tightly molded into one dramatic and passionate reality. An emotional DeVito fitted the facts into an incredible theory.

"Frieda," he told his wife as they lay in bed, "they're gonna say I'm crazy. They're gonna say I'm nuts. But it all adds up. Don't you see, I've spent my entire life preparing for this case. The years in the Army, the years in Germany were all training. All those years I was working for Immigration and filing papers and sitting there watching those crooks on the take were not in vain. Frieda, don't you see? It's no accident that I was chosen for this case."

When DeVito was convinced, he shared his secret with Schiano: "I now realize what we're up against, Vince. I'm certain of it. Vince, have you ever heard of an organization called Odessa?"

WHEN Oscar Karbach called and said, quite simply, that he had "some useful information," Tony DeVito quickly agreed to meet him that afternoon for lunch.

They met in an East Side restaurant where they ate well and talked a bit about the Ryan trial. Karbach, however, seemed to have forgotten the mysterious "useful information" he had to offer. The old man's talk was rambling, but still gracious; it was as if DeVito had called him to arrange lunch.

DeVito had first met Oscar Karbach, of the World Jewish Congress, when he started tracking down leads in the Ryan case. Karbach, a German-born scholar, had helped locate a few witnesses and had convinced other reluctant survivors of Majdanek to testify in open court. DeVito got on well with the frail, old man, liking his refined, rather formal manner: Like many European immigrants, Karbach was respectfully timid toward any representative of the government, even if the connection were only as an INS investigator. But this afternoon in the restaurant, as dishes came and were cleared and the ingratiating small talk continued, DeVito grew annoyed. He had passed up a meeting with Schiano for this lunch. Only later did he realize the old man in his soft, almost lilting voice had been efficiently interrogating him.

"Tell me, Mr. DeVito, why, if I may ask, are you so

interested in the Ryan case?" Karbach posed the question rather absently, simply a polite way of filling a pause after the soup.

"The woman's guilty. She killed people. It's as simple as that." DeVito was brusque when he talked about his work. He liked to talk like a cop.

"But really, all this time you're putting in. It's as if you had a special interest."

DeVito interrupted, "No, this case is nothing special. We treat 'em all the same."

"Oh come now, Mr. DeVito. You've really done an extraordinary amount of work. There *must* be some reason, I would think."

The afternoon was wasted. DeVito had missed his appointment with Schiano. And Karbach was so polite. DeVito looked across the table at the elderly, bald man, his skin not just pale but almost translucent. His fragility was affecting; it was almost tangible. And DeVito wanted to please the old man. He, too, would be gracious. So DeVito told him the other reasons. He told him how frustrating his job had been prior to the Ryan case. And he told him about Dachau, what he had seen and what he never would forget.

The old man just listened, never interrupting an intense and furious DeVito. The words came very quickly and DeVito gesticulated grandly as though he were conducting an orchestra.

They both remained silent for the rest of the meal, two solitary figures uncomfortably sharing the same space. Karbach sipped his tea slowly; apparently he had run out of time-filling chatter. DeVito took his coffee black and drank it quickly, eager to be going. It was as if the two men were sitting at separate tables.

When the waiter came with the check, Karbach spoke again. This time his voice was less vague. His tone was clipped, almost abrupt.

"Would you be interested in any other Nazi cases? Have you ever considered that there might be others like

Mrs. Ryan who had somehow managed to come to America?"

DeVito said, "Of course. That's my job." He was ready to leave. He still had not caught on.

"Sit a minute please, Mr. DeVito. I have something that may interest you." The old man reached inside his suit jacket and took out two sheets of white paper. He did not move easily, so that even simple gestures became very deliberate movements. The papers were folded in half and Karbach placed them, like a mysterious centerpiece, between the two men.

Now DeVito was interested. He sat upright in his chair, suddenly alert.

"Before I show you this, Mr. DeVito, allow me to recount some recent history. I have a certain fascination with numbers and dates, so you will please excuse me if I indulge myself." He smiled as he spoke, a sweet, pleasant smile.

"I am, Mr. DeVito, an immigrant. Your Mrs. Ryan is also an immigrant. Many people in this country are immigrants. It is very easy, Mr. DeVito, to come to this country. You sign a piece of paper saying you have never murdered anyone, and America lets you in. It was especially easy, Mr. DeVito, to come to this country after the war. Perhaps—if you will excuse my saying so—the United States felt a little guilty about how it had treated the Jews. When your troops liberated the concentration camps there were still somewhere between 90,000 and 100,000 Jews alive. A week later, there were only about 70,000 Jews alive. Before all the survivors died of typhoid or malnutrition, President Truman finally agreed to allow those who wanted to come to America. First he issued the Truman Directive of 1945. This law merely gave priority to refugees in United States occupied zones while still maintaining the existing quotas. Yet, under this law 41,000 refugees arrived by 1948. In that year, however, the United States truly opened its doors to the victims of the Nazis. In June of 1948, the Displaced Persons Act was passed by Congress and by 1952 nearly 400,000 European refugees had come to America."

As he spoke, Karbach waved the two folded white sheets toward DeVito, an unconscious gesture not unlike giving the scent to a bloodhound.

"Upon entering the United States," Karbach continued, "the government questioned you about your history, your character, about what you did during the war. But, it was a very confusing time after the war. It was easy, Mr. De-Vito, to change one's past. It was very easy to invent a new past. Hitler, you see, was wrong, Mr. DeVito: It is not always possible to look at someone and tell instantly whether he is a Nazi or a Jew."

DeVito smoked cigarette after cigarette and listened. As soon as one Raleigh was rubbed out in the ashtray, he lit another. He thought about the two years he had spent in Germany after the war. He remembered the disorder and confusion and silently agreed that anything was possible.

"What I'm trying to say, Mr. DeVito, is that not only Hitler's victims came to this country to start a new life. Many Nazis also escaped to this country. A Nazi didn't need to run to Argentina. America has been an even better hideout."

Karbach paused now, taking a sip of tea before continuing.

"These papers, Mr. DeVito, are a list, a list of 59 names, a list of 59 Nazis living in America. I did not locate these men. I am an old man. I am just—what should we say?— the . . . emissary. The real work, the hunting, was done by others. Their identities are unimportant. They have done their work and now, I think, would like to be forgotten. My information comes from many people.

"The Nazis on this list are an interesting group, Mr. DeVito. They have found America to be quite a comfortable home. One man is now a bishop. Another works for the government. Some are rich and some are poor. But all of them, Mr. DeVito, should not remain forgotten.

"If I gave you this list, would you be interested in bringing these men to justice?"

"Yes," said Tony DeVito immediately, "I would be very interested."

Karbach grinned a small, tight, satisfied grin. "Thank you, Mr. DeVito," he said. "We are counting on you."

DeVito did not respond. He knew it was not necessary. He simply took the list and placed it in his pocket.

THAT afternoon Tony DeVito sat in his office reading the strange, unpronounceable names on the list and wondering what to do next. Official procedure was clear: He was required to submit all new leads for investigation to the district director who would then determine whether an agent should be assigned to a specific case. But this time DeVito was reluctant to follow the rules. The specifics of rules and procedures now seemed less important—even dangerous—when challenged by his recent suspicions.

He made a mental accounting of the unanswered events of the Ryan case: the reluctance to prosecute; the unknown source of Mrs. Ryan's funds; the stolen files; the CIA disclosure; the mistreatment of government witnesses; the threats; and the strange call to his wife. These subplots swiftly led once more to what was for DeVito a now undeniable argument, an argument with a startling conclusion: The Service could not be trusted. Yet, DeVito had a list with 59 names and something had to be done.

He confided in Vincent Schiano. That evening the two men met and DeVito told his friend about the list and repeated the events of the Ryan case.

"You're no virgin, Tony," Schiano told him when he had finished. "You've been around long enough to know what rape is. If you give them that list, that will be the last time you'll ever see or hear those names again."

DeVito grimly agreed. Schiano had only confirmed what he had decided. The INS would—for reasons that were frustratingly unknown—never prosecute Nazis hiding in America. Unless—and this would be the thrust of his attack—it had to.

Late that night, unable to sleep, Tony DeVito was forced into another realization: He was the only man in the United States who had the position, the knowledge, and the power to bring these Nazis to justice. He wasn't scared by this realization; rather, he was excited and eager. He was determined that crimes be avenged. He, alone, would force the government to take action. By morning a simple, romantic strategy had emerged from his restless night: Tony DeVito—singlehandedly—would build the cases against the Nazis and when the damning evidence had been boldly assembled, the Service would not be able to avoid fulfilling its legal duty. Or Tony DeVito would make sure every newspaper in the country would be shouting, "Why?"

The next morning DeVito went to the office of Ben Lambert, assistant district director of investigations, and for the first time in his professional career, DeVito told a lie. DeVito explained that someone who wished to remain anonymous would soon be sending a list of names of alleged Nazi war criminals living in America. Lambert seemed uninterested. Lambert explained there had been reports in the past of Nazis living in this country, but the cases had been too difficult to prove. His instructions, however, were direct: When the list arrived, DeVito was to submit both it and the name of the person who had forwarded it to Carl Burrows, assistant commissioner for investigations. DeVito just listened, his mute rage building. He was very glad he had never mentioned that the list with 59 names was at that very moment in his back pocket.

DeVito waited two restless days before making his next move. The daily drama of the ongoing Ryan trial fed his resolve. He wrote a memo calculated, he thought, to ferret unmistakable signs out of the departmental woods. It said, in part:

"... a list of 59 names was furnished this office of per-

sons described as Nazi War Criminals and reportedly re-
siding throughout the United States. A Jewish organization supplied this list to criminal investigator Anthony J.
DeVito with the firm understanding that its source would
not be disclosed."

This vague memo, a direct contradiction of Lambert's
instructions, worked just as DeVito thought it might.
Lambert now called DeVito into his office and in the
presence of District Director Sol Marks insisted that De-
Vito disclose not only each of the 59 names, but also his
source for the list.

It was a request that—as far as DeVito was concerned
—fell like another remarkable piece into the stinking
puzzle he had been piecing together since the Ryan
investigation began over a year ago. He stared at Lambert
and Marks, men he had known for nearly all his professional career, and tried to decide why two Jews were
doing this. For DeVito, this was an important question.
Then for some unavoidable but unknown reason his mind
flashed on that scene in Dachau: the inmates in the awning
outfits attacking a fellow Jewish prisoner. DeVito stood
in front of his two superiors, furious, pacing the room in
anger. In his mind it was clear: One Judenrat had been
replaced with another; one generation of Jewish collaborators had been replaced with another. DeVito did not want
to speak. His hatred went beyond words. His would be a
very personal and private quest. He was a lone figure
calling for vengeance.

But he could not maintain control. "I know what you
guys are up to," he exploded. "You want to bury this list.
You want to make sure nothing is ever done."

Both of his superiors insisted DeVito was wrong. Tony,
they told him, you've been living with the Ryan case too
long. You're not thinking straight. You're paranoid.

DeVito, however, yelled above them. "Look," he continued, jumping from his seat, "in twenty-two years on this
job I've never taken a dime and I'm not going to start
now." He was out of control and did not really care. "If

you want me to give you those 59 names, you're going to have to make the request in writing."

DeVito stormed from the room, angry and wild, but certain of what he had done: It would be more difficult for the Service to bury 59 leads that had been formally requested. And no matter what happened, this written request would become part of the permanent record. It was all part of his plan: If necessary, DeVito would have written evidence when he built his own case against Immigration.

Two days later, the written request was received. DeVito promptly replied with a memo headlined, "Protest." He dutifully included the 59 names and their source, but he also included a lot more—his case and suspicions against the Service. He officially detailed for the permanent file—actually, both the records the Service kept and his own carefully hidden private files—the subplots of the Ryan investigation which culminated in his "strong feelings concerning the existence and operation of Odessa here in the United States, even to the point of possible infiltration into our own government."

And in emotional—perhaps desperate—language, language uncommon to a Service memo, he concluded:

"What difference would it have made if the list was received through the mail from an anonymous source? Are we not mandated by law to investigate allegations of illegal aliens in the United States whether they be Nazi war criminals, ship jumpers, or overstay visitors? Don't we owe an immediate inquiry to the six million Jews and some five million others who perished in gas chambers and crematoriums of concentration camps under the Third Reich? Why didn't we instead confine our discussion to best ways and means to pursue a relentless search for the reported Nazi war criminals and get an honest effort underway in that direction? This surely would have borne some fruit and certainly [been] more desirable in place of the girlish talk we engaged in, especially when it reached the point of useless schismatics as to revealing sources, dates, places, who or why or when?"

The Immigration and Naturalization Service now had its copy of the list with 59 names. And Tony DeVito still had his. His mind remained firmly set. The time for "girlish talk" was over. His "relentless search" would now begin. Tony DeVito was determined to bring 59 Nazi war criminals living in the United States to trial. And nothing was going to stop him. Not the Nazis. And certainly not his own government.

Part II

HUNTERS AND HUNTED

1

A Success Story

HAROLD Goldberg had been closely following Tony De-
Vito's career even before the two investigators met. For
months Goldberg had been collecting newsclips about the
Ryan case and carefully underlining DeVito's name when-
ever it appeared. And for months this public success of
Anthony DeVito had stalked Goldberg's fantasies.

The Ryan folder was not the only file Goldberg assembled in the small study of his suburban Baltimore
home. He also kept manila folders labeled, "Military Intelligence," "Narcotics," "Terrorists and Radicals," and
"Simon Wiesenthal." Harold Goldberg had been a New
York City police detective for twenty-two years and now
that he was retired and working for the Social Security
Administration in Maryland, his professional fascination
with mystery had become largely a passive hobby. Investigation was now just an old talent he played with at night
instead of watching television; like a vain, former athlete
he assembled the files as a workout, a mental exercise
to prevent flab.

But Goldberg's interest in his Ryan file was different: both personal and more complex. The simple reality that Hermine Braunsteiner Ryan had come to trial reassured Goldberg. This public and official retribution legitimized, he felt, his decision to take his old service revolver down from the closet and knock on strange doors in an unfamiliar city, asking questions many people were afraid to answer: material for a very special file.

Similarly, a newsclipping he deliberately kept as the top sheet of this special file also reaffirmed his decision. When he wanted to stop, when he felt like giving up because he was uncertain who was telling the truth or, if thirty years later, old truths still mattered, he thought of the trial and he re-read the news item. Like an experiment in physics, these two simple actions always resulted in the anticipated reaction: He had no choice but to collect evidence.

The clipping, from *The Paterson News,* a New Jersey newspaper, reported, in part:

> Tscherim "Tom" Soobzokov of 704 14th Ave., was presented with a framed citation by Michael Ardis, president of Teamster Local 945, "for the outstanding job he had done in aiding displaced persons forced out of their native country to find a new life and democracy in America."
>
> Among the list of notables was Harry B. Haines, publisher of the *News,* who said the presentation "was an inspiring occasion since our country is made up of little guys. Yet our honored guest is not really a little guy but really big in patriotism and having proven how you love this country and democracy . . ."
>
> Soobzokov, a Russian by birth, escaped from the Soviet Union after World War II and lived in Jordan before coming to this country in 1955. . . .
>
> Harry Schoen, counsel for the Democratic Party in Passaic County, said that many testimonials were phony, "but this one is sincere for Tom is truly deserving. He

likes the stars and stripes and has helped others to do
the same. . . ."

Fred Ardis, secretary to State Senator Anthony Grossi,
and Larry De Angelis, secretary-treasurer of Local 999,
praised the honored guest. The latter gave Soobzokov a
gold watch with the teamster emblem on it.

The citation reads:

". . . Be it therefore resolved, that Tscherim Soobzokov
is herewith bestowed the citation of Local 945, International Brotherhood of Teamsters, as a distinguished
servant of all mankind and has thus earned the gratitude
of his fellow man."

Harold Goldberg had read this news report hundreds of
times in the last three years, but still he never failed to be
infuriated by its horrible irony. This model immigrant
success story was based on lies, fears, and threats. He
knew the truth: This "distinguished servant of all mankind" had served as an Obersturmfuehrer in the Waffen-
SS, the equivalent of a first lieutenant in a Nazi mobile
killing unit that had participated in the murder of
1,400,000 Jews on the Eastern Front.

For the past three years, Goldberg's manhunt, started
by accident, had been a solitary adventure. At the start
he had been only officially interested in the little mysteries
hidden behind the rapid success of an immigrant who just
fifteen years ago washed cars at 90 cents an hour and
now served as chief inspector for the Purchasing Department of Passaic County, a respected member of the local
Democratic machine. But, Goldberg discovered that allegations of petty crimes buried larger ones; Soobzokov's
present life was only a continuation of his past.

Yet after three years of building his case against Soobzokov, Goldberg had also discovered that no one was
interested. The U.S. Attorney for New Jersey had promised an investigation; three years later his office was still
investigating. The Immigration Service also conducted an
active investigation, "active" for the past three years. And
Goldberg's boss at Social Security who had originally

initiated the investigation became less enthusiastic when an angry member of Congress arrived at Social Security headquarters in Maryland demanding that the case be closed. Now the official Social Security position insisted that the statute of limitations was in effect.

Harold Goldberg had been a New York cop for too long not to realize when the fix was in. It made his stomach turn to think that a Nazi SS man could get away with his past just because thirty years later he had become a faithful New Jersey Democrat.

When Harold Goldberg realized no one else cared about "Tom" Soobzokov's past, he took a day off from work and drove his Cadillac into New York City. The newspaper clips on the Ryan case gave him hope that at least one man would want to know.

Goldberg met Tony DeVito, during a recess in the Ryan trial, in a cubicle on the ninth floor of the Immigration Service building. DeVito listened to Goldberg's accusations.

"Okay, Harold, what do you have to go on?"

Goldberg put a black, imitation leather attaché case on the desk and withdrew three manila folders marked "Soobzokov." Each folder was as thick as a dictionary.

"Do you want to hear it all?" Goldberg asked.

"Every bit," said DeVito. "We're both New York boys so you can trust me."

Goldberg had decided to trust DeVito even before he met him. For over two hours Goldberg plotted out his case, talking in his firm, slow voice, the words slipping out of the side of his mouth; like many cops, he had affected a conspiratorial style which unconsciously hinted that even casual conversations were filled with secrets. Goldberg kept his hands tightly folded while he talked, the way children are taught to behave in school. Sometimes, for no reason, he rubbed the back of his neck with his two index fingers as though searching for an imaginary itch; it was an unconscious tic his wife had tried—unsuccessfully—to cure.

DeVito at first attempted to take notes, filling pages of a

yellow legal pad with a small, tight script. But he stopped after a while because there was too much. He just sat there behind a gray steel desk, chain-smoking, impressed by the professional way this former cop had put together his case. As Goldberg spoke, the constant tapping of type-writers outside the cubicle filled the background with a pattern of noise. The steady beats worked to give Goldberg's words an urgency: DeVito felt like he was listening to a news bulletin.

When Goldberg had finished, DeVito's brittle, officious attitude had been replaced by a broad smile. DeVito grinned and Goldberg could see that his teeth were a muddy yellow. The mouth of a corpse, Goldberg instantly decided. But Goldberg forgot about that very quickly because DeVito jumped up from his chair and started pumping Goldberg's hand, and then DeVito was reaching up to pat Goldberg, who was at least two heads taller, on the back. Somehow DeVito managed. Actually, he didn't pat so much as slap. He slapped the larger man's back so hard that Goldberg was startled and a bit confused.

DeVito was excited and in the mood to celebrate. Here was another Nazi case, a sure thing. Here was another case DeVito would bring to trial.

"Jesus Christ, Harold," yelled DeVito. "This case is made to order."

THE "made-to-order case" began by accident. It began in March 1972, when a man who didn't know he was dying went to see his doctor.

Suayip Kardan was simply worried that he was getting old. Forty years ago he had ridden in the Russian cavalry and now he became breathless after only climbing the front steps of his Paterson, New Jersey, home. This short-ness of breath was annoying, but he calmly accepted it as

another penalty of age. His wife, though, was more concerned. "Go see the *doctori*," she urged.

In Paterson, if one has a name like Kardan, there is
only one *doctori*—Dr. Jawad Idriss.

Since the early 1950s, Circassians had been immigrating
to Paterson in significant numbers. Originally descended
from the tribes that rode through and cultivated the mountains and valleys of southern Russia bound by the Black
Sea in the west, the Caucasus Mountains in the south,
and—if one is willing to believe the more aggrandizing
Circassian historians—stretching to the territory lying between the Don and Volga Rivers in the north, Circassians
still found it necessary and practical to preserve their
tribal qualities centuries later in New Jersey. Few, though,
of the perhaps three thousand Circassians in Paterson had
arrived directly from Russia. Dispersed first by the Russian Revolution and then a world war, one generation
of Circassians immigrated to American opportunity largely
from their fathers' temporary homes in Turkey, Jordan,
and Syria. Another wave of Circassians, running from the
horrors of World War II, came from displaced person
camps in Germany, Italy, and also the Middle East following the war of 1948. These Circassians first settled in
Paterson because it seemed to be a city where jobs were
available, but they continued coming to Paterson long after
the jobs were gone and all that was offered was a community that spoke the same language and ate the same
foods.

Paterson's history can be measured out in successive
waves of immigrants. Circassians and Puerto Ricans are
only the most recent arrivals to a city where more than
15 percent of the population is foreign born. Founded by
Alexander Hamilton in 1792 as the country's first industrial center, Paterson now displays little evidence of what
once was an impressive and even elegant manufacturing
city. There is a run-down, discarded look to the town,
a historical anomaly with neither the glamour and im-
portance of New York just sixteen miles away, nor the
suburban amenities of the surrounding New Jersey com-

munities. Yet everywhere there are brutal and uncomfortable reminders of Paterson's past industrial significance: its 150,000 citizens make it the fourth most densely populated city in the United States; one out of every eight persons is on welfare; and its inhabitants breathe the worst air of any city its size in the country. Life in Paterson came as an unexpected, nasty, urban struggle for the newly arrived Circassians. A succession of conquerors had vandalized their old world and now, still frightened, they again looked to the tribe for support and protection.

Most of the Circassians did manage to find jobs. Suayip Kardan worked steadily as a janitor of a local high school until he retired. He never found the work demeaning; rather, he was proud to be earning money and creating new opportunities for his family. Most of what he earned, he spent. He filled his life with possessions as if the more objects he owned in this new country, the more he would belong. The rooms he rented in an old Victorian house, whose grandeur was now subdivided into tight apartments, were a wild and curious melange of a foreigner's perception of American taste. A sharp and disturbingly futuristic glass and chrome dining set shared the same room with stocky made-to-look-old baroque carved sofa and chairs. The velvet upholstery established a bright orange scheme that continued in the orange-shaded lamps, along whose oversized base rows of frolicking gold cherubim dodged hanging amber glass pendants. Bold and confused liverish carpeting and drapes completed the room. Kardan and his wife were proud of their home: They had come to America with nothing; now look at all they had.

Dr. Jawad Idriss had not come to this country with nothing. When he arrived in 1955 from Syria, he already was an M.D. He came to do advanced work in internal medicine, decided to stay after marrying a Circassian biology student who had recently emigrated from Turkey, and within fifteen years was directing a twenty-five-doctor medical clinic in the Bronx. Though he practiced in New York, Dr. Idriss still lived with the Circassian community in Paterson. Actually, while most of the Circassians like Suayip Kardan rented apartments in downtown Paterson, Idriss lived in the nearby suburb of North Haledon. Here there were $100,000 homes, half-acre landscaped plots of trees and grass, and two-car garages. Every resident seemed to be on a casual, first-name basis with Success.

Idriss's low-slung ranch, so routinely American in its architecture with its picture window, low ceilings, and fieldstone chimney, disguised an interior that was a comfortable and inventive mixture of two cultures. The long living room—large enough to be filled with three full-size couches—had luminous Oriental rugs laid precisely end to end across the floor, as if on display, and conveniently scattered about were intricately pearl-inlaid tables. Mid-Eastern folk art hung from the walls. It was a home that accurately reflected Idriss's involvement in two worlds: his financial success as an American doctor and his position as a Circassian leader. "When people come into my living room," explained Idriss, "I want them to be impressed."

Idriss, not so much because of his relative wealth or position, but rather because of his active participation, had become one of the leaders in the Paterson Circassian community. He founded and promoted the Circassian Benevolent Association, a social group committed to maintaining the traditions and cultural heritage of the tribe. Dr. Idriss grandly contributed his time and his money, and all he asked in return was respect.

Idriss never doubted he should be leader of the Circassians, the head of the tribe. He was large and puffy-faced, a meticulous man who obviously considered each item in his elegant dress: The soft yellow of his turtleneck sweater, for example, would be muted tastefully by his brown slacks and camel blazer. He was also, perhaps because of his success, an annoyingly arrogant and dogmatic man. He did not converse so much as issue orders. When he spoke, his words were quiet and precise, his pronouncements trailing off into a long, hiss-like sound—the result of an awkwardly large space between his front teeth.

This hiss and his soft Syrian accent covered his speech and made his words seems sinister. And while his conversations uniformly began in a restrained, pedantic voice, they very often quickly gave way to an abrupt and disdainful tone. It was his style to slam down phones in midsentence or to end arguments by walking out of a room or simply turning his back. The doctor said what he had to say; you were only to listen. Understandably, even the most casual talk with Idriss could instantly escalate into an argument.

Yet, if a Circassian accepted him as head of the tribe, treating the *doctori* with respect by appealing for help and advice, Idriss would be genuinely gracious. He enjoyed this paternal role toward his less fortunate tribesmen. All he demanded in return was respect.

So when Suayip Kardan was having trouble catching his breath, he went to see Dr. Idriss. Idriss was only too glad to help. He listened to Kardan breathe and immediately insisted that the old man be examined by a heart specialist at Idriss's Bronx clinic. Of course, there would be no charge; the *doctori* was eager to be of service.

Dr. Charles Klein of the Clinton Medical Group examined Suayip Kardan on March 10, 1972. He was disturbed by what he found: a massive aortic insufficiency complicated by rheumatic heart disease. Dr. Klein concluded his report to Dr. Idriss with the warning "that there are certain risks involved both in surgery and postoperatively but that these risks are of less significance than the risk of leaving the patient untreated with this significant . . . disease."

Dr. Idriss met first with Kardan and then his patient's twenty-year-old son, Emin, a student at the Newark College of Engineering. He carefully explained the need for the operation and the risk involved. He also agreed to arrange for a room at Lenox Hill Hospital, in New York, where the operation would be performed. He even helped Kardan get his Blue Shield papers in order; Lenox Hill had already informed the Kardan family in writing that "the average fee for open-heart surgery is $2,000."

The operation took place on May 9. It was a success. Two hours later, Kardan started hemorrhaging internally. Oddly, in all the tests prior to surgery the doctors had never discovered that Kardan had a rare blood disease. By the end of the day, he had slipped into a coma. Two more open-heart operations were performed that week. Kardan never escaped from his coma and, on the evening of the seventh day, he died.

Three years later Kardan's son Emin was to remember, "It was my father's death which started this entire nightmare."

SUAYIP Kardan's legacy to his wife and two sons was the furniture that filled their apartment and a pile of bills. Nothing in Suayip Kardan's life had been so expensive as his dying.

Lenox Hill Hospital regretted that they had underestimated the costs. The actual bill, including the two emergency operations, was $21,362.19. An anesthesiologist was also demanding $1,400. Other attending physicians' fees totaled $425. And, the result of all this expensive medical attention, the funeral, cost $775. Suayip Kardan's widow now had debts of $23,962.19 and no prospects of paying.

Except Emin, the elder son, thought there might be a way. About a year before his father's death, Emin had accompanied his father on a business visit to an important member of the Circassian community. They went to see this man because Suayip Kardan was not receiving his entire Social Security benefits; it was well known to the Paterson Circassians that if there were any questions about the intricacies of any level of the government, this was the man to see.

Suayip Kardan's problem arose when he decided in

December 1963 to immigrate to America: He was too old. He was then sixty-six and even if he were allowed to come to America, where would a sixty-six-year-old man find work. So Kardan simply lied about his age, listing the year of his birth on his Turkish passport as 1912, instead of 1897, fifteen years disposed of with a few pen strokes. It was a common solution to a common problem, a lie told by many in the group of Turkish Circassians who came that year to Paterson.

Once in the United States and working, it did not take many of these Circassians long to discover there were truly tangible benefits for admitting one's actual age: Social Security payments begin at age sixty-two. Therefore, after settling, many of the Circassians filed to have their date of birth corrected. It would be a complicated bureaucratic process even for anyone speaking the language, but for most of these immigrants whose English was limited, the task was impossible. One member of the Circassian community, however, made it well known that he could grease the reluctant wheels of a confusing government. He would be glad to handle all Social Security problems. For a fee.

Emin listened as a deal was made with this man. His father agreed, filling out the required forms and paying $500 before leaving. This was the same price, Suayip later explained to his son, six of his Circassian friends had already paid this man for a similar service.

The Circassian with the government connections took an immediate liking to Emin, a bright, darkly handsome boy. He even offered Emin some work. He hired the college student to write Turkish "documents," birth certificates that would be used to help obtain Social Security benefits for other Circassians. Once Emin typed the "documents," the man with the government connections added an "official" Turkish seal and this proof of birth was submitted to the Social Security Administration.

But Emin's employment came to an end after his father's fight with this important Circassian.

"There is a problem," explained the well-connected

man at a meeting a week before Christmas. "We will need more than just $500. My friend is risking his job at Social Security. He requires more. It is not my fault, but you will have to pay an extra $150."

"But we agreed on $500," argued Suayip Kardan.

"I am sorry, but you must understand that someone is risking his job."

"No! No, I will not pay another dollar."

"Then nothing can be done."

And nothing was done. Kardan never received any responses to the papers he had filed. Then, within the year, Suayip Kardan was dead and there were over $23,000 in debts. Emin thought that if he could collect the Social Security money that was rightfully due his father, the family could begin to pay its bills. But this time Emin decided to avoid the Circassian with the government connections. That would be the way his father would have wanted it. Instead, Emin Kardan went to Dr. Idriss.

Dr. Idriss listened to Emin and could not help but feel sorry for the Kardan family. He had never dealt with the Social Security Administration, but Emin Kardan had appealed to him for help, he had shown respect, and now the doctor would reciprocate. It was his responsibility as self-appointed chief of the tribe. Dr. Idriss promised to solve the family's Social Security problems.

This proved not to be as easy as Idriss had imagined. He had naively anticipated the American bureaucracy responding immediately and decisively to any correspondence sent under the letterhead of the Circassian Benevolent Association and signed by a medical doctor. Social Security, however, did not respond. Dr. Idriss was not accustomed to such treatment. When his letters went unanswered, he personally appeared at the Social Security office in Paterson, and, when not satisfied with their vague response, he went to the main office in New York. The Kardan case, he was informed, "still remains under review."

This did not satisfy the doctor. Idriss now started a

lengthy correspondence with the Social Security Administration, letters written by an angry man. Each letter was meant to imply that Dr. Jawad Idriss was not to be taken lightly. For example, he warned the New Jersey Social Security district manager in a typical letter, "Both Mr. Nussbaum and Mrs. Hungo in your department were advised of the situation and our impatience and inability to understand the true motives behind the repeated procrastinations."

These "repeated procrastinations" left Idriss enraged and personally insulted. His inefficacy was demeaning. Infuriated, Idriss demanded Emin tell him if he had any suspicions why, after nearly two years, the matter had not been resolved.

"No," said the youth.

"Look, I insist you tell me. You must know something," said the doctor sharply.

"No, there's nothing."

But Idriss caught the boy's hesitation. The doctor shouted, "I really don't believe you. I'm going to wash my hands of this whole thing."

Emin decided he now had no choice but to tell the doctor about the deal and about the $500 his father had paid. Emin explained that many had paid the same fee, but he refused to disclose the name of the Circassian who had made the offer. That would be too dangerous. "This man has eyes everywhere," said Emin. "He would find out and finish me."

Armed with this new information, Idriss took Emin to the Social Security office in downtown Paterson and demanded to see Suayip Kardan's file. He now had a suspicion which, if true, would explain everything. When the file came, Idriss realized his suspicion had been justified. The Kardans' mailing address for all benefits had been crossed out and a new address had been written in: 704 14th Avenue, Paterson.

Idriss did not have to ask to whom that address belonged. It was very familiar. Now he knew to whom

Suayip Kardan had paid the $500. Now Idriss understood why he was having problems with the Social Security Administration.

Dr. Jawad Idriss knew the address belonged to the man he had described in an open letter printed as an advertisement in a local paper as a "pretender, a manipulator . . . and a perpetual troublemaker." The address belonged to the one man in the Circassian community who had either the confidence or the audacity to think that he, not Idriss, should be the leader of the tribe—Tscherim Soobzokov.

WHEN industry deserted Paterson, the biggest business in the city became politics. The Republicans and Democrats were not so much parties competing for control as two machines reaching for the spoils and payoffs from the federal- and state-funded programs that poured into Paterson. In a state with a national reputation for political corruption, Passaic County stood out as a home for wheeler-dealers, the base of many often indicted, but rarely convicted politicians. Up for grabs each election year were not only the control of the courts, the prosecutors' office—New Jersey cities do not have their own district attorneys conducting independent investigations—and the police, but also, more concretely, a $35-million county budget and fifteen hundred civil service jobs. The public has little to say in the actual division of these spoils. In fact, the only elected local official is the mayor. The victorious machine freely spends the county money according to its whims. In 1968, for example, county commissioners purchased a multimillion-dollar golf course while claiming that the county could not afford any sort of drug treatment program for Paterson.

The Democrats control Paterson by a seven-to-one voter registration majority and their party mechanism works diligently to maintain this numerical superiority. Local TV broadcaster and author Christopher Norwood accurately described a recent blitzkrieg of the machine through Paterson's electoral wards: "In the poor sections of the city, people were convinced that there were cameras in the voting booths and feared retaliation for making an independent choice. The Honest Election League of Paterson reported threats of the loss of jobs, public housing, and welfare. Some union members charged they could not obtain their paychecks without making a donation to the Democratic campaign. 'I can picture the Almighty God standing on top of Ganett Mountain and weeping over Paterson and Passaic County,' thundered Monsignor William Wall, the head of the Election League."

"Tom" Soobzokov, the success-oriented immigrant, meshed perfectly into this Democratic machine; first the rank-and-file recruit, then quickly the recruiter, and, in time, becoming another party regular, prospering and protected.

Before he arrived in the United States on the S.S. *Saturnia* on June 28, 1955, Tscherim Soobzokov had probably never even heard of the Democratic Party. Like most of the Circassians on board from Amman, Jordan, his voyage was paid for and sponsored by the Tolstoy Foundation, a White Russian philanthropic organization committed to the resettlement of the twelve hundred Circassians in Jordan; "sturdy, ardent anti-Communists," the Foundation bulletin promised, "people of integrity, imagination and independence." He arrived with his wife, two children, $3,000 in savings, and no prospect of a job. But he was determined to succeed in America and confident of his ability to maneuver his way to the top. "I knew that it would take hard work," Soobzokov later recalled, "and I was willing. I was eager to learn the American way."

Soobzokov's first job was in a car wash for 90 cents an hour. At night he took courses to become an insurance salesman. The profitable American way, though, seemed to be eluding Soobzokov and nearly two years after he arrived in Paterson he returned to the Middle East for six months' work as, he told friends, an antiques dealer.

It was on his return to Paterson that Soobzokov's career —and fortune—prospered. It was simply a matter of seizing the right opportunity. Soobzokov began working as a machinery operator in the local Colorite Plastics plant just as the Teamsters were trying to unionize the workers. Here was a volatile situation and Soobzokov tried to pick the winning side. He approached the Teamsters with a proposal: He would convince newly arrived Circassians to become dues-paying union men if the Teamsters would guarantee jobs. It was a practical, mutually beneficial arrangement. While most of the immigrants remained confused by life in New Jersey and spoke little English, Soobzokov had already smoothly managed to cement deals and connections. His English, too, was still awkward, a bit too formal, but he consciously filled his speech with slang. "Let's shake on it," Soobzokov would say with his quick, broad smile. Or, he would nod in agreement and offer a friendly "Okee-doo-kee." He wanted very much to seem like an American.

A friend remembers Soobzokov's "coming around to all the Circassian families on the night before a union election. If a family wasn't in, he would come back at twelve, one o'clock at night. If they were asleep or they didn't answer the door, Soobzokov would throw rocks at their windows until they would come downstairs and talk. Once he started talking, he wouldn't leave until you agreed to vote for the Teamsters. He would tell them that if they didn't vote as he instructed, the factory would be closed and they would be out of work."

By the time Soobzokov became a U.S. citizen in 1960, he had been elected plant chairman of Teamster Local 991. And, he was providing jobs for Circassians at other plants in the area. In 1969, for example, when the Universal Balance Company voted to become a union shop, it was the Circassian vote that provided the necessary margin. "The Teamsters never cared if the Circassians spoke English or if they were citizens," explains Soobzokov. "They were just interested in giving my people jobs. And in return I would ask my friends to back the Teamsters. It was a good deal for everyone."

The Paterson Democrats, an organization with eyes—and hands—everywhere, became quickly aware of Soobzokov's recruitment work for the Teamsters. "A local ward leader came to me and asked if I wanted to help the Democrats. I am a poor working man, so I agreed. It didn't seem right that my people were sitting by and not voting. So I became involved in citizenship and I helped register Circassians and got them to vote. People would come to my home seeking work and wanting to become citizens, and I would always try to convince them to vote Democratic. It was a fair shake all around."

Soobzokov soon became known in Paterson politics as "the man who could deliver the Circassian vote." In an electoral system where each victory insured the unhampered distribution of the spoils, each vote became—almost literally—money in the bank. And consequently Soobzokov's career became a good investment for the Democratic machine.

Soobzokov's name and picture now began appearing in the local newspapers. He was presented as a doer, a Circassian Horatio Alger. In 1965, Soobzokov was appointed a county purchasing inspector, a $20,000-a-year job, after his predecessor had been indicted, but—as is the way in Passaic County—escaped conviction. And just a year later another smiling picture of Soobzokov appeared when he received a citation from the Teamsters as "a distinguished servant of all mankind."

It was this picture of "Tom" Soobzokov being honored as "someone who has earned the gratitude of his fellow man" that years later was to infuriate and goad Harold Goldberg. But at the time the ceremony clearly demonstrated that after just eleven years in this country Soobzokov had maneuvered himself into the inner circles of the Democratic machine. Consider the company he kept that night: Michael Ardis, president of Teamster Local 945, who years later was to vanish, a victim, according to the speculation òf the papers, of "mob violence"; Fred Ardis, secretary to State Senator Anthony Grossi, who as state senator, Paterson tax assessor, a state public utilities commissioner, and county chairman directed the machine, while Fred Ardis, his former chauffeur, was now his "advisor," a man later to quit as a county purchasing agent after an investigation concerning double-billing, only to be indicted for fraud in another matter and plead guilty to a lesser charge of forgery; and Harry B. Haines, publisher of *The Paterson News,* the unofficial "mayor of Paterson," who ran the largest-selling paper in the county as an exercise in personal journalism, frequently editorializing against civil rights activity, the Communist conspiracy, and any local politician who dared to oppose him. From that evening on, "Tom" Soobzokov was officially one of the boys, a "made" Democrat.

As the machine pushed, Soobzokov's career and expanding network of influential connections moved smoothly ahead. In 1968, he was named to a five-year term on the Paterson Zoning Board of Adjustment, replacing a retired police captain who, according to the City Counsel, had been improperly appointed. Accepting the position, Soobzokov humbly told a reporter from *The Paterson News,* "I believe public service is vital to the community." The following year he was selected by Congressman Charles Joelson to head the congressman's New Americans program. Every Circassian in the area received a letter written by Joelson on House of Representatives stationery explaining:

"Many new citizens are bewildered by the law and by the new obligations they undertake as they swear the oath of good citizenship, and they need solicitous guidance.

"Under Mr. Soobzokov's direction, these folks will be able to seek counsel and guidance. If they require information about their roles in the community, or if they require contact with City Hall, the courts or any other official agency, he will be able to direct them so that they will not need to move about in bewilderment."

Joelson's letter neatly served to institutionalize Soobzokov's role as a sort of Circassian Godfather. Immigrants were informed by *a member of Congress* that if they wanted anything done, Soobzokov was the man to see. And Soobzokov, in turn, would provide the troubled with the magic words "so that they will not need to move about in bewilderment"—the Democratic Party. Coincidentally, or so he later maintained, Soobzokov now established a corporation called Paterson General Services "to translate documents from Circassian to English."

"I never accepted a fee for finding someone a job or helping with their Social Security," insists Soobzokov. "But if they want to repay me with a present to honor me, I cannot help that. There were five hundred people at my daughter's wedding. Many of them instead of giving my daughter $100, gave her $200 or $300 gifts. I cannot stop that and I appreciate the respect." The mayor of Paterson was also among his daughter's wedding guests.

After twenty years in Paterson, "Tom" Soobzokov was indistinguishable from the other politicians who roamed the downtown municipal buildings and courthouses. A "Circassian Carmine DeSapio" is the way one local Democrat described Soobzokov. Soobzokov's lawyer, Herman Steinberg, a man active in Republican politics, said of his friend and client, "He's a promoter. He learned the American way very, very fast. He didn't sit on his ass and wait for things to happen." Both men sincerely meant their characterizations as praise.

And, to the casual observer, it truly seemed as if Soobzokov were a man who deserved praise. At fifty-eight, a man who managed to keep in shape, he looked years younger. He was quick to smile, and facile with compliments, always noticing a new tie or a haircut. Like most of the Party boys, he dressed as a double-knit hipster, outfitted in suits of brightly colored synthetics, often with belts in the back, continental pants, and accented with wide ties and colored shirts. His hair had remained thick and glossy black, pomaded and carefully combed back on the sides, while on the crown it was brushed straight and flat, so flat that it appeared as if Soobzokov had actually pressed a heavy book against his skull. To complete his image, Soobzokov had artfully shaped "swinger" sideburns, and a bushy black moustache under his long, hawk nose. Still, when standing with his weary, balding, and paunchy political associates, Soobzokov clearly carried off these youthful excesses with a great deal more credibility.

His English was remarkably fluent and colloquial, though his broad Russian accent intruded, making his speech deeper and more gravelly. Actually this resonance, a sort of Cossack *brutissimo,* gave his words a distinguished, rather impressive tone, the way a public official should sound. To his acquaintances, Soobzokov seemed a prosperous politician, businessman, and family man.

He now had five children, three born in Paterson. His oldest son, Kazbek, already appeared to be following his father's public-spirited path to idealized success. *The Paterson News* ran a lengthy story reporting how "Kaz" Soobzokov, a dormitory advisor at the University of Bridgeport, "had engineered a peace between the students and the local motorcycle club, less affectionately known to the campus as the Huns." The lead paragraph of the story boldly insisted, "A new name has been added to the list of historical confrontations: Soobzokov and the Huns." The story also noted that the "senior Soobzokov . . . beams at the fact that his son is following the family plan of dedication to their country of adoption."

Soobzokov appeared to be a true Paterson success story: from rags to double knits. His past, if not an open book, was certainly public record. As reported in a 1968 *Paterson News* article, his earlier suffering made his recent prosperity more remarkable and more deserving:

Soobzokov came to Paterson in 1955 after a thirteen-year odyssey that began in 1942 when the German army captured the Russian territory of the Caucasus.

Soobzokov was shipped as a semi-forced laborer to Rumania.

"We were not exactly forced," Soobzokov says, "but we didn't have any choice."

Soobzokov worked as a transportation worker in Rumania and was later transferred to Hungary and Austria where he was when the war ended.

Refusing to return to the Russian-occupied Caucasus, Soobzokov went to Jordan which had a Circassian community. . . .

Many of the Paterson Circassians were troubled and insulted after reading this version of history. But still foreigners in a new land, they were reluctant to challenge a man whose picture appeared in the paper and about whom Congressmen wrote letters.

And so Soobzokov's past might have remained forever past if Suayip Kardan had not died and Dr. Jawad Idriss had not, therefore, been given another opportunity to avenge the accordion incident.

CIRCASSIAN folk dances are both menacing and romantic, a passionate mixture of leaping Cossacks, softly gliding veiled women, and brandished sabres. It seemed a good idea, then, when Dr. Idriss agreed to have the dancers of his Circassian Community Center perform at a folklore festival at nearby Montclair State College, the modest proceeds going to a scholarship fund for Circassian students. But it was a performance that erupted into a feud splitting the Paterson Circassians. The two self-proclaimed "leaders" now fought in public like petty chieftains for total control of the tribe.

It was a Friday evening, just a day before the performance, when Idriss, working late at his New York medical office, received a phone call from his wife. "She was crying," Idriss remembers, "and trying to tell me that Nabil Wazerman had just called to say he had to leave town and wouldn't be able to play the accordion tomorrow night.

She was upset because Nabil had practiced with the dancers for five months and no one was prepared to take his place. I was angry, too. I just couldn't understand why Nabil did that. Anyway, I got one of my patients, an Italian who plays in a band, to take his place. This man put on one of our costumes, practiced for a couple of hours, and the show went on. But for the next week I just sat around thinking why did Nabil do this to me. Really, I was very insulted. I couldn't understand.

"Then I hear from one person and soon from others that this Soobzokov is going around bragging. He is bragging how he showed the *doctori*. 'No one in this county can stand up to me,' he is saying. 'Not even the *doctori*. I got Nabil Wazerman to stay away.'

"So it became clear to me what had happened. It was not really Nabil's fault—he is just a young man—but I would have to fix him. He had insulted me. Soobzokov was trying to show that no one but Soobzokov could arrange any event representing Circassians. It was now clear. I would have to show our people that Soobzokov is nothing."

Idriss's revenge materialized in an advertisement in the April 15, 1971, *Bergen Record,* headlined as "An Open Letter to Tscherim Soobzokov":

Your recent attempts to disrupt the Circassian Folk Dance performance by ordering Mr. Nabil Wazerman to withdraw from playing the accordion at the eleventh hour, has revealed your true color once again . . . this letter was drafted on behalf of the Circassian Community Center and was endorsed by the Circassian Benevolent Association leaders, the same association in which you are and have always been a simple ordinary member, with the singular distinction of being a pretender, a manipulator of the Society's files and a perpetual troublemaker.

We protest your consistent, painfully tolerated behavior and demand an open answer.

Jawad S. Idriss, M.D.

The public message of Idriss's "open letter" was clear: Soobzokov was not and had never been a leader of the Circassians. This insult, above all, thought Idriss, would force Soobzokov to respond; his professional livelihood as the "man who delivered the Circassian vote" was threatened.

Two days later a letter from Nabil Wazerman appeared in the paper, explaining that "although I have high regard for Mr. Soobzokov, it was not he that stopped me from participating." Wazerman wrote he refused to play after "a relative said Dr. Idriss, who had the good fortune of obtaining an education in medicine in Syria, declined to help him on the grounds that he did not emigrate from Syria, but Jordan."

Idriss was cold with anger. "I do not know why that boy should say that about me. I really do not know," he repeated with furious indignation. And, as is the right of the chief, he set out to destroy Wazerman. His motive was not so much revenge; it was spite. On the stationery of the Circassian Community Center he wrote a letter to the Immigration Service that "Nabil Wazerman was admitted to the United States on a student visa. Through a false Social Security number, he applied and got a job at the Gulf Plastics Corp. . . ." Idriss's letter urged that the man who had insulted him be punished.

Other letters now appeared as sides were taken and many in the tribe prepared for an inevitable engagement with disaster. Laila Qualagan, a Circassian student who had helped Idriss organize the folk dance performance, wrote in *The Paterson News* that "I, myself, was threatened by him [Soobzokov] that if I did not stop participating in the CCC activities, he would see to it that I was expelled from college and deported from the United States." And Suhiel Quardan, Nabil Wazerman's uncle, circulated a letter quoting an unnamed "respectable leader," who was clearly Soobzokov, as saying, "The Jordanians . . . they are like a ring around my little finger . . . I can move them as I please, and whenever I wish . . ." The letter concluded, "When it is trash that fills a creature, nothing can hide it, be it a 'respectable leader' or a man in the gutter."

The Circassian community tensely waited for Soobzokov's response to these letters. But, he was strangely quiet. There was new talk, rumors that some of the Circassians knew secrets, secrets about Soobzokov's past, and would soon circulate another public letter. Then, quite suddenly, just two weeks after his attack on a "respectable leader," Suhiel Quardan was deported. The authorities had somehow learned Quardan had used a forged Social Security card to find work.

No one knew for sure who had informed on Quardan and convinced the authorities to take such immediate and definite action. But most Circassians suspected the same man. After the deportation, the letters and talk against Soobzokov stopped. No one spoke of those other, mysterious secrets hidden in Soobzokov's past. The tribe was frightened. Dr. Idriss, too, stopped publishing open letters. He realized his revenge would have to wait.

DR. IDRISS'S opportunity for revenge came nearly a year later when Emin Kardan told him about the $500 Soobzokov had charged his father. Now, thought Idriss, here was another chance to embarrass Soobzokov. This was most probably a crime. The government would have to act. But, bewilderingly, the local Social Security Administration refused to prosecute. Idriss became certain they were under Soobzokov's control. Still, he remained determined that Soobzokov be exposed. He was unwilling to give up. The cause at stake was now greater than the resolution of a widow's Social Security benefits. It had become a fight for the leadership of the tribe. If it now required a hundred letters, Idriss was prepared to write them.

So this time Idriss wrote to the Social Security's Bureau of Hearings and Appeals in Washington urging that an investigation be conducted of the Kardan affair because "without being appointed as a representative and without submitting the special fee form, money was collected in advance, cash, to speed up the processing of the case."

This letter was passed from department to department until it appeared in Baltimore on the desk of Harold Goldberg, claims investigator.

HAROLD Goldberg and his wife had just returned from spending a weekend with old friends in New York and he was sorry to be back. He hated Maryland. His new, suburban, small-town life left him uncomfortable and bored. Still a New Yorker, he was annoyed by such petty —but necessary—inconveniences as the twenty-minute drive to the shopping center for bagels. And worse, these Maryland bagels were unnaturally brown and wrapped in plastic bags as if they were exotic delicacies. He had left New York and the police department four years ago after putting in his twenty and then two more years for good measure. He had qualified for a half-pay pension and was still in one piece, so there didn't seem to be much point in pressing his luck. He found a job with the Social Security Administration in Baltimore, and, at his wife's urging, packed and moved. He agreed "for the sake of the children." Blacks were being bused into his daughter's school in Queens and this disturbed him. At the time, it helped convince him that "the city was going to hell and it wasn't safe to walk anywhere."

He wanted his children to have the best so Goldberg moved into a modern ranch home twenty minutes outside

Baltimore in a development known as Indian Village. They lived on a street with a genuine Indian name, a corner house at the intersection of another street with an equally authentic name. With the combined income from his police pension and his Social Security job, they were able to live better than they had ever lived before. Their house boasted a two-car garage with a vinyl-roofed Cadillac in one of the stalls, a paneled rec room, a master bath with a built-in Formica vanity and a hot towel rack, and a spacious living room filled with colorfully upholstered couches and chairs protected with plastic slipcovers. Still, Goldberg was unhappy. He was always embarrassed whenever he told friends from the precinct his new address. "Yeah, that's right," he would say when they laughed, "I live fuckin' right next door to fuckin' Pocahontas."

Uprooted at the age of fifty-two, Harold Goldberg felt as if he had become an immigrant, a foreigner living in a strange land. And like other immigrants in other cities, he turned to the tribe for protection and friendship. He had never been a religious Jew when he had lived in Queens, but his four years in his little bit of Good Housekeeping suburban America made him constantly aware of his identity. There was something, he instinctively felt, annoyingly *goyische,* foreign, about this cute, wholesome living. He decided, as a reaction, to send his eight-year-old son to a local Yeshiva. After a year at the Yeshiva his son, Bruce, went around the house wearing a gold yarmulke and speaking Hebrew, a language Goldberg had not read or spoken since his bar mitzvah nearly forty years earlier.

Goldberg's job was equally unsatisfying. For twenty years he had enjoyed being a cop, and then a detective. He had delighted in being an insider, of knowing how a certain case mentioned daily in the papers was really progressing. It had made him feel important and necessary. He also needed to be one of the boys, to go out for a couple of beers after work and trade gripes and stories.

Only now he was an "investigator" who sat at a desk in an office filled with strangers.

For the past four years Harold Goldberg had filed papers and made sure old men were getting their allotted $181 a month. They paid him well, gave him a title and a secretary to type his memos, and he hated it. He was an active man and he missed the intense, methodical discipline of tracking down leads in an important case. He had never before in his life sat behind a desk: This job made him feel unnaturally old. He had joined the police right after the Air Force. During the war, he had been a bomber pilot with the 94th Airborne, and he had been shot down and spent a rough year in a German POW camp. He was proud of this war record and, thirty years later, still wore a replica of a B-52 as a tie tack.

It had seemed natural that he become a cop; his presence could have been molded for the role. Even now in his fifties, he was still a large bull of a man, keeping his short-sleeved shirts rolled up a proper half-inch to display powerful biceps the way tough city kids do. His hair was gray, but he still combed it into a thinning pompadour. His face, though, was his best quality: bright, icy blue eyes and sharp features, the kind of expressive face that can transform in an instant; one minute heavy laughter, going along with the joke, and then—suddenly—there was a hardness, a grim, somber edge that warned the time for jokes and small talk was over. This was the technique he used on the job for twenty-two years and it had served him well. He had been, he was certain, a good cop and an especially resourceful detective, the kind of cop who could get people to talk. Still imposing and absolutely determined, this detective was reduced to keeping the files he assembled at home, his nights spent clipping items from obscure newspapers about Simon Wiesenthal, Military Intelligence, and Terrorists and Radical Activities. These were scrapbooks not of the past, but—somehow he still hoped—future glories.

So when the letter came to his desk alleging a Social Security payoff in Paterson, he jumped at the chance to

investigate. It was not so much the case that interested
him, but the location—Paterson was only sixteen miles
from New York. He told his boss he would spend three
days in New Jersey checking the allegations. And he told
his wife that this schedule would leave them free to spend
another weekend in New York with his friends from the
precinct. She was to take the train and meet him Friday
night at her mother's apartment in Queens.

Harold Goldberg interviewed Dr. Idriss and spent the
following days in Paterson asking other members of the
Circassian community questions. For two days he listened
and took notes in a small, black notebook and then he
called his wife and told her he wouldn't be stopping in
New York. On Saturday morning he drove directly to
Maryland. He spent the weekend writing a letter and
creating a new file, a file labeled "Tscherim Soobzokov."

On Monday morning he drove back to Paterson, but
before he left he did something he had not done since
he retired. He took his police service revolver down from
the closet in his study and strapped the holster around
his waist. If what he had heard were true, he decided
it might be best to wear a gun. Then he drove off, armed,
making only one stop along the way—the post office. He
mailed a special delivery letter to Berlin. He then pulled
onto the turnpike and drove his Cadillac as fast as he
could get away with to Paterson. For the first time in
four years Harold Goldberg felt not just happy, but also
excited and even a bit uneasy. This was the way it used
to be. Harold Goldberg was back on a case.

HAROLD Goldberg convinced the Circassians to talk.
He knocked on doors all over Paterson and spent hours in
strange living rooms assuring shaky, frightened old men
they would not be deported if they told him everything

they knew. "You've got nothing to fear," Goldberg argued. "I work for the government. I'll protect you. You have my word." And, after a while, most believed him. Goldberg, who somehow always managed to open his jacket and casually expose his revolver as if this were proof of his authority and power, would start each session of questioning with a controlled politeness. He would be gracious and sensible. And then, if a Circassian were reluctant or afraid, he turned into the "bad" cop, shouting, berating, bullying until he could get at the truth. After two more hectic weeks of these interviews, Harold Goldberg realized that he had stumbled onto a case involving something more terrifying than allegations about a cheap, local crook. He now considered adding another charge: war criminal.

On a warm April night he called a meeting at Dr. Idriss's house to get sworn statements from the men who had known Tscherim Soobzokov thirty years ago. When he presented this case to the U.S. Attorney, Harold Goldberg wanted his charges to stick. He also had another reason for calling an open meeting. He wanted to show the Circassians that Soobzokov's power and influence could be challenged. In America, he wanted this group of frightened men to realize you did not have to fear a Nazi.

Only ten men came to the meeting at Dr. Idriss's house. The other Circassians were afraid. But the testimony of these ten men, Goldberg was convinced, was enough to break Tscherim Soobzokov.

The men waited, fidgeting and nervous in the shiny luxury of Dr. Idriss's living room. These Circassians were working people, weary from a hard day, and yet in honor of the occasion of being in the *doctori*'s house, they wore ties and were carefully groomed. They spoke in turn, each now determined or simply resigned to tell what he knew.

Issa Hoket gestured enthusiastically as he spoke, the words said in a deep ominous voice; every syllable uttered as if it were part of a bitter curse. He knew little English and paused while a friend translated:

"I saw Soobzokov," Hoket began, his gold teeth shining, "in an SS uniform in June 1944, in Buzov, Rumania. Soobzokov was addressing a group of Circassian refugees I was in. He told us he was assigned to organize a Circassian troop unit to fight on a new front. The Germans have appointed him our leader, he said. I argued with him, saying we weren't going to fight with the Germans. I told him he was not our leader.

"Soobzokov left but quickly returned with two other SS officers, one a colonel, the other a major. The colonel spoke. He asked me my name and then said, 'Hoket, your *fuehrer* is Soobzokov.' He used that very word, *fuehrer*. The colonel said that for disobeying Soobzokov I would die. Soldiers came and grabbed me and took me away. They led me to a prison and Soobzokov followed behind me. They kept me in this prison for two hours. Then a Rumanian major, Bershack, a man I was good friends with, came and ordered me released. Soobzokov, he told me, had left with the other SS officers and some Circassian volunteers to fight in Hungary. It was safe to release me. If my friend the Rumanian had not released me, I would have been killed. There are other people living today in Paterson who witnessed my arrest.

"I saw Soobzokov again in 1965, when I came to this country from Turkey. He talked to me in a diner on Market Street. He had forgotten he had arrested me. Now he was very friendly. He tells me he can get me a job because he has a big position in the government. He says his friend is the mayor and he can do big things. And he tells me it will cost me $500 when he gets me this job. I tell him no. I don't need him. Another friend can get me a job as a mechanic. I have a skill. Besides, I tell him, don't you remember me. You had me arrested in Rumania. He became quiet and stares at me for a minute. You know, trying to remember my face. Then he says, 'You should forget what happened. It won't do you any good if you tell anyone. I am everywhere. I am very powerful in this country.' And then Soobzokov just walks away.

"It is a terrible thing, I tell you. People were scared of Soobzokov all through the war and they're still scared."

Kassim Chuako spoke next. His English was slow and deliberate, his eyes fixed in a dull, blank stare as if he were concentrating very intently on each word.

"I deeply believe in God and don't like my people to be fooled and lied to. And I don't like my people to be terrorized. Soobzokov, he said that he was in the Russian army and that he was captured by the Germans. I *know* him. He was working before the Germans came as a tax collector. I lived ten miles from him in the Caucasus. When Germans came he went to secretary of police and asked to join. We all talk about him. We saw him going into the villages with the Germans and rounding up people—Communists and Jews. I saw him with the SS troops that took people away. In 1943, I saw him again in SS uniform in Rachovich in White Russia. He was talking to secretary of refugee camp, telling him that he wanted to take his relatives out. When the secretary said no, he pulled his gun out of the holster and led his family out by gunpoint.

"I see him again in this country. He brought me to Universal Company and told me he get me a job. But I have to give him my first pay check. I pay him and then I get laid off. He tells me if I pay him again he'll get my job back. I tell him no and go to work as a janitor instead.

"Please, Mr. Goldberg, I am not scared. I am up to here. But should anything happen to us, will you protect us?"

"You don't have to worry," Goldberg told him, "this is America."

And so the evening continued. Perhaps, Goldberg decided, these immigrants had accepted the intimidations and threats of Soobzokov in Paterson because after what they had experienced in Russia and during the war, they almost needed to depend on an element of persecution without which life would be unpredictable and, in a way, less safe. As the investigator listened to each detailed, open confession, he hoped these men were finally liberating themselves from the past, and past fears.

Mahimid Neguch, a meticulously dressed old man in a well-pressed suit, V-neck sweater, white shirt, and tie, told how he first met Soobzokov:

"Soobzokov's father-in-law introduced me. And then Soobzokov walks up, head high, and he is in full uniform, an SS uniform. Then I see him weeks later. He is with a group of SS men taking prisoners from two towns in the Caucasus, Edepsuikay #1 and Edepsuikay #2. Three boys were killed from that town and Soobzokov was there with the group that executed them. We were all witnesses.

"I been in this country since 1969," he continued, his right hand nervously playing with an unlit cigarette. "I work in A & P, you know, the Atlantic & Pacific Company. But I no believe America is a good, *democratische* country. In world war America and Russia have same trouble with Nazis. So how come, Mr. Goldberg, they let Soobzokov live in this country? America must know about him."

The evening's testimony gave Goldberg a solid case: four men who had personally paid Soobzokov fees for employment or Social Security assistance, eight witnesses who had personally seen Soobzokov in an SS uniform, plus the names of others living in Paterson and Russia who were also familiar with Soobzokov's activities in World War II.

But Goldberg was not satisfied. He wanted these Circassians to see how justice really works in this country. He insisted these men should immediately inform the Immigration Service of what they knew.

"But you don't know Soobzokov," Hisa Torchako argued, his words quick and alarmed. "He will take care of anyone who says a word about him. He says he is a Mason and that the Masons are very powerful. He says the Masons can kill people and get away with it."

Goldberg wanted to laugh, but he realized the man was serious.

"Look," Goldberg said, raising himself up from the couch to look as large and as imposing as possible, "I told you there's nothing to worry about. This is America. You don't have to fear Nazis or Masons or anyone."

"Thank you. Thank you very much, Mr. Goldberg. I knew you would help . . ."

"Look," Goldberg interrupted. His face was now flushed. He was yelling. "You and your friends don't have to thank me. I'm not doing this for you. I'm doing it for six million other reasons. If any of you were honest, a shit like Soobzokov couldn't have ever become your leader."

Then Goldberg got his papers together and, without saying another word, walked out the door.

THE next day Harold Goldberg interviewed "Tom" Soobzokov. For nearly a month Goldberg had been concerned about this inevitable confrontation: Would he be able to control himself sitting directly across from a man he was certain had served with the SS?

The meeting, though, was empty of catastrophe. It was only puzzling.

"Yes, Mr. Goldberg, I heard you were asking questions about me. There can be no hush-hush among our people. I just wish you had come first to me. I am sure I can answer whatever questions you may have," said a calm Soobzokov, smiling as he spoke. He appeared open and gregarious, as if he couldn't have been happier at meeting an investigator from the Social Security Administration.

Goldberg toyed with him, asking vague questions about his past history and his assistance to his fellow Circassians. He did not want Soobzokov to think he had anything more than suspicions.

"In the war, one did many things to stay alive," Soobzokov explained with his ferocious smile. "I was forced to join the Germans. But I didn't fight. I was a transportation worker."

Goldberg did not object. He only listened.

"Of course, I've never taken money for helping with Social Security problems. I just wanted to help my people," Soobzokov continued.

As Soobzokov talked, Goldberg noted that he was very convincing. Goldberg had not expected this. He had imagined some sweaty little man who would break into tears at the first bit of pressure. Instead, Soobzokov's speech was reasonable and steady.

Only toward the end of the hour did Soobzokov betray a simmering anger. "You may hear some things about me, Mr. Goldberg. I hope you will not believe them. They are the lies of one arrogant man, a Dr. Idriss. I assume you have spoken with him, yes?"

Goldberg remained mute and noncommittal.

"That man," Soobzokov shouted, "is the devil. He wants to ruin my people."

But an embarrassed Soobzokov quickly recovered from this outburst and resumed his smiling, confident way. Goldberg thought that for a moment Soobzokov even looked ashamed that he was capable of such uncontrolled rage.

When the meeting was over, Goldberg extended his hand and thanked Soobzokov for his time; it seemed the only natural way to behave, Goldberg decided.

The ride back to Baltimore that afternoon was spent sorting strange and confusing thoughts. Soobzokov had seemed so secure, so confident. He had acted so . . . so normal. It didn't seem possible that he had served in the SS. Perhaps, at worst, he was a politician making a few quick bucks. But a Nazi?

Idriss, Goldberg thought as he continued down the highway, was another matter. The doctor behaved more like the arrogant, belligerent Nazi one expected. The doctor was a character from a von Stroheim movie. Could Idriss have gotten those ten Circassians to lie? He doubted it. But Goldberg was no longer sure. Perhaps Goldberg had been duped into playing a role in a tribal dispute. Like the unfortunate accordion player, one camp was using him against the other. Perhaps Idriss, not Soobzokov, was the villain. Goldberg was not sure about anything anymore. It was all very bewildering.

He arrived in Baltimore at about six, his car creeping with the rush-hour traffic. But before going home Goldberg decided to deposit his files at his office. He was at his desk rummaging through his papers when he noticed the letter. An airmail letter from Berlin had arrived in his absence. He quickly opened it and read the reply by the Berlin Documents Center to the letter he had written weeks ago:

"Dear Mr. Goldberg:

"I refer to your letter . . . requesting information on Mr. Tscherim SOOBZOKOV. In our custody there is a roster from the Personnel Office of the Waffen-SS dated March 13, 1945, concerning the transfer of former officers of foreign armies to the Waffen-SS. According to this document SUBJECT, born 1 January 1918, was assigned effective 4 January 1945 to the *Kaukasischer Waffenverband der SS* as *Obersturmfuehrer* which is equivalent to First Lieutenant. Copy of document is herewith enclosed."

Goldberg anxiously scanned the list and found, on the fourth line from the bottom, Soobzokov's name. His hand was trembling as he read the rest of the letter which concluded:

". . . based on similar cases it can be assumed that SUBJECT prior to his official takeover by a regular Waffen-SS unit (4/1/45) was not assigned to regular units of the Waffen-SS but rather performed services with organizations such as *SS Bandenkampfverbaende, SS Einsatzgruppen,* or similar irregular forces."

Goldberg knew enough about the Third Reich to realize these were the antipartisan and mobile killing units, the squads that executed Jews, Communists, and other "misfits."

Goldberg read the letter two more times, each time his excitement and anger increasing. And strangely, he felt frightened, as if some enormous horror was close and threatening. Suddenly he remembered that just a few hours ago he had politely shaken hands with Soobzokov. He thought about that for a minute and then he put the letter from Berlin in his pocket.

From that moment on, Harold Goldberg no longer had any doubts about who was lying. From that moment on, he was determined to get "Tom" Soobzokov.

FOR the next six months Harold Goldberg occupied himself with interviews and official documents, prying and pushing into the past, questioning anyone he could locate who had ever met Tscherim Soobzokov. When Goldberg was done, the blanks and pauses had been filled, the vain posturings and cynical half-truths had been corrected. An entire life was assembled in Goldberg's files.

Here was the biography of a remarkably persistent individual, a man who, despite the demands of three radically diverse cultures, had been able to maintain an awful continuity of personality and behavior. As Goldberg's Social Security report detailed, it was the biography of a rogue, a crook, and a war criminal.

Soobzokov restructured and altered his visible behavior as the times and the countries demanded, but his actions were always grounded in a well-established mechanism that insisted he strive for success and public recognition. He needed to be thought of as a leader. Obsessively, and perhaps inevitably, he chose corrupt, coolly pragmatic paths to the top. It was a conspiracy of historical fates that gave Soobzokov the opportunity to join the Nazis and then, years later, a Democratic machine. Yet, he never determined—or judged—the ethics of either party. He objectively chose and instinctively followed men he thought would be winners. If he ever felt an excuse were necessary, perhaps Soobzokov could plead he was only following his own orders, motivated by an amoral and compulsively success-oriented psyche.

Soobzokov's life, Goldberg discovered, was filled with a pattern of government service, a succession of public roles that were unanimously clouded with charges of larceny. As a young man in the Caucasus town of his birth, Tachatamukai, Soobzokov worked as a county clerk and tax collector. Soobzokov volunteered and Paterson Circassians confirmed this information. However, the reason for his subsequent dismissal and imprisonment are debated. On his application for an immigrant visa to the United States written from Jordan in 1955, Soobzokov admitted he "was arrested by the Soviet authorities in 1940 for about two months and a half under pretext of a political offense. . . ." Settled in Paterson, though, Soobzokov insisted he was imprisoned by the advancing German army after he "protested giving them lists of local Jews." On other occasions, Soobzokov unself-consciously changed this story, explaining he had been arrested for "throwing a rock at a judge who had imprisoned my older brother." What had his older brother been convicted of? "I forget, honestly," Soobzokov says. Perhaps this revenging assault was just an act Soobzokov dreamed of committing. The reality was more conventional. Soobzokov had been arrested by the Soviets for embezzling farm tax funds. "The Germans," remembered Hisa Torchako, "gave many of the prisoners an opportunity to be released if they would join the occupation forces. In Tscherim Soobzokov they found a man they could use and they used him."

Soobzokov never denied he served with the Germans; he simply altered the specifics of his service to fit his audience. In an interview with *The Paterson News* following his appointment to the zoning board, Soobzokov explained he had been "shipped as a semi-forced laborer to Rumania" in 1942, where he "worked as a transportation worker and was later transferred to Hungary and Austria." Again, on his immigration visa application written from Jordan, he was more candid: "1943 to 1945 moved with the retreating German army until I finally reached Villach, Austria, in 1945."

The image Soobzokov tried to create was of a victim, a man captured and forced to serve. The reality, as confirmed by testimony from Circassians and the official Nazi records, is different: Only volunteers from occupied countries served in the SS.

When the German armed forces invaded Russia on June 22, 1941, the Wehrmacht troops were accompanied by small, mechanized killing units of the SS. These SS Einsatzgruppen troops were to operate in front-line areas, moving from town to town executing Jews, Communists, and "partisans" on the spot. Years later, as the horror became more routinized and sophisticated, the Jews of central, western, and southwestern Europe would, instead, be transported to killing centers; in these opening phases of the "final solution," though, Russian Jewry was to be overtaken and killed immediately.

Contemporary history often conveniently forgets that large numbers of local police, civil servants, and other volunteers eagerly joined these advancing Einsatzgruppen forces of the SS. These men were welcomed by the SS officers because they spoke the local language, were familiar with the surrounding terrain, and—not unimportantly—often brought to these pogroms a traditional enthusiasm that the German SS lacked. The great majority of the German Einsatzgruppen officers were professional men: At least one was an opera singer, a few were physicians, and a large number were lawyers. These men, as Goldberg read in Raul Hilberg's *The Destruction of the European Jews,* "were in no sense hoodlums, delinquents, common criminals or sex maniacs." These men were trained, efficient killers. The local SS volunteers were often another sort. Hilberg quotes a former Einsatzkommando chief, speaking after the war: "We were actually frightened by the blood-thirstiness of these people."

As part of these mobile killing operations in Russia, SS chief Heinrich Himmler also organized the SS Bandenkampfverbaende, the supposedly antipartisan units. Actually, these troops were a supplement to the Einsatzgruppen units, another rationale for invading civilian areas and hunting down Jews.

Soobzokov, according to the official records and the testimony of eyewitnesses, joined these Einsatzgruppen units and was observed participating in the capture of civilians who were then immediately executed in the towns of Edepsuikay #1 and Edepsuikay #2. The specifics of any other crimes Soobzokov might have committed while a member of these extermination troops eluded Goldberg: Nearly all the eyewitnesses were dead. Goldberg told himself, however, that a man does not rise to become an Obersturmfuehrer, a first lieutenant in the SS, by shirking duty. And Goldberg's imagination struggled with the details of the crimes the Einsatzgruppen committed in the name of duty: SS activities in Russia were responsible for the murder of 1,400,000 Jews.

The SS, though, was just a springboard, another practical alliance for the ambitious Soobzokov. The Circassian Obersturmfuehrer, Goldberg decided, had a grander strategy. The SS colonel who arrested Issa Hoket had revealed these plans: "Soobzokov is your *fuehrer*." Soobzokov, as he would during other stages of his life, had convinced the authorities he was a leader of the tribe, the chief who could deliver foot soldiers (or, years later, votes). It was also during this period that Soobzokov made the obligatory marriage for a man determined to play a major role in the New Order. His wife was the daughter of a Circassian Vlasov colonel, an officer in the Wehrmacht-equipped army of renegade Russians.

The Thousand Year Reich lasted just four more years and Soobzokov's grandiose scheme and career were ruined. Worse, he was a wanted man: The Russians were searching for any Soviet citizen who had served with the Germans, and the Allies on April 26, 1945, issued a directive ordering the automatic arrest of "all Waffen-SS down to the lowest noncommissioned rank." An SS Obersturmfuehrer would be a fairly sizable catch.

Soobzokov was quickly captured by the British, according to evidence Goldberg discovered in the Tolstoy Foundation files, but he also quickly escaped. On the run, Soobzokov and a small group of Circassians were again detained, this time by the French. By now Soobzokov had shed his incriminating SS uniform and had managed, once more, to portray himself as a Circassian leader. Fearful he would be repatriated to Russia, Soobzokov ingeniously convinced the French authorities he and his band of Circassians had originally been settled in Greece. The French obligingly allowed these collaborators to return to Greece through Italy. Once Soobzokov reached Italy, however, he abandoned all plans of going to Greece and, instead, went to the Turkish Consulate in Naples hoping to emigrate. From Naples, Soobzokov was sent to the Turkish Embassy in Rome where, as self-proclaimed spokesman for all Circassian refugees, he argued for their resettlement in Turkey.

The Turks were not interested in allowing the Circassians to settle, but Soobzokov was not deterred. He remained in Rome until 1947, knocking on other embassy doors, describing himself in those early days of the Cold War as the head of a Circassian refugee contingent that refused to return to a Communist-ruled homeland.

Finally, in October 1947, the readily adaptable Soobzokov made the right connection. Now portraying himself as a representative of Moslem Circassian refugees, he convinced the Egyptian government to send him to Cairo. From Cairo he was sent to Jordan where he met with King Abdullah, a rather difficult monarch known to end negotiations by ordering that the supplicant's skull be transformed into a polo ball. The glib Soobzokov avoided this fate and returned to Italy literally a new man. He was now calling himself Abuel-Karin in deference to his new homeland and he had decided to become a devout Moslem. Most importantly, he had convinced King Abdullah to accept an unlimited number of Circassian immigrants.

Soobzokov, despite his newly found religiosity, was not prepared to wait until the next world for his reward. A fellow Circassian now living in Paterson remembered some of Soobzokov's money-making ventures on the boat trip from Italy to Jordan: "Soobzokov was smart all right. Right away he learned Italian so that he would have to act as our spokesman. He tells us the Italian captain of the boat is really taking us to Russia, not Jordan. But this captain may be persuaded to change his mind if he is given enough money. So Soobzokov goes around the boat collecting whatever he can get. He doesn't realize that my wife is Italian. She speaks to the captain and he just laughs. I tell this to Soobzokov and he tells me to keep quiet or he will kill me.

"Then I notice another thing about Soobzokov. Always in the middle of the meal he returns to his cabin. I ask him why and he shows me. Inside his cabin is a pile of silverware he has been stealing. He never missed an opportunity."

In Jordan, Soobzokov once more returned to public service, working in the city of Amman in the office of the controller, and, later—significantly—in the office of employment. It was in Jordan that Soobzokov first earned his reputation as a man who could provide other Circassians with jobs—for a fee. And it was also in Jordan that Soobzokov started feuding with established Circassian leaders. Like Idriss, these were educated and successful men who looked down on the embarrassingly ambitious civil servant.

The Mufti family was Jordan's most distinguished Circassian family. They were doctors, lawyers, and scholars and they served in high government positions: A Mufti had been both prime minister and president of the Senate. When members of this family heard reports that a Circassian, a recent immigrant, was introducing himself as leader of the tribe, they became infuriated. A petition was circulated throughout the Circassian community of Amman denouncing Soobzokov as "a troublemaker and a Communist." While the latter charge was not true of Soobzokov—why should he join the Party? The Communists were not a powerful factor in Jordanian politics—it might have been true of his brother who eventually returned to Russia and worked in the Soviet bureaucracy. This petition led to a formal investigation by the Jordanian Political Bureau. Brigadier Ozeir Ayub found the charges groundless, a rumor inspired by tribal antagonisms. His characterization of the public Soobzokov, though, might just as accurately have been written by a superficial observer twenty-five years later in Paterson: "He is a conspicuous leader who likes leadership and loves to help people in a manner that arouses the envy of those around him."

Soobzokov's arrival in Jordan coincided with the first Arab-Israeli war and, according to sworn statements Goldberg received from Paterson Circassians, Soobzokov made another practical alliance; the Palestine refugee organizations could be a promising connection for an ingenious man. Mahamet Perchich in his statement to Goldberg wrote: "During my stay in Jordan, it was 1949, I was witness of a conversation between Tscherim Soobzokov and the head of the Palestinian Arabs refugee camp, when Mr. Soobzokov told the Arabs about his activities during World War II. As part of his story Mr. Tscherim Soobzokov told the Arabs that if all those Jews he liquidated during World War II were now in Palestine, all the Arabs in the camp would not be enough to drink the blood of all those Jews. The same day the head of the camp gave an evening of festivities in honor of Mr. Tscherim Soobzokov." And Danil Gussov in his statement wrote: "While in Jordan Mr. Soobzokov used to show Palestine refugee Arab leaders his documents with photos certifying his membership in Nazi execution commandos and that he was a killer of Jews in World War II, for which Mr. Soobzokov received material help from Arab leaders. I am witness of many cases while in Jordan when Mr. Tscherim Soobzokov and his brother used to come home with food provisions which they received from Palestine refugee organizations."

It was also during this period that Teymuraz Bagration of the Tolstoy Foundation first came to Jordan. Bagration, a sharply featured, aristocratic White Russian, who, despite the demands of travel in a primitive country managed to confront each new day displaying a precise half-inch of freshly starched white pocket handkerchief, offers another view of the resourceful Soobzokov: "Back then I was running the Foundation office in Amman. We were trying to help those Circassians who wanted to settle in Jordan or who preferred to immigrate to the United States. It was a very exciting time, a sort of Lawrence atmosphere. You know, all those Arabs running around in their costumes. Anyway, I did not know how I was going to set up an office. And then on my first day in the space we rented in the Anwan Building, Soobzokov arrives. He asks me, 'Do you need any typewriters? Do you need any interpreters?' I don't know how he did it, but he got me typewriters that very afternoon. Oh, he's a very colorful character, that Soobzokov."

By 1955, Soobzokov decided to leave Jordan. Reflecting on the decision twenty years later, he explained with candor, "I left because Syria had just established diplomatic ties with Russia and if Jordan was to follow suit, I knew I might be in trouble. And there just seemed to be so many more opportunities in America. Jordan was a poor country."

Soobzokov, sponsored by the Tolstoy Foundation, arrived on the S.S. *Saturnia* with a large group of Jordanian Circassians in April 1955. And, as Bagration observed, the always adaptable Soobzokov did not wait long before publicly trying to re-establish his leadership: "I usually met the Circassian refugees as they came off the boat in New York. This time, when I got there, I find Soobzokov in a large glass booth with the immigration and customs people. He was assisting the officials, working as an interpreter. And he had been in this country for just two minutes."

Soobzokov, though, apparently had a difficulty in quickly making the right connections in this country. He worked at a car wash, while at nights he studied to be an insurance salesman. After a year of this work, Soobzokov openly admitted defeat. He complained to friends of the long hours and miserable salary, and said he was returning to the Middle East to work as an antiques importer. Actually, as Goldberg discovered, the expedient and convincing Soobzokov returned to the Middle East as a government employee—Soobzokov was now working for the CIA.

After a conversation with officials of the Tolstoy Foundation, Goldberg checked Form 941A in the Finance and Accounting Office of the U.S. Army Civilian Payroll Section. According to the information on this form, employee number 37–30–9646, Tscherim Soobzokov, was paid $4,600 for the quarter ending September 30, 1957. The Army Civilian Payroll Section, Goldberg learned, has traditionally been a conduit for paying low-level CIA employees.

An amused Bagration was even more specific about Soobzokov's work for the government in the Middle East: "First you must remember that Soobzokov was not even a citizen when he was sent to Lebanon. I find it amazing that he was able to make the contacts so quickly. I guess he always kept in touch with people in the Jordanian Defense Department and perhaps they put him in touch with the right people in this country. Anyway, that man is really something.

"Soobzokov, as I remember, was assigned to Beirut just after the Marines landed in 1958. He was then sent to Jordan. His job was to get local labor leaders to cooperate with the Americans. He would act as a glorified interpreter and he also distributed cash to those in the labor movement whom the United States was trying to woo."

Alexis Wrangel, another aristocratic émigré Tolstoy Foundation official who was stationed in the Middle East in 1957, offered a further account of Soobzokov's actions in Jordan. Wrangel, the socially well-connected son of a czarist general famous for leading a regiment against the Bolsheviks, had a career of drifting in and out of work for the Tolstoy Foundation and the U.S. government. An Air Force pilot who was forced to give up flying "because it made me dizzy," he then—ostensibly—devoted his life to his true passion—riding. While head of the Tolstoy Middle Eastern office in the 1950s, he appeared to be spending the majority of his time riding with the president of Lebanon, another devoted equestrian. And after leaving the Foundation, Wrangel worked for the U.S. Embassy in Buenos Aires under Ambassador Robert McClintock, an ambassador known affectionately in diplomatic circles as McHorse. But, it now appears that Wrangel, who has since retired to his own stud farm in California, had other things on his mind besides horses. During a conversation with Goldberg he let slip, "It was I who had Soobzokov booted out of Jordan in 1957. I just wrote a letter to Allen Dulles and a week later Soobzokov got the boot."

Wrangel first admitted he was a CIA operative while working for the Tolstoy Foundation, but later decided, "I wrote the letter because I was a good, personal friend of Mr. Dulles. If Soobzokov were CIA, I would have laid off.

"I wrote the letter because Soobzokov was a pain in the ass. He was becoming involved in local politics and I couldn't afford to keep such people around when the Mid-East situation was so explosive. It was a very delicate situation. People were chucking bombs at King Hussein every day. So when people smelled wrong, we tried to get them out of the situation. Soobzokov was one of those professional refugees who was just a bad egg."

Bagration also remembers Wrangel's fury at Soobzokov: "Wrangel's sister was married to the British Ambassador in Jordan so he knew just about everything. Anyway, according to British intelligence, Soobzokov was meeting with the Palestinians when the Americans were supporting Hussein. Wrangel was frantic. He even called me up to complain about Soobzokov's cheek. Then he writes to Dulles and has Soobzokov pulled back to this country."

Soobzokov vehemently denies that he ever worked for the federal government or the CIA. He insists he was just an antiques dealer in the Middle East in 1957. Both the Defense Department and the CIA also deny ever having employed Soobzokov.

On his return to Paterson, Soobzokov finally succeeded in establishing himself in local government for the third time in as many countries. His American incarnation proved to be his most successful. Here was a political bureaucracy designed for opportunists. Abuel-Karin quickly and gracefully made the change to "Tom," the Democrat.

But, as in Jordan, Soobzokov again became involved in a feud with another established leader. Except this time the resulting investigation was not conducted by a superficial and indulgent Jordanian brigadier.

"I didn't give a shit about some petty Circassian dispute," said Harold Goldberg. "My job is to talk to people. At first I didn't believe what they were telling me. But when I was convinced this guy was a Nazi war criminal, I made up my mind to nail that bastard to the wall."

Harold Goldberg had now assembled three thick files of evidence. His job, he was certain, was over. He would present his case against Tscherim Soobzokov to the Social Security Administration, the Immigration and Naturalization Service, and the U.S. Attorney in Newark.

Said Goldberg, "I did all my work. Now I just want to sit back and watch justice be done."

THE five Circassians were enthusiastic and hopeful when they received the official notice from the Immigration and Naturalization Service asking them to appear at the Newark office at 10 A.M. They had followed Goldberg's instructions and had written a long letter to the INS detailing Tscherim Soobzokov's World War II activities. At first they had been reluctant to write, but Goldberg had insisted. He argued, "You don't have anything to be afraid of. This is America. That bastard can't touch you." They did not flatly agree with Goldberg, but they trusted his intensity; it made them braver and more confident. And, they *wanted* to believe they no longer had anything to fear.

On the morning of the interview, the five Circassians seated in a long corridor in the INS offices had forgotten they had ever been reluctant to testify. American justice, just as Goldberg promised, had responded promptly. They were now exuberant, eager to tell the INS all they knew: names, dates, and locations.

Askar Chesseby, a handsome, prematurely gray-haired man, was called first. He remembers, "I gave a Mr. Sieb from Immigration a sworn statement telling all I knew about Soobzokov. While we were talking, someone opened a side door and I saw a man sitting on the other side of the door. He looked like he was taking notes. I didn't pay any attention to him at the time. Only later did I wonder who that man was and why he was listening. Anyway, when I'm done and Mr. Sieb is thanking me, that door opens again and the man who was listening calls Mr. Sieb over. They talk for a minute and then Mr. Sieb tells me I can go. I join my friends in the hall outside Mr. Sieb's office. About five, ten minutes later, this Mr. Sieb comes out and says, 'There will be no more interviews today. I am sorry, but we will get in touch with you again very shortly.' So we all leave. We were, you can understand, confused and upset. I don't want to give up, though. I call Mr. Sieb two times in the next two weeks and ask him when are the others going to testify. He tells me not to worry. Three weeks pass and I call him again. This time he tells me, 'I cannot pursue this Soobzokov matter anymore. If you still wish to pursue it further, I suggest you speak with the U.S. Attorney.' And then he hangs up. That was the last we heard from him."

In the weeks that followed, these Circassians grew anxious and uncomfortable. The strange behavior of the INS became, in their minds, another example of Soobzokov's total control. Any man who was friends with congressmen, Masons, and teamsters, they were convinced, would have no trouble controlling the Immigration Service. Each time they told the story of Chesseby's interview, Soobzokov's

power expanded until, in one version, it was Soobzokov
who was seated in the next room taking notes.

Goldberg again told them that their fears were unfounded. He said there must be a good reason why Sieb
had not interviewed the others. It all would become clear
in a while. But this time Goldberg was not very convincing. He, too, was puzzled that the INS had refused even to
hear eyewitness testimony about Soobzokov. And the
Circassians, frightened to the edge of panic, waited, wondering what would happen next.

They did not have to wait long. Hisa Torchako received
the first call.

"Torchako, do you plead innocent or guilty?" the midnight caller demanded in Circassian.

Torchako asked, "What do you mean?" But he was only
bluffing. He had no doubt what the caller meant and as a
deep voice continued in Circassian, Torchako wrote down
every word.

"Why did you go to the Immigration people?"

"I didn't," Torchako insisted.

"Don't lie. Soobzokov and the congressman have received a full basket of reports. If you have decided to live
in this country as Soobzokov's enemy, you will have to live
in fear. Anytime you go in your car, something could explode. Nobody can help you, Torchako. Soobzokov can do
what he wants."

And then the caller hung up.

Other Circassians also received phone calls that week.
When Goldberg visited, they now explained they could
not talk because they were sick or were too busy. Others,
through their wives or children, simply insisted they no
longer spoke English.

Mahomoud Chucko, though, told Goldberg he was "too
old to be afraid." "What," he asked, "can anyone do to an
old man like me?" Chucko's wife provided the answer.
According to Mrs. Chucko, "On October 14th I was walking home with my two grandchildren. We were crossing
the street when suddenly a car comes straight at us. I

thought it was going to hit us. I pull my grandchildren back and jump back on the sidewalk. If I hadn't jumped away, that car would have killed my two grandchildren and me. I look up and the driver of the car is just sitting there laughing." Mrs. Chucko submitted sworn testimony to the FBI that the amused driver was Tscherim Soobzokov.

Hisa Torchako also experienced more than anonymous phone threats. Whether he was the attacker or he was attacked is still debated. But the legal reality, as defined by the Municipal Court of Passaic County, is clear: Hisa Torchako, a fifty-one-year-old man, was guilty of assault against two husky men in their twenties.

Both sides agree some sort of incident occurred when Kazbek Soobzokov and his friend Halil Yavus encountered Torchako at a Circassian Benevolent Association party. According to the police record, for no apparent reason, the fifty-one-year-old man grabbed Kazbek's left arm, punched him in the chest, and then shoved him backward. After polishing off Kazbek, Torchako turned on Halil who was shoved and pushed in the neck. The police record does not mention that both of the quickly subdued youths were taller and heavier than their middle-aged attacker. And, of course, the police report does not mention that the easily intimidated Kazbek Soobzokov was the same youth *The Paterson News* had described as "confronting" an entire motorcycle gang.

Torchako's version of what happened that night is less eventful: "Kazbek started shouting at me, 'You are dogs. You are dogs.' Then his friend throws a drink in my chest. No one ever came close to me. They just turned and left. The next day two policemen come and arrest me. It cost me $200 just for the bail. Then there are legal fees and fines. And when it is done, I am a criminal with a record. It is a very sad situation. The law in New Jersey belongs to Soobzokov."

The New Jersey law also caught up with Soobzokov's fiercest rival. Dr. Jawad Idriss was charged and convicted in a Passaic County court with "carelessly driving an automobile" with intent of "obstructing, molesting, or interfering" with three women. The three women were Soobzokov's wife, daughter, and daughter-in-law.

Two completely contradictory stories were presented in the courtroom of Municipal Judge William Rosenberg. Sarah Sinforossa, Soobzokov's daughter and the wife of a Paterson police officer, testified that on a Saturday afternoon she and her mother and sister-in-law were shopping in a small grocery on Belmont Avenue in Paterson. It was a popular store among the Circassians because it stocked Mid-Eastern foods and magazines; the wooden shelves were filled with cans of tahini and humus and loaves of pita bread. Searching for a particular item, Mrs. Sinforossa testified, she went back to the back of the store and discovered Dr. Idriss standing nearby. Then, "Mr. [not Dr.] Idriss turned to me and said, 'I got your father and now I'm going to get you.' He got me so upset I went back to where my mother was standing and I asked her to please hurry up." Of course, she explained to the judge, she recognized Idriss: "For the past three years he's been conducting a very vicious smear campaign against my father. . . ." The three women immediately left the store. "We got into the car . . . I then proceeded to move my car down the hill. Mr. Idriss came around the corner at a high rate of speed and directed his car into my direction causing me to slam on my brakes. Otherwise I would have contacted with him. I went home. I was so upset I don't even remember how I got home and I called my husband who advised me to call the police."

Dr. Idriss told the court a more innocent story. He had gone to the store to buy a 93-cent package of pita bread. While waiting to be served, he passed the time reading a Lebanese newspaper. He did not talk to or even notice anyone in the store. After paying for the bread, he drove home without incident.

What had occurred? It was, quite simply, a case of Soobzokov's daughter's word against the doctor's. The judge, however, was easily convinced: "I find, beyond any reasonable doubt whatsoever, and I don't believe the doctor's testimony quite frankly." The doctor was convicted and fined $200.

But after reading the transcript, Harold Goldberg had more than a few "reasonable" doubts. He wondered if the incident were even possible. According to the courtroom testimony, Soobzokov's daughter's car was parked up a steep hill around the corner from the grocery. They had entered the store after Dr. Idriss, who had been parked in the middle of the block fronting the store. When the three women left, Idriss, according to the testimony, followed a minute or two later. How could he have known where the women were parked? It was impossible to see through the brick building.

Then there was the question of the cars. Idriss drove a four-cylinder, 1,600-pound Datsun. The Soobzokovs drove a full-size Chevrolet, at least twice the weight of the doctor's import. Could Idriss have rushed into his car, turned the corner, and, while driving uphill for less than "the distance of three car lengths" have already accelerated to "a high rate of speed"? And, why would the doctor try to ram a car when he was going uphill, especially when the car he was driving was half the size of his "victim"? It was Mrs. Sinforossa who testified she "slammed on the brakes." If the doctor's intent were to drive uphill into a collision, her braking would not have prevented any accident. Goldberg knew Idriss to be arrogant and haughty, but he was also shrewd. If the doctor wanted to attack someone, Goldberg was certain he could devise a more effective strategy than ramming his car into another twice its size, a car traveling downhill at, most probably, a faster speed. Idriss could be unpleasant, Goldberg knew, but he was surely too concerned with his own self-importance to be suicidal: The certain victim of the crash as portrayed in the courtroom would have been the Datsun's driver.

There had been a time when Goldberg had argued with the Circassians, telling them their fears were foolish and inflated. That sort of terror might be possible in Russia or under the Nazis, but certainly not in this country. Except now Goldberg had his own suspicions. He, too, began to fit incidents into a pattern, a pattern of premeditated intimidation and terror. When anonymous phone calls wouldn't suffice, the courts—was this possible?—seemed ready to do the dirty work. He was confused. Stories had become twisted and illogical. What seemed clearly lies to him were accepted as true by the courts of New Jersey. Could Soobzokov have this much influence? Goldberg wanted to laugh at himself. He tried to tell himself to cut it out before he also started believing the Masons were a secret group who could kill with impunity. If he hung around these Circassians long enough, he would become as gullible as they were. And yet, he also knew there was no easy explanation for the two court convictions and the INS's inaction. Unless . . . Things were just different, he decided, in Paterson. In that city reality was a subjective state, perceived and defined only by men of power. Truth had become a practical, political question. And when necessary, this "truth" chose powerless men as its victims.

But Goldberg was no backward immigrant who could be pushed around and told day was night. Let them play whatever games they could get away with in Passaic County. This was still his case and he was still determined to see it through. He would confront the authorities and they would have no choice but to listen. Harold Goldberg was not about to be intimidated by any Nazi. No matter who his political friends were.

"I THINK we should have a talk," Goldberg's boss in the Social Security Administration told him. "Right now!"

Goldberg listened as his superior announced that he just had met with two visitors. "A Mr. Soobzokov came to see me and he didn't come alone. He brought a friend with him. A congressman—Congressman Robert Roe. They both came all the way down to Maryland to talk about *you.*

"Soobzokov was very polite and very friendly, but his friend, the congressman, was a little annoyed. He said you've been making trouble. Something about spreading a lot of lies about this Soobzokov being a Nazi. What about it?"

Goldberg explained that while he had been conducting a Social Security investigation, he had uncovered hard evidence that Soobzokov had served with the SS.

"Now you listen," his boss shouted, "this is the Social Security Administration you're working for. You're not here to play cops and robbers. You just pay attention to Social Security cases. You got that?"

Goldberg nodded.

"You'd better get it, because if I hear one more complaint about you calling someone a Nazi while you're working for the government, you've had it. I don't need some congressman telling me he's going to start asking questions in Washington about this department's terrorizing innocent people. You stick to your job. Understand?"

"Yes," said Goldberg.

Goldberg stuck to his job. He submitted a lengthy report detailing all the Social Security violations he was convinced Soobzokov had committed. Goldberg documented incidents of Soobzokov's obtaining duplicate Social Security cards for individuals and his charging fees for helping others receive illegal benefits.

And, on his own time, Goldberg presented his case against Soobzokov to the U.S. Attorney in Newark and to officials of the New Jersey office of the Immigration Service.

It was not long after Goldberg met with the U.S. Attorney that Congressman Roe, a New Jersey Democrat who previously as state commissioner of conservation and economic development had his department come under the scrutiny of special legislative inquiry, held a small ceremony. He presented "Tom" Soobzokov with an American flag in honor of the Circassian's contributions to his adopted country. A picture of the smiling Soobzokov holding his American flag and standing next to his friend, the congressman, appeared in all the Passaic County papers.

IT is nearly two years since Goldberg first submitted his reports to the authorities.

After eight months of considering the charges, the Social Security Administration informed Goldberg that "the statute of limitations is in effect." The charges against Soobzokov, regardless of their validity, were no longer applicable.

The New Jersey office of the INS tells Goldberg whenever he calls that "we are still trying to review the evidence and gather witnesses."

The U.S. Attorney's office also says "the case is still active." But the deputy attorney in charge confided, "This case will never get beyond the preliminary phase."

And Emin Kardan, whose father's death started the investigation, has still not received the Social Security money he had anticipated. The medical bills remain unpaid. When he finishes college, Emin plans to return to Turkey. "American democracy has been a nightmare for me," he complains. "I wish Dr. Idriss and Soobzokov would have a duel and kill each other. They are splitting our people in half. If they want to fight, I'll be glad to supply the pistols."

Dr. Idriss is also depressed. He, too, sometimes talks about leaving the country. "America has been good to Soobzokov," he says. "Already three of the witnesses against him have died. If they wait long enough, all the witnesses will die. Soobzokov will be free forever."

This week, though, Idriss is paying for another ad in the local newspaper. This ad will announce that Tscherim Soobzokov has been expelled from the Circassian Benevolent Association.

Only Soobzokov appears happy. He is happy because he has a new plan. He tells this plan to anyone in Paterson who will listen. "I have many friends in the Middle East," he explains. "I am respected there. Only I could make a deal for the Jews. I love Israel and would like to help that country. I could talk to the Palestine Liberation Front and make them listen."

"Does anyone know Meir Kahane?" Soobzokov asked whomever he cornered at a recent Masons' meeting. "That man is a fighter like me. If I could meet him, together we could settle the Middle East situation. We could save Israel. Do you know him?"

AFTER all else had failed, Harold Goldberg met with Tony DeVito in New York. For three years he had lived with the knowledge that the chief purchasing investigator of Passaic County had been an SS officer, and for three years he had not been able to convince any of the legal authorities that this was a crime worthy of punishment. During these years, Goldberg had suffered more than Soobzokov. Soobzokov had moved on to new schemes and new plans. But Goldberg still lived uncomfortably with the past. He spent his nights sifting through the evidence in his Soobzokov files, hoping that this intense, even obsessive scrutiny would uncover a new detail that could be expanded into a major fact.

Tony DeVito was Goldberg's last hope. Goldberg was not disappointed. DeVito told Goldberg he had brought one Nazi to trial even though they had tried to stop him, and now with the help of Goldberg's files, he would succeed in another case. As soon as a verdict was reached in the Ryan case, DeVito promised to concentrate on Tscherim Soobzokov. The Ryan trial, DeVito explained, was only the first; other trials would follow.

In the meantime DeVito wanted to convince his new friend Harold that he was serious, so he made some preliminary phone calls. He first called the New Jersey INS office. He wanted them to send him the file on Soobzokov. And he wanted to speak to the agent assigned to the case. He wanted to know how thoroughly Goldberg's leads had been pursued.

Two days after his call, DeVito received an answer. There was no agent in charge of a case involving Tscherim Soobzokov. In fact, there was no file, and, therefore, no case.

Before the Ryan trial, DeVito would have been surprised. But not any longer.

He called Goldberg at home that night. "I'm gonna tell you something and I want you to listen. Harold, Odessa has struck again. This is another Ryan case. I can tell a mile away that the fix is in."

Goldberg had no trouble believing DeVito. After hunting Soobzokov for so long and watching him slip away, he told DeVito he could believe anything.

The next day DeVito decided it was time to start an official INS investigation of Soobzokov. He sent copies to the New Jersey office of all the documents Goldberg had given him and instructed that these papers be placed in a file marked "Tscherim Soobzokov."

During the next three weeks DeVito was occupied with the Ryan trial. But in a lull in the proceedings, he called up the Newark INS office.

"Could you get me the file on Soobzokov?" he asked. "There's something I want to check."

The agent left the phone and returned in a few minutes.

"Tony, I got the file . . ."

"Yeah?"

"But, Tony, you're not going to believe this."

"What do you mean?"

"Tony, the file is here all right. But there's nothing inside. It's empty."

2

The Bishop and the Dentist

THERE were so many calls. Everyone seemed to know a Nazi.

A woman from Brooklyn suspected her butcher. Why, DeVito asked. "Well, he has this accent. You know, like a Nazi. But the real giveaway was watching him cut the meat. He just stands there with this sly grin whenever he is slicing through red meat. It's disgusting, all that blood and fat and everything, but he's just smiling to beat the band. And besides, he's a rotten crook. He tried to cheat me out of a dollar." Another lady didn't like the way a Forest Hills baker shoved his bread into the oven. And then there was the tailor from the Bronx who had suspicions about his rabbi.

"It got so after a while that I just wouldn't take phone calls from strangers," explained DeVito. "It seemed like every nut in New York was discovering a Nazi under his bed."

Dr. Charles Kremer also tried calling Tony DeVito at

the Immigration Service. He, too, had a name. For twenty
years Dr. Kremer had been on the trail of one man, a man
who had come to America in 1950 as a displaced person
and settled in Michigan. And for twenty years the authorities had insisted they were not interested. Now, when Dr.
Kremer called the much publicized Tony DeVito, he was
informed, "Mr. DeVito is out" or "Mr. DeVito is in
court." To Kremer, these excuses were obviously trans-
parent; here was further proof that the cover-up had
reached every level of the Immigration Service. Still, he
did not stop calling. He called not so much to ask for
help—he was convinced that was useless—but to issue a
warning. He wanted to notify the government he would
not give up. Each time he called, Dr. Kremer left the
same message: "Tell DeVito that Charlie Kremer has still
not forgotten about Valerian Trifa."

Yellow message slips with that strange name, Valerian
Trifa, were shoved daily across DeVito's desk. DeVito
would be working or on the phone and he would absent-
mindedly glance at one of the slips, an unexplained intruder into his routine. There was something familiar
about that name. Trifa? Could it be? On a whim, DeVito
checked his list with the 59 names and there it was, page
two, near the bottom: "Trifa, Valerian a.k.a. Viorel."

"I figured this guy Kremer was on to something, all
right. The name he gave me was on the list. But to tell
you the truth, I ducked him," DeVito later said. "I was in
the middle of the Ryan case and then there was Goldberg
who was going on about Soobzokov. And I still hadn't
figured out what was happening to all the files. I didn't
know who I could trust anymore. So I ducked him, clear
and simple.

"Once I got the answers to a couple of questions, I
was going to get back to Kremer. I figured that I could
only handle one Nazi at a time. It wasn't that I didn't know
his problem. If he had waited twenty years, he could
surely wait a few more months. I was certain there would
be plenty of time to get back to Dr. Kremer."

But, Dr. Charles Kremer was not the sort of man to

wait idly. And Tony DeVito never suspected that his time with the Immigration Service was rapidly running out.

THE bishop was celebrating. Today, May 13, 1957, Bishop Valerian Trifa had become a United States citizen. Champagne corks popped and toasts were proposed by the priests assembled in the large dining hall. As the festive evening continued and the participants became caught up in the free-flowing liquor and champagne, the priests became louder and more joyous. They were also celebrating: If their bishop's secret was safe, so was their own. But the short, stocky man at the end of the long wooden table turned quiet as the evening progressed. Perhaps the champagne had made Bishop Trifa reflective. He sat silently, absently fondling his black horn-rimmed glasses.

At least one person at the table decided Bishop Trifa was considering his good fortune. Only seven years before it had seemed remarkable that Trifa was even allowed to enter America as a displaced person, that his obviously invented autobiography had remained unchallenged by the Immigration authorities. And now today, his past seemed truly past, protected—if not endorsed—by the government which had granted him citizenship. Trifa had arrived from Italy as a penniless history teacher, a layman who had taught at a church school. This evening he sat at the head of the table in a wood-paneled room of his twenty-five-room house, the main residence of his two-hundred-acre estate in northern Michigan. He was surrounded by old friends, friends from Bucharest and Buchenwald. And, most remarkable of all, these men were now priests and Trifa was their bishop.

The man who thought he understood Trifa's silent musings was the only person at the table not dressed in dark clerical robes. His clothes, considering the surroundings, were conspicuously jaunty and bohemian. He wore a dark beret, a red foulard tied loosely around his neck, and open-toed sandals. This outfit, though, was indulged and probably expected by the bishop and his priests: Constantin Antonovici was an artist, a well-known sculptor. Antonovici, a born Rumanian like all the men in the room, had been spending the past six months at the Vatra (as the bishop's estate is called) completing two church commissions: a ten-foot high, carved wooden cross and a room-long iconostasis decorated with carefully carved geometric forms from Rumanian folk art.

The champagne, too, had gone to Antonovici's head and loosened his tongue. It made him aggressive. He approached the silent bishop and asked what many in the room might have been thinking.

"Don't you think that someday the Americans will find out about you?" the sculptor demanded in his high, almost squeaky voice.

The bishop was not annoyed. He was among friends. "Don't be stupid, Antonovici. Who will tell them anything?"

"Many people know," the sculptor persisted. His tone was clearly belligerent. Like the bishop, Antonovici was a short man, but he stood above the seated Trifa trying to look fierce and imposing.

"Oh, you are a fool. I am a bishop. Who can touch me? Things don't fall on my head." The bishop started to laugh and the priests at the table joined him. It was a happy, drunken chorus.

But the sculptor was insistent. "Perhaps you are wrong, bishop. Perhaps someday your past will catch up with you."

The bishop stopped laughing. He no longer was in the mood to indulge this strange little man. He shouted at Antonovici, "With my luck, nothing will ever happen. I have friends in the government. The FBI knows all about me. Hoover protects me. I have been very lucky. Things don't fall on my head. Now you leave me alone, Antonovici. This is an evening to celebrate."

Another toast was quickly proposed and more bottles of champagne were passed around.

Antonovici went back to his chair, no longer light-headed. He sat there, wanting very much to run from the room. But he did not. Instead he drank more champagne. Art, he reminded himself, not politics, was his concern. This was the same excuse he had repeated ever since he had arrived at the Vatra. Usually, it was a sufficient rationale. Tonight, however, was different. He blamed the wine. He blamed Trifa sitting there in his bishop's robes, now a U.S. citizen. But whatever the cause, this evening Antonovici could not repress the memory of another night, a night in January 1941, when he had seen Trifa lead an execution squad into a cell filled with Jews. The scene inside the Bucharest police station remained clear in his mind: the sharp, definite reports of a pistol, and then the uncontrolled fire of many guns rumbling through the concrete building, a loud, curiously anonymous noise, only a backdrop to the lacerating screams of cornered men. But this evening, in the United States as in Bucharest, there was nothing Antonovici could do. Who would punish a bishop? Trifa was right; with his luck, nothing would ever happen. Antonovici was another cornered man; his screams would also be futile.

Antonovici sat with the priests, drinking until early morning. He drank with determined excess, but it was useless. He could not forget. Worse, as dawn approached he sat stunned, though resigned to the inevitability of Trifa's success: The Iron Guard would be re-established in America, protected and sponsored by a bishop of the Rumanian Orthodox Church.

THE next day began late for Antonovici and his drinking companions, but in New York a sixty-year-old dentist was up early. Dr. Charles Kremer's first patient was scheduled for nine, so he had to work quickly to finish typing the letter. Since dawn he had been working intensely at a small desk shoved against the wall in the hallway waiting room of the West Side apartment that served as both his home and office.

Late the night before, Dr. Kremer had received a call from a friend in Detroit. "Charlie," the friend said, "they approved the bastard. They bought his story lock, stock, and barrel. He's now a U.S. citizen and . . ."

"If they think they can get away with this, I'll show them," the dentist immediately yelled into the phone. "They couldn't have done it. They just couldn't have done it. I'll show them," he repeated and then abruptly hung up. After seven years of pursuing Trifa, he interpreted this latest action by the Immigration Service as a private defeat. Like many egotists, he personalized larger and more complex events: The government had chosen to believe Valerian Trifa, war criminal, rather than Charlie Kremer, dentist. A man of ambition accustomed to measuring his accomplishments in superlatives—the first, the best, the only—Kremer refused to believe that Trifa's citizenship was irrevocable.

By early morning Kremer had drafted a letter—this was only his most recent effort; over the past seven years he had written, he estimated, five or six hundred letters about Trifa—to the Immigration Service. He wrote first in blue ink, fast, furious script interrupted by words written in capitals and entire sentences underlined three or four times for emphasis. Then, he corrected this draft with a red ballpoint. The final copy, however, was typed. He typed with only two fingers on an old Remington, searching carefully for each key; this slow, awkward work required much concentration and served as a governor on his emotions.

The dentist was still typing when his first patient arrived shortly after nine.

"Have a seat. You're going to have to wait. This is something terrific I'm doing. Wait till you see what ammunition I put in this letter."

The patient knew about Dr. Kremer and his letters. And he also knew it would be useless to explain he was in a hurry. He had no choice but to sit and wait.

The patient sat on a small, green vinyl couch and passed the time studying the pictures the dentist had hung for public display on the graying, once-white walls of the hallway waiting room. This was not the sort of dentist's office that provided magazines. On one wall, hanging from a gold curtain rod, was a large—at least a yard long —cardboard blow-up of a photograph of the Warsaw Ghetto Monument. Opposite this was a framed photograph of Golda Meir with a yellowed *New York Times* article taped to the bottom corner. The article was headlined, "Mrs. Meir Says Tension Marked Talk With Pope," and the dentist had neatly underlined a statement by the Israeli prime minister: "The Christian cross is a symbol under which Jews were killed for generations." Scattered about the other walls were framed autographed pictures from President Eisenhower, Vice President Nixon, and the chief rabbi of Israel. Other framed pictures had typed captions: "Dr. C. H. Kremer (r) presents Torah" or "Dr. C. H. Kremer at Lod airport." Also, there were framed citations embellished with intricate script honoring Dr. C. H. Kremer from such diverse sources as the United Jewish Appeal, the state of Oklahoma, and the Masons.

At the end of this memento-filled hallway, the patient could look into the dentist's bedroom. Actually, the dark room—its two windows faced a solid, sooty brick building wall—also served as the dentist's dining and living room. It was a good-sized room, but bulky wooden antique furniture—Kremer's share of a divorce settlement—was crammed into nearly every inch. The drawers of a handsome mahogany dresser were flung open, as if vandalized, exposing a disorder of shirts and underwear. Next to the dresser stood a wooden bookcase filled with other mementos: a row of silver tankards, plaster casts of teeth, a small green buddha, and a silver-colored candelabrum fitted with orange light bulbs. A bed, that also by necessity was a sofa, was covered by a mess of papers and manila folders, part of Kremer's evidence against Bishop Trifa. In the middle of the room, opposite a huge television, was a round wooden table piled with dirty dishes.

"Come on, what are you looking at?" Dr. Kremer yelled to his patient. "Did you come to get a tooth filled or are you from the Board of Health?"

The patient followed the dentist into the front room. Here was a rather neat dental office—all the required equipment and the usual chair—except for a tall steel filing cabinet in the corner of the room. Most of the drawers of the cabinet were open, revealing rows of manila folders wedged haphazardly into spaces much too tight. The drawers had literally popped out of the cabinet like buttons off a tight shirt and many manila files lay scattered on the linoleum floor. This cabinet (and floor) held the details of Dr. Kremer's case against Valerian Trifa. On top of the cabinet was a human skull colored a decaying, earth brown.

Without much ceremony or any questions, Dr. Kremer opened his patient's mouth, poked around a bit, and then started drilling. While he drilled, he stood over his patient and talked.

"This letter is really going to shake those bastards up. Wait till they read what I got. They think they can get away with it, but Charlie Kremer will show them. Won't he?"

The patient, helpless, a drill buzzing in his mouth, could only nod.

"I just asked these *gonifs* a couple of good questions. I asked them how come they let Trifa become a citizen if the law specifically states that anyone who belonged to the Iron Guard before 1952 is excluded from U.S. citizenship. Let them answer that one. And if they tell me they don't believe he was an Iron Guardist, they're full of shit. I sent them proof, eyewitness evidence. I sent them eighty-eight pieces of documentation. Eighty-eight exhibits! Now, gargle.

"Oh, they want to forget all right. But I won't let them.

I can't forget and I'm not going to let them. You see that skull?"

The dentist pointed to the head on top of the filing cabinet and the patient, his mouth now filled with cotton, again only nodded.

"I keep that skull as a reminder. That skull is something terrific. It reminds me of that bastard Trifa and all the people he killed. Any time I want to give up, I just look at that skull and I know I can fight anyone.

"They think they can give me the business, those sons of bitches. I told them they had better send me a copy of Trifa's naturalization hearing. I want to know what questions they asked and how he answered them. I'll show them. He may be a citizen, but it's not over yet. There's an old Rumanian proverb, 'Every bird dies by his tongue.' And Trifa's one bird that's not going to fly away. I sent the Immigration people every speech he made in 1941. It's his own words. When they read what Trifa said, that bastard is going to be sorry Charlie Kremer ever heard his name. I can document everything Trifa did in 1941."

ON the evening of January 20, 1941, a husky young man dressed in the dark green military breeches and tunic of the Iron Guard, a wide leather bandolier across his chest and a pistol on his hip, mounted the pedestal of the statue of King Michael in University Square, Bucharest, Rumania. Over six thousand students and Iron Guardists, many also armed, filled the square eager to hear what the speaker would say about the assassination of a German major, part of the Nazi "advisory" contingent in Bucharest. The crowd quieted as twenty-six-year-old Viorel Trifa (the name would be changed to Valerian ten years later to symbolize his "entering monasticism"), president of the National Union of Christian Rumanian Students, and leader of the Iron Guard student movement, began his speech.

The political events culminating in this 1941 rally actually started in the 1930s with the rise of the pro-Nazi and anti-Jewish Iron Guard, the combat arm of the Legion of Archangel Michael, a mystical fascist movement. These Iron Guard legionnaires were the Rumanian equivalent of Hitler's "Brownshirts," a major political and social force which pushed Rumania into a closer alliance with Nazi Germany and advocated strict laws against the country's 800,000 Jews. (By the end of the war, Rumanian Jewry, once the third largest Jewish community in Europe, would be reduced to 300,000 survivors.)

King Carol II was ruling Rumania when the war began, and he found himself caught between the domestic agitation of the Iron Guard and the advancing Russian army. When, in June 1940, the Russians occupied and then demanded the cession of northern Bucovina and Bessarabia, King Carol, on Germany's advice, agreed. By July 1, 1940, Carol proclaimed a reorientation of Rumania's foreign policy as "a neutral ally" of the Axis. To placate the legionnaires, in August 1940, laws against the Jews were proclaimed, laws which later would be instrumental in the routinized destruction of Rumanian Jewry: Jewishness was legally defined, and economic restriction and ghettoization measures were enacted.

The Iron Guard, though, would not be satisfied with anything less than a Nazi Rumania. Taking advantage of the humiliating cession of the northern part of Transylvania to Hungary in September 1940, the Guardists escalated their public agitation against King Carol. This led to a bloodless coup and a new government—the "regime of the legionnaires." Carol's son, Michael I, became King and General Ion Antonescu, long a supporter and associate of the Iron Guard, became *conducator* (leader) of Rumania. This government was largely staffed by Guardist leaders: The vice president was Horia Sima, the chief Iron Guard commander, while other legionnaires were ministers of the Foreign, Labor, and Interior Departments.

Under this "regime of the legionnaires" all political parties and movements except the Iron Guard were outlawed and 120,000 Nazi troops entered Rumania as "a military advisory mission to protect Rumania's oil fields." In November 1940, Rumania formally joined the Axis.

In these first few months of power, the legionnaire government passed two additional anti-Jewish laws: a decree dated October 5, 1940, which authorized the state expropriation of Jewish agricultural property, and a decree dated November 16, 1940, which outlined the gradual dismissal of Jews working in private commerce and industry. Radu Lecca, commissar for Jewish questions in the Antonescu government, directed the ghettoization and deportation of Jews, while Jasinclia, the Iron Guard commander of Bucharest and the government's labor minister, supervised the "Rumanianization" of Jewish property.

It was in this period of political turmoil that an ambitious theological student, Viorel Trifa, joined the Iron Guard. As a high school student in Sibiu, Trifa had already established himself as an effective and fiery orator through his speeches as president of the St. George Orthodox Christian Association. After high school, he attended the Theological School in Chisinau, where he once more rose to a position of power after being elected president of the students in theology and president of the Students' Association of Chisinau. It was while at theological school that Trifa was recruited into the Iron Guard, becoming an active member and quickly rising to the rank of commandant. The Guardist leader, Horia Sima, later remarked that he saw in Trifa "a young man who could recruit Rumanian youth, the future of the movement."

Presumably, Trifa's initiation followed Guardist ritual: A new legionnaire sanctified the occasion by sucking blood from a slash on the arm of every member of his "nest." Then the recruit wrote in his own blood an oath to obey the instructions of his superiors, even if the order were to murder.

As Guardist fantasies became actual horror, the legionnaires would prepare for pogroms with another atavistic ritual. Each Guardist let an ounce of his own blood from a cut on his wrist flow into a goblet. This blood-filled goblet was then passed around like a sacrament, each legionnaire drinking "his strength."

By 1936, Trifa was no longer a theology student, but a full-time legionnaire and "student leader." Elected president of the students at the University of Bucharest in 1936, after conducting an Iron Guard–sponsored campaign, he attended a legion congress in Targu-Mures. At this conference, according to eyewitnesses, Trifa spoke in support of a Guardist "death commando" squad that would liquidate "Jews and other enemies of the state."

But when Rumania's first pro-Nazi regime of Prime Minister Octavian Goga fell in 1937, the Iron Guard leaders were arrested. Rumanian records still exist indicating "mandat de arestare No. 65660" for Viorel Trifa. Apparently Trifa was already considered a significant Guardist leader. The legionnaires, however, were quickly released and in the September 1940 coup Trifa and his fellow Guardists came to power. His official position was president of the Union of Christian Students of Rumania, a title which institutionalized Trifa's role as head of the student wing of the Iron Guard.

With the adoption of the "regime of legionnaires'" anti-Jewish decrees, special Iron Guard squads rushed to enforce these laws, confiscating property and conducting "spontaneous" pogroms. Twenty years later, eyewitnesses would testify that Valerian Trifa not only participated in, but also directed a pogrom on November 26, 1940, in Ploesti.

The evening of January 20, 1941, when Trifa climbed to the pedestal of the statue of King Michael in University Square, though, had been planned to be Trifa's greatest moment. This was not to be just another speech or rally. His speech, Horia Sima and other Guardists were later to testify, had been chosen as the signal for a new revolt. The legionnaires had long been dissatisfied with Antonescu

and the relative slowness with which the general was instituting the Iron Guard revolution. Now, an assassination
on the streets of Bucharest provided the legionnaires with
an excuse to overthrow the general. And Trifa had been
designated to initiate this putsch.

The assassination had occurred two days earlier when
Major Boering, one of the 120,000 Nazi military advisors,
had been shot while strolling along a Bucharest street by
a member of the Greek underground. The Iron Guard,
skillfully opportunistic, immediately responded to the
assassination, insisting that such violence necessitated the
need for Nazi troop reinforcements and harsher restric-
tions against the Jewish agitators. Just hours after the
murder a proclamation signed by Viorel Trifa, president
of the National Union of Christian Rumanian Students,
was plastered to walls throughout Bucharest, and the next
day it was printed in newspapers and broadcast on radio.
The proclamation attacked "the defenders of the murder . . . the kikes" and issued a series of demands: "We
demand the replacing of all Masonic and kike sympathizers in government; we demand a Legionnaire government . . . the Rumanian students cannot tolerate the
murdering of German soldiers in the streets of the capitol
by agents of Britain." This proclamation established the
rationale for the Iron Guard revolt.

From the statue of King Michael, Viorel Trifa delivered
the speech which he and Sima had hoped would initiate
a new revolt. Trifa, according to eyewitnesses, began cautiously, talking in a steady, calm voice. Below him, the
square was packed with six thousand listeners and the
crowd continued to increase.

"This war started," Trifa began, "with the French Revolution. The origin of the old world was these miraculous
words—liberty, egality, and fraternity. These words liberated the people from one tyrant who had enslaved them
and, instead, delivered them to hundreds of thousands of
tyrants exploiting these principles.

"People were never equal. Not even in the first days of
the Revolution. These ideas of equality served a category

of people who enslaved others and profited by these confused ideas. These ideas of equality served the kikes. The kikes of Europe have intensified their struggle for emancipation at the moment when the revolutionary spirit reached the Rhine. . . . The leadership of the people has fallen into the hands of a group of kikes and Jew lovers who are ruling everything, especially history. The League of Nations has served the interests of Jewry to dominate the world. London has become the center of world capitalism. On the shores of the fabulous Albion, Jewry has found a good place from where it will spread its spider web over the entire world. . . ."

Trifa's voice now rising, the crowd intermittently shouting and applauding ferociously, he concluded his hourlong speech in a hoarse scream:

"Even if Adolf Hitler had done nothing else than wage this huge struggle of National Socialism, which leads to the unmasking of the fight against Judaism, he would still have risen to great peaks of history, as he blazed a new path."

When the applause subsided, Trifa ordered the crowd to form columns. Then, following the strategy he had formulated with Sima, Trifa led his marchers through the streets of Bucharest. First the demonstrators marched to the king's palace and then to the Italian and German Embassies where they cheered the assembled foreign ministers. By now the crowd had swelled, according to witnesses, to nearly ten thousand and, as planned, Trifa led the marchers to the steps of General Antonescu's palace. The crowd surged forward and government troops and tanks started firing. The Iron Guard revolt had begun.

By late evening the revolt had degenerated into a pogrom. Raul Hilberg, drawing on interviews with eyewitnesses, wrote in *The Destruction of the European Jews:* "Iron Guardists had stormed into the Jewish quarter, burning down synagogues, demolishing stores, and devastating private apartments. For miles around the city the Guardists had left traces of their revolution. On January 24, travelers on the Bucharest-Ploesti road discovered at Baneasa over a hundred Jewish bodies without clothes. Gold teeth had been knocked out of the mouths of the dead. . . . On the road to Giurgiu passers-by stumbled upon another eighty bodies of Jewish slain. In the city itself the German military attaché was busy collecting casualty reports. 'In the Bucharest morgue,' he wrote, 'one can see hundreds of corpses, but they are mostly Jews.' Jewish sources report that the victims had not merely been killed; they had been butchered. In the morgue bodies were observed hanging like carcasses of cattle. A witness saw a girl of five hanging by her feet like a calf, her entire body smeared with blood."

During the three-day Iron Guard revolt, the Rumanian press reported that 118 Jews were killed and 26 were wounded. The true death toll, as estimated by Jewish sources, was between 4,000 and 6,000 in Bucharest and nearly 10,000 throughout the country.

Twenty years later many people were still alive who could remember hearing Viorel Trifa's proclamation against "the kike sympathizers" broadcast hourly over Rumanian radio. But those who actually saw Trifa during the pogrom were few; most witnesses were dead, victims of the slaughter.

Twenty years later, these few survivors would try to avenge ten thousand deaths.

WHILE Trifa was leading demonstrations through the streets of Bucharest, Dr. Charles Kremer was fighting pettier battles in the courts of New York—the dentist was divorcing his wife and, in what was to be a landmark action, making a rather extraordinary demand for custody of his five-year-old son, Lewis.

As Kremer tells the story, the divorce started over a newspaper: "I was reading the paper and all of a sudden

she decides she wants it. Boom! She grabs it right out of
my hands. But you know Charlie Kremer. Once I make
up my mind, you know I'm going to get the paper. I got
the paper all right, but I also got a divorce.

"She's an outstanding woman. She was an outstanding
psychiatrist with a large practice. It just didn't work out.

"When she wanted the divorce, I gave it to her. But I
made up my mind not to make things easy for her. I was
forty-four and I had established a good practice. I was
making good money. But I'm not the type of dentist who
pays alimony. Not Charlie Kremer.

"When I told her I was demanding custody of the boy,
she laughed. Her lawyer told me I didn't have a prayer,
that a father had never before obtained custody of a child
when the mother was a responsible citizen. She fought me
for five years, taking me to the appeals court. But you
know Charlie Kremer, when I set out to do something, I
do it. I won all right. I want you to know I had thirty-nine
witnesses. She had one. That was really something, thirty-
nine to one."

This custody dispute was, however, just another char-
acteristic preliminary to the major battle which would
soon dominate the dentist's life. Annoyingly—if not compulsively—combative, Kremer had and would continue to
clutter his life with the debris from many small but intense
squabbles: He could look back upon nasty fights with the
draft board, college fraternities, Jewish organizations, and
landlords. Still, he fought every argument fortified by an
arrogant certitude and a romantic egotist's commitment to
challenge what others said was impossible. He was a man
who enjoyed the relentlessness of grudges, a man who
mocked those who accepted events and followed paths of
least resistance. His arrogance was pervasive; in restaurants, for example, he addressed waiters, "You're to bring
. . ." A bit of a curmudgeon who incessantly complicated
daily events, he seemed to pursue disputes so he could
someday inevitably boast—all in a tone of curious, third-
person detachment—"But you know when Charlie Kremer sets out to do something, Charlie Kremer does it."

And if "doing it" required the meticulous accumulation of testimony from thirty-nine witnesses, Charlie Kremer found the necessary compulsive energy, intelligence, and discipline. Kremer had portrayed his own life for so long as a series of epic struggles, it was almost as if he were a self-styled hero in search of a cause of heroic proportions.

An emergency meeting of the United Rumanian Jews of America in February 1941, just a few months after his custody victory, provided Kremer with the dramatic cause which would occupy the rest of his life.

The organization, a fraternal group of Rumanian-born Jews, usually spent its monthly meetings conducting the "official business" of card games. The possibility of an emergency meeting would have been ludicrous if not for the recent headlines from Rumania. Twenty men seated themselves around a wooden table in suite 702A of a decrepit building on West 40th Street in Manhattan. They were prepared for grim news.

"I have here," the president explained, "a report issued by the Jewish Telegraphic Agency. The dateline is Sofia, January 29, 1941. I want you all to hear it.

"The report filed by correspondent Leigh White begins, 'This, I believe is the first eyewitness account to reach the outside world of the Iron Guard horror in Rumania. It was necessary for this correspondent to come to Sofia to send out details because of Bucharest censorship. . . .

"'On Wednesday afternoon,'" the president continued reading, "'the Guardist general staff ordered the destruction of the Bucharest Jewish quarter and the murder of its inhabitants.

"'Storming through the Jewish quarter in a mad orgy of killing and destruction, armed Guardist gangs killed or beat up every person they saw who appeared to be Jewish. The test seems to have been whether persons encountered by the frenzied Guardist gangs were willing to participate in the massacre. The pogrom, which cost the lives of at least a thousand Jews in Bucharest, was not accidental but an integral part of the Guardist insurrection and had been prepared in advance. . . .

" 'Perhaps the most horrifying single episode of the pogrom was the "kosher butchering" last Wednesday night of more than two hundred Jews in the municipal slaughterhouse. The Jews, who had been rounded up after several hours of Iron Guard raids, were put into several trucks and carried off to the slaughterhouse. There the Greenshirts forced them to undress and led them to the chopping blocks, where they cut their throats in a horrible parody of the traditional Jewish methods of slaughtering fowl and livestock. . . .

" 'Some mangled bodies were disposed of by pouring them down manholes to the sewers usually used to carry animal remains. Other naked, headless bodies were hung on iron hooks and stamped *Carne Kosher:* kosher meat.' "

The organization president had to stop; he needed to compose himself before continuing.

" 'The general staff,' " he finally resumed, " 'which ordered the massacre consisted of Vice President Horia Sima, chief of the Greenshirt Legion, Dimitry Groza, boss of the Legionnary Workers Corps, and Viorel Trifa, leader of the frenetic Greenshirt student movement.' "

The men listened to the president without interrupting. When he had finished reading, there was some discussion, but the talk reached an agonizing realization: Protests would be futile and action would be impossible. Nothing could be done.

Before leaving, though, Kremer asked the president if he could keep the news dispatch. He took the Jewish Telegraphic Agency report home and re-read it many times that night. His parents still lived in Braila, Rumania, and he worried about their safety. It was after midnight before he went to bed. Sleep was impossible. His mind was filled with the horrors he had read. Desperate to do something, anything, he rose from bed and went to his desk. He took the dispatch and underlined the last paragraph in red ink. He then drew frantic circles around the three names in that paragraph—Horia Sima, Dimitry

Groza, and Viorel Trifa. It did not help, but at the time Kremer did not know what else to do.

Thirty years later he still had the original dispatch with the circled names. He kept it in the top drawer of a filing cabinet in his dental office, a filing cabinet with a skull on top.

THE Iron Guard revolt had been over weeks before Dr. Kremer first learned of its atrocities. The revolt lasted only four days. Of course, the Guardists blamed their defeat on the Jews. Horia Sima complained to Himmler, "General Antonescu did not realize that he was simply used by the Jews and the Masons."

The victorious Antonescu troops, though, found no trace of the Guardist leaders. Trifa, Sima, and others in the "command group" had been given refuge in the German Embassy in Bucharest. They remained hidden in the Embassy till March 13, 1941, when, disguised as German officers, they boarded a troop train and arrived in Berkenbruck, a town outside Berlin. This command group stayed in Berkenbruck while nearly three hundred legionnaires gathered in the north German city of Rostock. The Guardist-German relationship was comfortably pragmatic. The Nazis were eager to protect the Guardists because this Rumanian government in exile was a constant warning to Antonescu: If he did not enthusiastically adopt the policies of the Reich, he could be easily replaced. And, the legionnaires had little choice but to remain in Germany.

On June 15, 1941, the leaders of the revolt—Sima, Trifa, and eight others—were tried *in absentia* by the newly consolidated Antonescu regime. The verdict: "The most severe punishment, namely hard labor for life." Trifa was specifically singled out by the court for his role in the revolt:

"Viorel Trifa, commandant of the student Iron Guardists, on January 13 called together the presidents of the students' societies. He organized the student corps, he gave orders and he conducted this corps in the rebellion of January 20 to 24, 1941.

"He released the manifestos. . . . The leaflets were distributed throughout the entire country and were broadcast over the radio.

". . . as commandant of the student Iron Guard corps, he has organized this corps and supplied it with arms, a fact confirmed almost in unanimity by all the accused who were present.

". . . the accused was at the head of the demonstration on the night of January 20, 1941, a fact which was confirmed by Panaitescu, Biaia and others including Professor Chirnouga. He released an instigating manifesto. From the affidavit of Angel Mihai, witness, it is observed that this accused was among the commandants at the Rome headquarters (later to be identified as the scene of anti-Jewish atrocities) on the day of January 22, 1941."

Trifa, though, was safely protected from the avenging Rumanian government by the Nazis. According to official papers now at the Berlin Documents Center, he was even offered a university position by the Germans. Survivors have also testified that Trifa made pro-Nazi broadcasts into Rumania over Radio Donau and that he actively recruited Rumanians to fight with the Nazis on the Eastern Front. This easy alliance with the Germans, however, reached an impasse toward the end of 1942.

Horia Sima, as skillful a diplomat as he was a revolutionary, tried to negotiate a secret agreement with Mussolini which would give the legionnaires a greater role in the New Order. This secret agreement was never secret and it never became an agreement. Sima was called back from Italy and an infuriated Hitler ordered that constraints be put on the Rumanian legionnaires. On December 18, 1942, Heinrich Himmler personally issued an order that the legionnaires be kept in confinement. Thirty years later, Trifa would claim that he was a political prisoner in

Buchenwald, another victim of the Nazi concentration camps. This was never true. The Guardists were not kept in Buchenwald, but Fichtenheim, an "isolation camp," according to the official document signed by Himmler, "erected for immigrants and refugees to be financially coordinated with Buchenwald." The Buchenwald SS guards also lived in this facility and, witnesses interviewed by Simon Wiesenthal reported, "the legionnaires could have radios, exercise as many hours as they wanted, or they could work for pay. Food and medical care were the same as for German soldiers. Married men were allowed to live with their wives in a sector reserved for families." Also, Trifa was specifically allowed to continue his radio broadcasts.

On August 24, 1944, as the Russian army broke into Rumania, the Antonescu government surrendered. The Nazis now released the legionnaires and sent them to Vienna where Trifa was given an official position in the Guardist government in exile. Trifa remained in Vienna working, according to the testimony of former legionnaire Vasile Arbor, as an agent of the German secret police with "the special mission of verifying the movements and cargoes of all trains from Rumania."

When the war ended, Trifa fled Vienna. Portraying himself as a victim of Nazi political persecution arrested in Rumania and interned in Buchenwald, Trifa now sought asylum in Italy. It is conceivable that the specifics of Trifa's story were never seriously examined. Many in the Italian Catholic Church (Bishop Alois Hudal who ran a postwar underground railroad for Nazis from Italy to South America, for example) were willing to make excuses for Nazis and Guardists; fascism seemed to be a powerful and, therefore, acceptable weapon against Godless Marxism. Trifa, though still a layman, found a position teaching history at a Catholic college in Pesaro, Italy. He hid quietly in Italy for four years, but all the time he was teaching history, plans were being made for Viorel Trifa in the United States: plans that one day would restore him to power.

John Trutza, a priest from Cleveland who had studied with Trifa in Rumania in 1940, filed the necessary forms for Trifa's admittance as a displaced person to the United States in the fall of 1949. On July 19, 1950, Trifa finally arrived in New York.

Like all refugees arriving under the 1948 Displaced Persons Act, Trifa was interrogated by the Immigration authorities. But the short, balding history teacher gave all the correct answers. Immigration examiner Leo M. Jaremko asked, "Did you ever make any speeches or give any lectures that might be construed as being anti-Jewish or anti-Semitic?"

Trifa replied, "No, I cannot say. I don't believe so."

The examiner then asked if Trifa had ever been a member of the Iron Guard, a membership which would disqualify him from entry into the United States.

"No," said Trifa flatly.

Five months later in sworn testimony given in an Ohio court case involving dissident church factions, Trifa revealed more of the fictitious biography he had probably offered the Immigration examiner.

Q: Have you come directly from Rumania, or from another country?

A: From Italy.

Q: When did you leave Rumania?

A: Five years ago.

Q: For what country did you leave Rumania five years ago?

A: For Italy.

The past was quickly obliterated with a few glib lies. Who would know about the pogroms and the years in Germany and Austria working for the Nazis? He could, if necessary, wound even the most aggressive accuser with the nastiest epithet of the 1950s—Communist. Besides, the United States did not even have an extradition treaty with "Red" Rumania. Trifa's nine-year odyssey was finally over. He had been a man without a home or country since the failed revolt in January 1941. Now, safe in America, he could prepare for the future. He settled first in Cleveland where he ostensibly was employed on the Rumanian-language newspaper, *America*. Actually, Viorel Trifa and his supporters were working full time toward the restoration of his power.

IN 1947, while Trifa hid in Pesaro, Italy, as an anonymous history teacher, Dr. Charles Kremer returned to Rumania in ceremony and triumph. He arrived as treasurer of the Rumanian-American Medical Relief Organization, bringing, at his own expense, crates of penicillin. Leaders of the Bucharest Jewish community greeted him at the airport with speeches of praise and a seven-foot-high hillock of gladioli. The homecoming was particularly emotional for the dentist because just twenty-six years ago he had escaped from Rumania hidden under a pile of burlap bags in the dark hole of a freighter.

Kremer enjoys telling the story of his flight from Rumania and his subsequent success in America; it is another story about how "Charlie Kremer did what nobody else could have done."

"I was born in 1897 in Yasi, Rumania," Kremer quickly begins. He takes an instinctive delight in telling stories; the longer the tale, the longer he can dominate the conversation. A large man, tall and broad, he talks with equally large, expansive gestures, his sentences punctuated with broad sweeps of a long arm, the pounding of clenched fists, and the insistent pointing of an aggressive finger.

"My father was a shoemaker, but he was very interested in the whole *shtetl*. You know, like me he was interested in community affairs. Anyway, he wanted his son to be more than just a shoemaker. His son was going to be a doctor. So I went off to medical school in Bucharest. But you couldn't learn anything there. There was just one body for all the students and it had a big red line down the middle. There would be twenty, thirty Jews on one side and just six *goyim* on the other. Then the *goyim* would sometimes come around and beat up the Jewish students. But they never beat me up. I was the biggest kid in the class. They couldn't tell I wasn't a *goy*.

"It was terrible, but I stayed. When they wanted to take me in the army, though, that was it. My father said, 'I was never in the army and you won't be either.' He tells my brother and me that he's going to send us to America. He knows a man who exports wheat and this man has promised to take care of us.

"So on the seventh of August—I still remember the exact date—we go to the dock. It was very hot, but both my brother and I are wearing two suits, one right on top of the other. Anyway, before we get to the boat, there's policemen shooting at us and we're arrested. We're thrown in the cellar of a police station in our two suits and Charlie Kremer figures he has had it. I'm certain they are going to shoot us. The next morning, who opens the door to our cell, but my father. He was a politician all right. He just gave the policeman a *schmeer* and we're free.

"We went home, but the next night we went back to the dock. This time we weren't caught. We got to the boat, but this lousy boat just sits there for three days. Do you know how hot it was in the hold of that boat? During the day we would just sit there naked, it was so hot. The perspiration came like water. We had to use the burlap sacks to wipe off all the sweat.

"On the third day the boat finally moves. We made friends with this sailor and he hid us in a toilet. All we ate for ten days was figs, crackers, and water.

"Finally the boat reaches Port Said in Egypt. The plan is that we're supposed to leave the boat before it docks. So late at night with just one candle as light, we climb down from the ship into an empty rowboat. We were very high up and we had to go down this rope one by one in the middle of the night into this little boat and who has to go first? You guessed it, Charlie Kremer. Charlie Kremer goes first and then I pull down my brother, Harry, and another fellow. It was really something. Anyway, we get the rowboat to shore and I start running off in the middle of the night. To this day I'm still running.

"But back then we're in Egypt and we're still wearing our two suits and it's August and, oh boy, is it hot. We're just wandering around and I pass a hotel that says 'Carmel' so I figure the owner must be Jewish. I guessed right and we rent a room.

"After I'm in Egypt two weeks wondering how I'm gonna get to America, I see a store called Solomon's Department Store. I go in and start talking Yiddish to the owner. Then I show him a letter introducing me from the president of the Zionist Association of Rumania. He reads the letter and finds out Charlie Kremer is no nobody. He tells me to come back the next day and he'll put my brother and me on a ship to England.

"The next day my brother and I come over and this Solomon takes us in the largest carriage you've ever seen to the English consul general. I couldn't speak a word of English so Solomon did all the talking. Anyway, it worked. We got jobs as sailors on a boat to England. We get on the boat and when it docks at Malta the chef gets drunk and lands in jail. What do you know, but Charlie Kremer becomes the chef. It was really something terrific.

"When we get to London, first thing I find a synagogue and show the rabbi my letter from Rumania. Right away the rabbi is impressed. He takes us to Liverpool and gets me a job on a boat going to the United States. My brother decides to stay in England until he saves some money. I got a job as an interpreter on the S.S. *Baltic* and they paid me thirty English pounds—a fortune! Even funnier, I didn't know a word of English. But you know Charlie Kremer, he can do anything."

Kremer is genuinely enthusiastic about his own story, talking nonstop, sentences rapidly following sentences as if he, too, is hearing the story for the first time and is eager to learn how it will end.

"When we get to New York, Charlie Kremer has a new problem. The boat docks at East 23rd Street and I have

an aunt and uncle in New York, but how do I get off the
boat? I'm scared. I figure if I jump ship, they'll arrest me.
But I take a chance. I wait till it's dark and then I just
walk down the gangplank, down the pier, and no one stops
me. I see an El and I keep stopping people until I find
someone who speaks Yiddish. This man gives me directions to 158th Street. I get there, all right, and I'm looking
all over and finally I see the name of Avrum Markowitz
on a mailbox. I knock on the door and my uncle answers.
'I am Leon Kremer's son,' I tell him and he starts to cry.
Everyone was so happy to see me. It was something terrific. I'll never forget that evening as long as I live.

"Anyway, right away I enroll in City College. I don't
know English, but I make up my mind to learn and in
two, three months I can speak fine. I still wanted to be a
doctor, but my aunt tells me, 'Don't be a doctor, Charlie.
All the doctors here have died of influenza. Be a dentist,
Charlie. It's an easier life.' I'm just a kid and I'm in a new
country so like a dope Charlie Kremer listens to her.

"So I win a YMCA scholarship for a course in dental
mechanics and I complete the course in record time. Before you know it Charlie Kremer is ready for dental
school. The University of Pennsylvania will accept this
course as a qualifying exam, but when I go up there they
tell me I can't get in. Registration was closed three weeks
ago. They should have known better than to tell Charlie
Kremer he can't get in. I go to the dean and I give him a
whole story about Rumania and of course I get in. I
worked all night as a waiter and then in the morning I
went to classes and what do you know—Charlie Kremer
gets the highest marks in the class. All the big dental fraternities want me to join I'm such a big shot. I was the
only Jew they ever asked and I'm the only Jew they ever
will ask. But you know Charlie Kremer. I don't join, I
found organizations. I founded my own dental society.

"Look, I got something terrific here about my school
days." Kremer reaches over to his desk and buried in the
midst of a pile of papers he finds a yellowed news clipping.
The article has been mounted with white masking tape to

a piece of his dental stationery. Its headline: "Studies Dentistry at Penn and Human Nature As Waiter/Young Rumanian, Despite Handicap, Achieves Highest Scholastic Average in Class." Across the bottom of the short article a classmate wrote fifty years ago, "You're all right, Kremer. We all know you're good. The trouble is you know it, too." The dentist is very proud of his classmate's observation, and has been careful so that the words were not hidden by the uneven, masking-tape frame.

After graduation Kremer returned to New York and established a practice on Manhattan's West Side. He paid a boy a few dollars each month to place an orange card in West Side mailboxes. The card announced:

Good Teeth are an Asset to Good Health
Good Looks and Good Breath
If You Are Afraid of Pain and Want A
Gentle Dentist
Come and See Dr. C. H. Kremer
The Neighborhood's Surgeon Dentist
Open 9 A.M. to 9 P.M.
Sundays by Appointment

"You got to work hard to make money," Kremer explains. "My wife would say, 'Take it easy, Charlie,' but she never knew anything. I'd put in ten, twelve hours a day and Sundays, too. I made good money, all right. You know, Charlie Kremer just had to go out and make it big."

This was the Charlie Kremer who returned to Rumania in 1947. He found that his family in Braila had survived the war. And they found that their twenty-two-year-old son had grown up into a middle-aged man, an American who looked like he "had made it big." He was tall, at least six foot two, and rather stocky, always dressed in freshly pressed white shirts, dark suits, and colorful ties. His face had filled out, becoming rounder and fleshier, but his jaw remained sharp and firm. The dentist would smile a great deal and talk with infectious energy. His hair had thinned out a bit and turned an even, soft gray and he brushed it straight back, hoping to cover the bald spots. When he stood tall, people noticed a large, handsome man; his was an impressive appearance and one was always aware of the dentist's presence.

Kremer's reunion in Braila with his relatives lasted only a week and then he went to Bucharest for business. The business was a series of secret meetings to discuss plans for getting Rumania's surviving Jews to Israel or the United States. Political regimes had changed since 1919, when Kremer had left, but life for the Rumanian Jews remained unfortunately similar. The meetings with Jewish leaders continued for nearly two weeks and at least once a day Kremer heard stories about the Iron Guard, men describing how they watched helplessly as their wives or children or friends were slaughtered by the legionnaires. And whenever the Guardists were discussed, two names were uttered like a curse—Horia Sima and Viorel Trifa. The same names Kremer had circled with red ink six years ago.

"What ever happened to those bastards?" Kremer asked. "Have they been killed or are they rotting in jail?"

No, Kremer was told. Horia Sima had escaped to Spain. He lived comfortably in Madrid, wealthy and respected. Trifa? No one knew what had become of him. Perhaps he had been killed in the war. Perhaps he had escaped to South America. He just seemed to have disappeared.

THE gray farmhouse was surrounded by shouting men. A rock crashed through a window. Other stones slammed against the front door and roof. Stefan Feraru tried to call for help, but it was useless: The telephone lines had been cut.

At least a hundred men crowded the finely shaven green lawns stretching from the road to the main house. Most were just observers, up from Detroit for a fine summer's day in the country. The crowd, though, had been drinking and the alcohol and sun mixed to make them restless and aggressive. Many, waving their bottles in the air, started chanting in a tough, loud cadence: "Com-mun-ists . . . Com-mun-ists . . ." At the head of the lawn, directly in front of the farmhouse, was a more menacing group of approximately thirty men. They were neither drunk nor merely restless. They had planned the assault on the Rumanian Orthodox Episcopate in Grass Lakes, Michigan, as if it were a military operation: first the phone lines would be cut, a barrage of rocks, and then the final push— the seizure of the Vatra. In fact, many of these men were trained soldiers. They had been trained twenty years ago in Rumania when they fought with the Iron Guard.

These men, some brandishing broom handles, advanced toward the house. A priest's new Buick directly in their path became an easy target: Windows were smashed and tires slashed. Another volley of rocks was thrown as they moved closer.

Inside the farmhouse, Bishop Moldovan and his priests began to panic. "We were scared," Stefan Feraru remembered. "We had come to the Vatra a few days early to prepare for the annual church congress. We knew there would be some discussion, some debate, but we never expected an attack. These men were wild."

Father Oprean, a short priest with a long, gray beard, decided he could stop the assault; he believed no one would attack a priest dressed in his black cassock, a cross hanging from his neck. He walked out to the front porch and raised his arms, appealing for quiet. "Fellow Christians," he began. But before he could continue, he was dragged from the porch. Clutching the priest's beard, the attacker spun the priest as if he were a child's top into the crowd. Men surrounded the priest, pushing, punching, and kicking until Father Oprean fell to the ground. He lay dazed, a small, old man, his black cassock spread about the green grass like a discarded rag.

Bishop Moldovan had no choice but surrender. If a

battle were to be fought, he would have to wage it in an American court. On Independence Day—July 4—1952, he surrendered the two-hundred-acre Vatra in northern Michigan to the priests and supporters of the newly chosen dissident bishop—Valerian Trifa.

The Reverend Vasile Pascau, Bishop Moldovan's secretary, had been inside the farmhouse during the assault and later wrote: ". . . a group of Iron Guardist hoodlums . . . invaded our property . . . beating an old priest . . . creating terror among our women, children, and old people, exactly as Hitler did once in Germany against the Jews. After this kind of ordeal, they took over our property by force, chasing us out."

The attack on the Vatra began over a canonical dispute rooted in Cold War politics, a dispute which grew bitter as it was further twisted by fear and opportunism. For twelve years, since the start of World War II, the American Rumanian Diocese had been without a bishop. Then, in 1950, the Rumanian patriarchate in Bucharest summoned a priest from Akron, Ohio, Andrei Moldovan, to Rumania where he was consecrated bishop of the diocese in America. But church and state were not firmly separated in the minds of many Rumanian-Americans. If Bishop Moldovan had been appointed by a Communist government, then, he, too, was—if not an actual Communist—certainly suspect. Like many immigrants and first-generation citizens, these "Midwest" Rumanians often displayed anxiety over establishing roots, over becoming part of their new, American hometown cultures. And in the 1950s, one word symbolized the entire un-American and foreign threat—Communism. These Rumanians decided they could not have a bishop who would impugn their patriotism.

Here, then, was an opportunity. The episcopate was leaderless. A layman with many friends—Viorel Trifa—was chosen to oppose Moldovan. Trifa would be the "non-Communist" bishop. In January 1941, a "spontaneous" revolt erupted in Bucharest ostensibly because of the assassination of a German major by the Communists. Eleven years later, on July 4, 1952, another "spontaneous" demonstration against the Communists occurred in Grass Lakes, Michigan, two days before the annual Rumanian Orthodox Church Congress.

This time what had failed in Bucharest succeeded in Michigan. In mid-July, Bishop Valerian Trifa and his priests moved into the twenty-five-room house on the two-hundred-acre estate. It had taken eleven years, but the Iron Guard had finally been restored to power. The future of the legionnaires in America seemed assured.

FOR five years since his return from Rumania, Dr. Charles Kremer had been fascinated by one mystery—what had happened to Viorel Trifa. Then, just months before the attack on the Vatra, the mystery was solved. The answer came by accident from an unexpected source. Only now, Kremer found no one else was interested.

In the winter of 1952, two clerics addressed the executive committee of the United Rumanian Jews of America. Father Glicherie Moraru said they had come to New York to appeal for the help of Rumanian Jews. The problem, as explained by this intense, scholarly father, seemed primarily a Church dispute. A dissident faction of the Rumanian Orthodox Church was trying to appoint a layman, "a wanderer and a heretic who had never as much as served as an altar boy," as bishop. Canonical law insisted, the priest explained, that only the patriarch in Rumania can anoint bishops.

"Look, I don't want to appear rude," a voice interrupted, "but why come to us? We're Jews. What do we know from bishops and canonical law?"

The other cleric, Bishop Moldovan, was clearly agitated: "We thought the identity of this impostor bishop might interest your group. We thought you might like to know that this man cannot return to Rumania because he faces life imprisonment. We thought you might like to know this man served as a commandant during the Iron Guard revolt when thousands of Jews were slaughtered. We thought you might like to know that this bishop's name is Viorel Trifa."

Dr. Charles Kremer was sitting in the back of the room as Moldovan announced the dissident's identity. "I heard that name and I thought, oh boy, I've got him. Trifa is finally caught," Kremer recalled. "I had been thinking about this man for years and then, out of the blue, I suddenly find out what had happened to him. I was excited something terrific."

But Kremer's excitement was not shared. The members of the executive committee—lawyers, doctors, the owner of the drygoods store, a pocketbook manufacturer—did not want to get involved. "This is still Church business," a member protested. "It doesn't concern Jews." And there was another argument, unspoken but perhaps more influential. These were practical men. The American government had allowed this Trifa to enter as a displaced person. There must have been a reason, many of them decided. If a Jewish group were suddenly to challenge the government, wouldn't that make all Jews seem somehow foreign and unpatriotic? The horrible memory of the concentration camps intimidated these men. American Jews needed their government as a friend and a protector, not as an adversary.

Charlie Kremer, though, did not care about offending anyone or any government. "We must get involved," he shouted, jumping to his feet. "Jews were killed by Trifa. Why shouldn't we get involved?"

The other men were more cautious. A vote was taken to decide whether the organization should formally protest Trifa's presence in the United States. The United Ru-

manian Jews of America voted nineteen to one—not to
protest.

The one dissenting vote, Dr. Charles Kremer, stormed
from the room. They're nothing but a bunch of scared old
men, Kremer told himself as he waited for the subway at
Times Square. The hell with 'em. Charlie Kremer doesn't
need anybody. Charlie Kremer can do it all by himself.

It was a short subway ride to Broadway and 72nd
Street and then just a two-block walk to his apartment.
But it was long enough for Kremer to reach a decision
which would dominate the rest of his life. Kremer swore
to himself that he would force Trifa's deportation from
the United States. Charlie Kremer, he swore to himself,
would personally make sure Trifa spent the next thirty
years in a Rumanian jail. He reached this decision because
it was right: "Trifa is a Satan, he killed my people." And
he reached this decision because he "wanted to show a
bunch of old men that nobody tells Charlie Kremer he's
wrong."

It was not as easy as the dentist had imagined. He went
to the Anti-Defamation League, then to the American
Jewish Congress asking for support. "Kremer," they told
him, "don't rock the boat. America has been good to the
Jews. Leave well enough alone." Yet every time the dentist
was told not to interfere, his commitment became more
personal and more intense. After each meeting with these
cautious and practical elders of Zion, Kremer grew more
impetuous and rebellious. He was determined to prove
them wrong.

When no Jewish organization offered to help, he decided "to shake up the old men." He spent the next
months writing letters and making phone calls to the few
hundred members of the United Rumanian Jews of America. This campaign worked: Charlie Kremer was elected
president of the organization. And with the title came the
one benefit he most wanted—the stationery.

The formal letterhead of the United Rumanian Jews of
America, Kremer felt, commanded immediate political at-

tention; elected officials would respond immediately to a vociferous Jewish interest group. But the dentist was wrong. He wrote letters to the President, the Vice President, and most of the Cabinet. When he received vague responses thanking him "for your interest," he wrote to senators, congressmen, and mayors. The replies were generally the same—Kremer's letters concerning Trifa would be forwarded to the Immigration and Naturalization Service. And when Kremer wrote the INS, he was informed, again by a form letter, that "the matter would be looked into."

Then, on April 23, 1952, Kremer received a call from a Rumanian priest telling an incredible story: In just four days, Trifa, a layman, would be consecrated as a bishop. Trifa's supporters had devised an ingenious canonical strategy to challenge the Rumanian-designated (and, therefore, "Communist") Bishop Moldovan: Trifa would be annointed by the archbishop of the Ukrainian Orthodox Church, the ecclesiastical logic being that the laying on of hands of a prince of *another* Orthodox church would legitimize Bishop Trifa.

Immediately after the phone call, Kremer sent a telegram from the United Rumanian Jews of America, Inc., Dr. Charles H. Kremer, president, to the Immigration Service:

"We are informed that Viorel Trifa, a man who never was a priest and is responsible for tens of thousands of Jews killed in Rumania in Antonescu regime in 1940, 1941, will be consecrated as bishop by Archbishop M. Stanislaw and Bishop Ioan on Sunday morning April 27 at the Ukrainian Orthodox Church, 128 Grace Road, Bala Cynwyd, Pennsylvania. We urge you advise both Archbishop Stanislaw and Bishop Ioan not to consecrate Viorel Trifa until your own investigation is completed."

Two days later, Kremer received the Immigration Service's response:

"Receipt is acknowledged of your telegram of April 23, 1952, regarding the consecration of VIOREL TRIFA as a bishop on April 27, 1952. I regret that your request that we intercede to prevent the consecration of Mr. TRIFA as a bishop cannot be granted. . . ."

"I was depressed, all right," the dentist remembered. "Everyone was telling Charlie Kremer they couldn't interfere, that requests couldn't be granted. I felt like that bastard Trifa was laughing at me. Here I was beating my head against the wall and that bastard was now in bishop's clothing. Think of it! They let him become a bishop. It was just unbelievable."

The dentist had never met or even seen Trifa, but he was convinced the bishop was laughing at him. Kremer's concern with Trifa became total. He would cancel appointments with patients, telling them, "Go away, I've got work to do." His work consisted of writing letters. He wrote to columnists, editors, and church officials. He made frequent calls to Detroit Jewish groups who kept him informed of Trifa's every move; if the bishop traveled to a church parish in Ohio, the editor of the local newspaper would be sure to receive a letter about "mass murderer Viorel Trifa." After two years of letter writing, the dentist had received only one positive response. On February 3, 1953, the Yiddish daily, *The Day,* reported, "One of the worst Rumanian Nazis and Jew-baiters who helped to murder 6,000 Jews in Rumania is at this time a bishop in America."

No one else seemed to be interested. But the dentist resolved to make them interested. "They say they need evidence. I'll give them evidence, all right," he announced to his son Lewis, now a college student. "I'll show them that when Charlie Kremer sets out to do something, he does it. Nobody can do what Charlie Kremer can do. Nobody laughs at Charlie Kremer."

It seemed only natural to the dentist that in 1954 he shut down his practice, sell his dental equipment, and go abroad. Some of his friends thought Charlie Kremer had given up, that he was going to Europe and then to Israel to retire at age fifty-seven. They were wrong. "I went abroad," remembers Kremer, "with only one thought—to get evidence on that bastard Trifa. Every day I woke up and heard that bastard laughing at me. I wanted to make sure Charlie Kremer had the last laugh."

WHILE Kremer traveled through Rumania and then Israel in a small car he had bought in England, Valerian Trifa solidified his power as bishop. He now controlled an episcopate with forty-six churches, mostly in Ohio, and ten thousand parishioners.

The Vatra, which his supporters had taken by force, was now officially his: Bishop Moldovan's legal challenges were defeated. An Ohio District Court—reaching its decision in the midst of the McCarthy era—decided, "The . . . Communistic government of Rumania . . . was dictating appointment of its Bishop [Moldovan], and the American diocese was entitled to revoke its 1936 by-laws and . . . elect its own Bishop [Trifa]."

As a bishop and a fierce anti-Communist who had fled his native land supposedly to escape Red oppression, Trifa moved in influential circles throughout Cold War America. He made broadcasts over Radio Free Europe to Rumania, broadcasts he bragged were arranged by "my good friend, J. Edgar Hoover." He sat on daises with the Governor of Michigan and his picture appeared in newspapers shaking hands with a smiling Hubert Humphrey.

On Wednesday, May 11, 1955, Bishop Trifa had the honor of offering the opening prayer before the U.S. Senate: ". . . Almighty God . . . who has made America trustee of priceless human liberty and dignity, look down from Heaven upon Thy servants now present before Thee, and bless them, that they may remember in their discussions and decisions Rumania and all the oppressed nations who are still longing for 'a government by the people, and for the people.' . . ."

Bishop Trifa's presence had been requested by Vice President Richard M. Nixon.

At the time, Kremer said, "If I had been in the country, they never would have let Trifa into the Senate or on Radio Free Europe." But years later, after the revelations of contemporary history, the dentist had become more cynical. He now believed Hoover had been aware of Trifa's past, but, in the interests of anti-Communism, was willing to make a practical alliance with an Iron Guard commandant. Just as the newly formed CIA quickly and expediently forgot past grudges to draft Nazi spy chief Reinhard Gehlen's agents, Hoover could have sought out and protected Trifa. Significantly, Kremer was to learn, following the collapse of the Antonescu regime in 1945, Trifa had worked in Vienna as an agent for Gehlen's spy network.

Also, Kremer decided it was no political accident that Richard Nixon invited Trifa to the Senate. It seemed more than coincidental that Richard Nixon had a rather incriminating history of involvement with another Iron Guardist who had also immigrated to America—Nicolae Malaxa.

IN his June 1941 trial, Viorel Trifa was identified as "commandant of the student Iron Guard corps; he has organized this corps and supplied it with arms." But it was another trial held that same month which named Trifa's source for the tanks, guns, and munitions used in the revolt and pogrom. The source was Nicolae Malaxa, the chief contributor to the Iron Guard and the wealthiest man in Rumania, if not all Eastern Europe. Both Trifa and Malaxa were convicted and both shared the same eventual fate—sanctuary in the United States.

During the 1930s, Malaxa had perceptively invested a sizable loan from the Rumanian government intended for his locomotive factories in other industries. By 1939, he had purchased controlling interests in numerous steel, rubber, munition, and artillery factories; Malaxa had seen the future of Europe and had realized the next decade's profits were to be earned from guns, not butter.

Malaxa, though, was not just a businessman. He also was a political force in Rumanian politics, an agent who actively worked and conspired with the Nazis and the Iron Guard. From his factories, Malaxa hoped, would come the weapons which would win the New Order.

In 1936, Malaxa went to Berlin to meet with Reichsmarschall Hermann Goering and the two men parted as business partners. This personal agreement became formalized in the 1940 Wohlstadt Pact which integrated Malaxa's industries with Germany's. Directing this new Nazi industrial coalition were Nicolae Malaxa and Albert Goering, younger brother of the Reichsmarschall.

Malaxa's partnership with the Nazis also intruded into domestic Rumanian politics with his staunch support for the Iron Guard. A telegram sent on January 8, 1941, by the German minister in Rumania to the Foreign Ministry in Berlin accurately documents the financier's relationship with the Guardists: "In this fight between the General [Antonescu] and the legionnaire command, one man plays a role who even earlier played a secret part in Rumanian politics: . . . the present financial mainstay of the legionnaires, N. Malaxa. The legionnaires let the clever, big industrialist finance them. He has in his plants the leader of the legionnaire labor organization, Ganeu, and their green flags flutter above his factories. . . . Malaxa has even again supplied with arms the legionnaire police. . . ." Just two weeks after this secret diplomatic telegram was sent, the Iron Guard revolt broke out, and Malaxa's complicity became even more conspicuous: His house served as the Bucharest Guard headquarters and munitions depot.

Malaxa, however, was more successful in business than politics, and after the revolt failed he was convicted and jailed by the Antonescu government. He remained in jail for only six months and, under pressure from the Nazis, the Rumanian officials were forced to begin returning Malaxa's industrial properties. By April 1945, all of Malaxa's holdings were restored.

With the defeat of the Nazis, the adaptive Malaxa was ready to make new alliances. Grady McClaussen, head of the American Office of Strategic Services (OSS) in Rumania, signed personal contracts and became an employee of Malaxa's while still stationed in Rumania as an agent of the OSS. These contracts stipulated that McClaussen would be paid certain sums once Malaxa arrived in the United States. Ten years after these contracts were signed, Immigration officials would argue that these agreements were actually bribes: money to be paid to the OSS agent *if* McClaussen got Malaxa into the United States.

Malaxa's dealing with the OSS did not preclude, however, his making similar overtures to the Russians. For reasons never disclosed, the Communist government of Rumania in April 1945, issued a decree without precedent: Malaxa received $2,460,000 in American money for steel manufacturing plants which had been appropriated by the new Rumanian government and then given to the Russians as a reparation payment.

But, despite this ability to make unique deals with the Communists, Malaxa remained intent on immigrating to the United States. On September 29, 1946, Malaxa arrived in New York as part of a Rumanian government trade mission. He was never to return to Europe.

In 1948, Malaxa formally applied for permanent residence in the United States, appealing for admission under the Displaced Persons Act. For the next ten years Malaxa was to fight a legal battle to remain in America—the best legal battle his money could buy.

Malaxa's first step was to claim millions of dollars which had been deposited before the war in the Chase National Bank in the name of one of his corporations. These funds had been frozen as enemy assets during the war by John Pehle of the Treasury Department. Normally, such funds are used for postwar compensation to American companies (such as Standard Oil) which had property confiscated by Rumania. However, John Pehle had since returned to private practice and Malaxa shrewdly hired the law firm of Pehle and Loesser to argue his case. This time, Pehle and Malaxa won.

Similarly, Ugo Carusi was United States Immigration commissioner when Malaxa first attempted to enter as a displaced person. When Carusi resigned his job, Malaxa hired him. Other former government officials and their associates were recruited—and compensated—to assist in Malaxa's legal suits: Secretary of State John Foster Dulles's law firm of Sullivan and Cromwell; former Air Force Secretary Thomas K. Finletter's law firm; and the firm of former Undersecretary of State Adolph A. Berle, who personally testified on Malaxa's behalf before a Congressional Subcommittee on Immigration.

The briefs of these lawyers, though, were no match for the vivid eyewitness testimony detailing Iron Guard atrocities which were heard at every Immigration hearing. A victim of justice, Malaxa tried, instead, privilege. At Malaxa's urging, the junior senator from California, Richard Nixon, introduced a private bill in 1951 which would allow Malaxa to remain permanently in the United States. Congressman Emanuel Celler, head of the House Immigration Committee, later said on television, "I saw something suspicious about the bill . . . I held up the bill. The bill was never passed."

The bill was defeated, but it was not the end of Nixon's involvement with Malaxa. The Rumanian (or one of his lawyers or advisors) now had a new scheme. In May 1951, at the height of the Korean War when all industry was under war-time control, Malaxa organized the Western Tube Corporation. The company, of which Malaxa was treasurer and sole stock owner—a thousand dollars' worth—planned to manufacture seamless tubes for oil refining. Although most similar manufacturing was done in the East, Malaxa's plan was to construct facilities on the West Coast, near the California oil fields. It had taken Malaxa five years in the United States to locate what he insisted was the perfect site for new industry—a small suburb east of Los Angeles, Whittier, California. And for Malaxa's purposes, the site *was* perfect. It was, coincidentally, the hometown of the then junior senator from California, Richard Nixon. This was, for Malaxa's purposes, just the first of many perfect coincidences.

Western Tube's California address was 607 Bank of America Building, Whittier. This was the same address as that of the law firm of Bewley, Kroop & Nixon. Throughout his Senate career, Nixon's name remained part of the official firm title and Nixon used the office on his vacations in California.

Thomas Bewley, Nixon's long-time friend and law partner, was secretary of Western Tube.

Herman L. Perry, the vice president of Western Tube, was an old Nixon political supporter, the same "family friend" whom Pat Nixon credited as the man who "got Dick . . . to oppose Congressman Jerry Voorhis."

On May 17, 1951, the Western Tube Corporation filed for a "certificate of necessity" to give top war-time priority to its materials and personnel. Also, the company filed a petition seeking "first preference quota" for its treasurer, Nicolae Malaxa, on the grounds that he was indispensable to the operation of Western Tube.

These two applications were personally promoted by Senator Nixon. Nixon telephoned the executive assistant to INS Commissioner James Hennessy to plead for Malaxa's permanent entry. And a letter sent by Nixon to the Defense Production Administrator marked "Urgent" insisted, "It is important strategically and economically, both for California and the entire United States, that a plant for the manufacture of seamless tubing for oil wells be erected . . . urge that every consideration it may merit be given to the pending application."

Both appeals were successful. The application for Western Tube was quickly approved and on September 26, 1953, Malaxa was admitted from Canada under a special first-preference petition as a permanent resident.

Yet, once Malaxa obtained permanent residence in the United States, nothing further was ever done to make

Western Tube a reality. Neither Malaxa nor Nixon nor any of the corporation's other sponsors ever again concerned themselves with Western Tube. Congressman John Shelley of California was later to observe, "It is impossible to discover any reasons for creating Western Tube and seeking a certificate of necessity other than to give Malaxa a springboard for entry into the United States."

A year after becoming a permanent resident, Malaxa visited with Juan Perón in Argentina. Malaxa also met in Buenos Aires, according to the CIA, with Otto Skorzeny, the Nazi parachutist who had rescued Mussolini in 1943. Skorzeny, now settled in Madrid, remained a close associate of other Rumanian exiles, including Horia Sima, the head of the Iron Guard.

When, ten months later, Malaxa attempted to re-enter the United States, he was challenged once more by the INS. In 1958, after two years in the courtroom, Hearing Officer Arnold Martin ruled against Malaxa and ordered him deported. Malaxa appealed the decision and won. Another Nixon friend, U.S. Attorney General William Rogers, affirmed the Immigration Appeals Board's ruling.

"How interesting," Congressman Shelley noted with judicious understatement, "that this man . . . found sanctuary in the United States thanks to the special favors accorded him by Mr. Nixon and Mr. Rogers. This was at a time when thousands of deserving displaced persons, victims of Mr. Malaxa's Nazis, Iron Guardists, and Communists, were unable to obtain admission. Maybe they would have done better if they transported plunder and been friendly enough with Richard Nixon to obtain his personal intervention in their behalf."

But Dr. Charles Kremer was not concerned about "thousands of displaced persons." He was only concerned with one—Valerian Trifa. Had Nixon personally intervened in Trifa's case? The dentist knew Nixon had invited Trifa to make the opening prayer at a Senate session in 1955. But, had he actually spoken to the Immigration authorities on Trifa's behalf as he had done for Malaxa? Had Malaxa first introduced Nixon to the bishop? After the Western Tube fiasco became public, Kremer's imagination raced.

Kremer also wondered about Malaxa's relationship in the United States with his Guardist associate, Trifa. Had Malaxa made sizable tax-deductible contributions to Trifa's episcopate, money which Trifa would use to help "priests" immigrate to the United States? Had Malaxa met with Skorzeny in Buenos Aires to discuss, as he claimed, "engineering business" or Guardist business? Was Skorzeny relaying instructions from Sima to Malaxa? Was this a conference of Guardist leaders to establish policy which Trifa, the respected bishop, was to initiate?

These questions and suspicions tormented the dentist. "I thought about what it all meant day and night for so many years," says Kremer. "Nixon, Hoover, Malaxa, Trifa—why did all those *gonifs* just happen to get together? It was obvious what it all meant, but I didn't want to believe it. Sure, you could give a *schmeer* here and there, but not until the Western Tube affair did I really believe you could buy senators or the big men in Immigration. But I figured out what had happened. Charlie Kremer put it together, all right. If anyone wants to call Charlie Kremer crazy, that's their problem."

Kremer's theory was incredible: Sima, Malaxa, and Trifa, planners of the Iron Guard revolt in 1941, had never given up their dream. Malaxa bought and used U.S. officials to help himself and Trifa with only one goal in mind—the restoration of the Iron Guard in America.

Only one man, Kremer realized, could ever be forced to confirm this theory. Both Sima and Malaxa were beyond the law, Sima safely in Madrid and Malaxa now a corpse; he had died a decade after his return from Argentina. Only one man remained.

The two years Dr. Kremer spent in Europe and Israel incessantly pursuing this man's past would have to provide all the clues. The dentist sifted through Valerian Trifa's former life for the evidence which would force the bishop's future plans to crumble.

"I HAD him. I got stuff on Trifa no one else could have gotten. I told myself, 'Charlie Kremer, you've really done something terrific. You've got that bastard cold,'" said the dentist, remembering how he felt when he returned to New York in 1956, after his two years abroad.

"But I was naive. I didn't know what kind of friends Trifa had. But they were naive, too. They thought Charlie Kremer would just give up."

Like a lawyer preparing a case, Kremer had carefully organized his evidence. Each document was alphabetized; when he reached the twenty-seventh, the dentist simply started numbering what he called his "exhibits." He returned to New York with cartons filled with eighty-eight exhibits, each meticulously labeled and included in a master index. "Here was the ammunition," Kremer hoped, "to shoot down Trifa."

The United Rumanian Jews of America, however, had elected new leadership during Kremer's journey. "They told me they were no longer interested in Trifa. I told them that's fine with me. Who needs those old men? Charlie Kremer isn't a joiner, anyway. Charlie Kremer is a founder." In the fall of 1957, the dentist resigned from the organization and started his own group, the Rumanian Jewish Federation of America, Inc. This group, at first consisting of only Dr. C. H. Kremer, president, and boxes of stationery, had just one purpose—the deportation of Valerian Trifa.

Under this new letterhead, the dentist mailed copies of his eighty-eight exhibits. He sent copies to the President, the Secretary of State, Immigration officials, Rumanian Christian societies, the forty-six parishes in Trifa's episcopate, New York and Michigan congressmen, the mayors of Detroit and Grass Lakes, and any newspaper he thought should be interested.

"I sent it all out and then I waited. I said any day now, Charlie Kremer, you'll be reading about the government kicking that bastard out. I really had terrific stuff."

The "terrific stuff" had not come easily. In Rumania Kremer had spent weeks searching through newspaper morgues. "I'd get up in the morning and spend the day in a hot room just looking for articles that mentioned Trifa." He found them. Bucharest newsclippings reported Trifa's speeches and there were many photographs of the twenty-six-year-old commandant in his Iron Guard uniform. "I looked at those pictures and I said, oh boy, Charlie Kremer, let Trifa now tell people he was never in the Iron Guard." And the dentist also discovered anti-Semitic proclamations signed by Trifa which had been published in the Iron Guard newspapers, *Buna Vestine* and *Porcuna Vremei.*

Photographs, though, were not enough. Kremer wanted witnesses. Taking names from court records, he searched for other members of the Iron Guard who had served with Trifa. These men had not forgotten their commandant. "Certainly he was in the Iron Guard," said Traian Boeru, a friend of Trifa the student leader. Other legionnaires, some who had spent up to fifteen years in prison for their participation in the 1941 revolt, found the question ridiculous. "They looked at me like I was crazy," remembered Kremer. "It was like asking an American if FDR had been our President." Kremer questioned these men without animosity. He was unconcerned with their crimes, their participation. His fixation on one man was complete.

"But for my case to stick, to throw the net over that Satan so he really couldn't wiggle out," the dentist decided, "I needed eyewitnesses who had seen Trifa during the revolt. People who would implicate Trifa in killings." This was more difficult. None of the Guardists would admit that either they or Trifa had participated in any killings. And the victims had been silenced.

"I thought it was a dead end. But everyone I spoke with said, 'Go to Israel. You'll find Rumanian Jews there who will remember Trifa.' So I went. It was a trip of how many thousand miles? Three thousand? Five thousand? I didn't even think about it. I just knew it might help me catch that devil, so I packed and left. And wouldn't you know Charlie Kremer found what he was looking for."

In Israel, Kremer quickly made contacts among the Rumanian immigrants. There were many who could never forget.

Marcu Iosif told Kremer about his imprisonment in the Iron Guard headquarters with other Jews who had been rounded up from the Ploesti Synagogue. Iosif still recalled the precise day—November 10, 1940. Sixteen days later, the jail was inspected by an Iron Guard party headed by Sima and Trifa. Iosif remembered that following their inspection, nine Jews were taken to the forest and shot.

"I was doing by then fatigue duties imposed on the detainees and I heard all the telephone calls being made in the name of or behalf of Comrade Trifa," Iosif told the dentist. "It was he who approved the deals, money against freedom, as well as the plunder being done by the special squads of the Iron Guard."

In Tel Aviv, Kremer met with Moshe Maur-Schur, a newspaper editor: "I happened to be in the center of Bucharest the very day the Trifa-Sima instigated pogrom started . . . At approximately 3:30 I saw from the shop Trifa arrive on a motorcycle. He parked it in front of the Choral Synagogue and went inside to inspect.

"I was able to recognize him because I had seen him so often at press conferences and at the university. Fifteen minutes later he emerged and left on his motorcycle. I left the shop and went home through back yards. The following day I entered the Choral Synagogue. I saw torn Torah scrolls on the floor and the whole place was a shambles."

Maur also introduced Kremer to Rabbi Hersh Guttman. The rabbi was an old man with a long, silver beard. He told Kremer, rather matter-of-factly, "Trifa, I will never forget that man. He destroyed my life." And the rabbi spoke slowly, but without hesitation, into Kremer's tape recorder:

"It was January 1941. The legionnaires were masters of our country. . . .

"A group of legionnaires broke into my house in the dark of night and arrested me and my sons. They brought us together with some hundreds of Jews. They beat us until our blood ran like a stream and late in the afternoon they took us to Jilava forest and shot us two by two.

"I shouted, *'Shema Yisroael,'* and I felt that my sons were dead. I stayed with them the whole night covered with snow and my blood mixed with the blood of my sons."

The bullets had somehow only wounded the rabbi and when the war was over he immigrated to Israel where he established a small Tel Aviv synagogue named for his two dead sons. "Put Trifa behind bars," the rabbi told Kremer. "My heart won't be quieted, but my conscience will be satisfied."

Often during the next ten years the dentist played and then replayed the rabbi's tape. He was always fascinated by the resignation in the rabbi's voice. Rabbi Guttman was beyond hate. After so many years, the words became unimportant to Kremer. He played the tape only to listen to the sound of the rabbi's voice. The tone was as flat and steady as a horizon, the Yiddish quiet and controlled. There were no shouts or screams for retribution. Each time he heard the tape, Kremer swore to himself that he would not quit "until that bastard Trifa paid for his crimes." The tape was not so much a sort of psychic boost, an inducement to continue; Kremer did not need encouragement. The dentist listened to the tape and heard a warning. This is what it sounded like to lose. Guttman was not a survivor; the rabbi had been another victim murdered in the forest. Kremer, though, was determined to be a victor.

The dentist thought his eighty-eight exhibits would guarantee his victory. He was wrong. "My evidence didn't do a God damn thing," said Kremer.

Nearly all the government officials had forwarded Kremer's exhibits to the Immigration Service. And Immigration officers in Washington, New York, and Detroit replied to the dentist. The addresses and signatures were different, but the responses were always identical:

"Subsequent to Bishop Trifa's entry into the United States, charges against him were received by this Service. An extensive investigation of all such charges was thereafter conducted over a period of years. Although the inquiries were exhaustive in scope and nature, they failed to establish any ground upon which Bishop Trifa might be removed from the United States. . . ."

"Exhaustive? Extensive? The hell they were. Those bastards were believing every lie Trifa told them. Didn't they care?" It made no sense to the dentist.

"When I heard about Trifa becoming a citizen, I knew something was fishy. Anyone who had even just been in the Iron Guard was excluded from citizenship. The law was as simple as that. And certainly Charlie Kremer had at least proven that Trifa was in the Iron Guard. I knew from that moment on that someone had been paid off. I realized Immigration people were involved in one of the greatest cover-ups of all time."

Kremer's failures fired his anger. He remained determined not to lose, not to quit. He began a new campaign of letters, again mailing his evidence that Trifa had served in the Iron Guard. This time he received a new version of the old response: "In the course of the naturalization proceedings, all avenues of inquiry into the charges brought against him were again thoroughly explored."

"It was nothing but a pack of lies," the dentist yelled. "They gave me the business about all avenues of inquiry being thoroughly explored. Who are they kidding? Don't they think I know this is just one big cover-up? Don't they think Charlie Kremer knows someone is on the take? I gave them eighty-eight exhibits. What else do they want?"

For ten more years the eighty-eight exhibits stayed in a filing cabinet in the dentist's office, a cabinet with a human skull on top. During those ten years Dr. Kremer continued to write letters and gather more evidence. He was a man obsessed by the bishop he had never even seen. He could not stop his pursuit.

And for ten years the one piece of evidence he needed to complete his case was, unknown to Kremer, just two miles from his home. The evidence was in the crypt of the Cathedral of St. John the Divine.

CONSTANTIN Antonovici worked days and nights in a dark, forty-foot-high stone room underneath the main floor of the massive gothic Cathedral of St. John the Divine in New York City. Mostly, he worked on his owls. He sculpted the birds in bronze, marble, and aluminum. He created sleeping owls, owls on pedestals, owls in relief, baby owls, owl queens, and owl princesses. "I find something human in their expression," he once wrote, attempting an explanation. Critics praised the "essential mystery" of Antonovici's owls, a "symbol of the Good which has dominated his work for thirty years," and observed that Antonovici's "preoccupation with this symbol has shaped his personal style."

The owl seemed an appropriate symbol for Antonovici. There was truly something owlish about the short, old man, something hidden and mysterious. It was as if, after all the years, the mystery in his work and the secrets he knew had merged, each fertilizing the other. Constantin Antonovici isolated himself in this dim, stone crypt—the chamber had been designed as a tomb—because of the burden of his knowledge: He knew an Iron Guard commandant, a man he had seen lead an execution squad into a prison cell, had become a bishop. But what could he do? He was a private man, an artist. He hoped to create new worlds, rather than rectify old ones. Like his birds, An-

tonovici remained silent, consumed by what he knew and
the futility of this knowledge.

When Antonovici had immigrated to America in the
early 1950s, he thought he had finally succeeded in blot-
ting out Trifa and the war; it was a repressed secret which
only manifested itself unconsciously in his art. Yet retri-
butive fate or perhaps just casual accident forced the
sculptor to confront the past. Antonovici was working in
New York during the winter of 1956, when the call came
from the Rumanian Orthodox Episcopate offering him a
commission for two wood sculptures. It was natural that
they sought Antonovici; he was a Rumanian sculptor of
international reputation. And, it was natural that the
sculptor accept; he was an Orthodox Christian and he was
eager to create art for his church.

In the midst of a bitter north Michigan winter, Antonovici arrived at the Vatra. Excited about the challenge of
carving a wooden iconostasis for the chapel, he immediately asked to meet the bishop who had approved his
commission. He wanted to thank Bishop Valerian and
hear his comments on the sculptor's plan to decorate the
structure with Rumanian folk art symbols. "You will meet
everyone at the evening meal," explained the priest who
showed him to his upstairs bedroom in the large farmhouse.

Many of the priests were already seated when Antonovici entered the dining room that first evening. They
were talking in Rumanian. He sat down and noticed that
the seat at the head of the long wooden table was empty.
The bishop had not yet arrived. Politely, he conversed
with the priest to his right about the winter beauty of the
Michigan countryside. He talked, but all the time he concentrated on the priest's face. It was somehow familiar,
yet disturbing. He thought he recognized it, but no, he
told himself, that was impossible. He decided he was tired
from his journey; his fatigued mind played tricks. Then,
he noticed another priest across the table. Antonovici was
certain he recognized him. His mind was surely not de-
ceiving him. What was happening? Suddenly, the room

became respectfully quiet. Bishop Valerian Trifa took his seat at the head of the table. This was incredible! Antonovici wanted to shout. He wanted to run from the room. But he just sat there.

"Welcome to the Vatra, Constantin Antonovici," said the smiling bishop.

Antonovici stared and only nodded. He could not speak. This bishop was the same man he had seen sixteen years ago dressed in an Iron Guard's uniform. This bishop was the same legionnaire who had entered the Bucharest jail cell only moments before the Jewish prisoners were shot in cold blood. Antonovici was also certain he had recognized the two priests. They, too, were Guardists, members of the same legionnaire group which had arrested him in Bucharest.

After sixteen years, these men had forgotten Antonovici. His had just been another face in a crowded jail. But he could never forget their faces.

During the next few months Antonovici did his work and avoided the bishop. He considered telling someone about Trifa, but whom could he tell? Who would care? It had happened long ago in another country. Also, the sculptor was frightened, a man living in terror. If these men recognized him, Antonovici was certain he would be killed.

On the night of May 13, 1957, though, Antonovici made the mistake of drinking too much champagne at the party celebrating the bishop's citizenship. The wine had overpowered his fear and caution. The next moments remained with Antonovici forever; a conversation which, in time, the sculptor remembered as a threat.

"Don't you think that someday the Americans will find out about you?" he demanded of the bishop.

The bishop laughed. Antonovici's threats were unimportant. The priests laughed. "Who can touch me?" Trifa asked. "Things don't fall on my head."

By summer, Antonovici's work at the Vatra was completed. He was eager to return to his studio under St. John's Cathedral. He left confused and baffled. He had gone through this once before. These were the very men who had forced him to flee from Rumania and now, sixteen years later, he felt as if he were escaping again.

Not long after he had first arrived in America, Antonovici sculpted an intricate white marble tomb for William Manning, tenth bishop of New York. The Cathedral of St. John the Divine was so enthusiastic about this Rumanian immigrant's work that it gave him a studio in a basement crypt. Antonovici returned to this spacious room, its dense stone walls reaching forty feet to a vaulted red brick ceiling—support for the floor of the main cathedral above. The room was dark and as cold as moist stone, and the sculptor deliberately made it even darker by muting the two hanging light bulbs with improvised aluminum foil shades. The only effective color and light in the room was from his work: the high gleam and polish of the aluminum, marble, and steel owls, all displayed on wooden shelves like birds perched on branches about the room. He worked night and day, so he kept a short-legged cot—just inches off the cement floor—in a corner of the studio. Across from the cot was a hot plate and some food piled on a fragile card table: two loaves of white bread, an aspirin bottle, a container of milk, Sanka, crumpled paper towels, and a few slices of toast kept fresh in a plastic bag. It was here that Antonovici worked, a short, jaunty man, always dressed in sandals, a brown beret, and a long, soiled smock. It was here that Antonovici hoped to finish his career, living with his owls and his secret.

Once Antonovici had grander plans. "A young artist is overwhelmed by grand dreams of glory, of conquering the world of art," he had written. When Antonovici had graduated from the Academy of Fine Arts of Yasi, Rumania, in 1939, he decided only one man could help him "conquer the world of art": "At any price, and at any risk, I should go to Paris and continue my studies in the studio of the revolutionary Brancusi." It was an ambition that would take eight years to fulfill, an ambition hindered by men concerned with conquering more tangible worlds.

Antonovici was first arrested during the Iron Guard revolt in 1941. He escaped, fleeing to the studio of the Yugoslav sculptor Mestrocovic in Zagreb. He was in Zagreb only one day before the Gestapo arrested him. He was taken to Belgrade: "I was thrown into a small, damp and dark prison cell, approximately five by eight feet. Although it was winter, the cell had no heat, and the only food was a slice of bread and ersatz coffee for breakfast, at lunch two boiled potatoes, and one for dinner. No sugar. In the meantime, they were asking me, 'Do you accept liberty and go to the front?' My answer was always the same, '*Nu*.' " After six months in this cell, Antonovici was sent to Vienna. In Vienna the local Gestapo were more lenient. They required that he register at the police station every morning, but allowed him to enroll at the Academy of Fine Arts. "My thoughts," he wrote, "were only on art, not Hitler's war."

It was 1947 before Antonovici reached Paris and Brancusi. The master was now seventy-one years old and crotchety, but he accepted Antonovici as a pupil. Just months before he died in 1951, Brancusi officially selected Antonovici as his only protégé. "I certify," wrote Brancusi, "that Mr. Antonovici, Constantin, possesses much talent for sculpture and works with dedication." "To me," said Antonovici, "all my diplomas have no value to compare with Brancusi's certificate."

Glad to leave a Europe which he associated with wars, murder, and imprisonment, Antonovici came to America in 1951, determined "to think only about art." But a chance commission in Michigan abruptly shoved him into the past. The past, once uncovered, could never remain past. "I did my work. I work harder than ever. But no matter how much I work, I cannot forget about Trifa," said Antonovici. "I cannot forget that he is a killer and no one can do anything about it."

For thirteen years he kept his secret. Then in April 1970, another chance incident informed Antonovici that someone else knew about Trifa. Antonovici was in his studio, resting after an exhausting morning of chipping marble, when he read an article in a Rumanian-language paper about a Manhattan dentist who was accusing Bishop Valerian of being an Iron Guardist. Antonovici, still dressed in his sculptor's smock, immediately ran through the cathedral and out into the street looking for a telephone. On the corner of Amsterdam Avenue he found a phone and called Dr. Charles Kremer.

The sculptor and the dentist did not get along. Antonovici was a soft-spoken European gentleman, the sort of man who immediately shook hands or kissed a lady's hand when being introduced. He found Kremer to be "very aggressive." "He likes to insult everybody. I tell him, 'You are not polite. You are a dentist. You should act different.' But Kremer just antagonizes people. I go to meeting with him and he tells people to shut up. He acts like a man who is not educated."

Still, Kremer and Antonovici made an alliance. The dentist pushed the sculptor into action. Kremer, quite literally, dragged a reluctant man from his tomb. "I told him," said Kremer, "that between the two of us we could get Trifa cold. 'Stick with me,' I told him, 'and watch Charlie Kremer get everyone to jump.'"

The two men wrote a new series of letters and went to Jewish and Rumanian organizations asking for support. Kremer now had an eighty-ninth exhibit—the testimony of Constantin Antonovici:

"During the revolt in January 20, 1941, I was eating in a restaurant in Bucharest when I was arrested by the Iron Guard. They came at me like wild beasts and brought me to a cell in the basement of the Iron Guard headquarters. From my cell I heard sobbing. I asked the guard what was the trouble and he answered me, 'Those are Jews who will soon be shot.'

"At this police headquarters there was an officer named Ilie Stanga with whom I was a friend from the time I was student at Yasi. Through the guard I send him a note. . . . After fifteen minutes, four policemen appear in my cell saying that Officer Stanga wants me in his office.

"While I was walking in the corridor along the cell

block and surrounded by the four police, three Iron Guardists appeared at the entrance to a cell. I recognized them and quickly covered my face so they would not recognize me. The policeman who was leading me said, 'The Commandant has come to liquidate the Jews.' They mentioned the names of Trifa, Talnaru, and Acrivu. The three Guardists arrived at the front of the cell and I heard them order the guards to open it. Immediately I heard pistol shots being fired and cries from the people being killed. I had not reached the end of the corridor before I heard more begging and shots into the next cell. My guards said, 'They will kill all the Jews who are in those cells.' Another added, 'Poor men. They are not guilty.' Another answered ironically, 'You heard what Trifa ordered. Either we are victorious or we die.' The policemen laughed."

Kremer realized that for the first time he had testimony directly implicating Trifa in murder. He was certain his eighty-ninth exhibit would finally force the government to prosecute Trifa. "When I have you give your testimony in a courtroom," he told Antonovici, "your friend the bishop will shit in his pants."

DURING the thirteen years when Kremer incessantly wrote letters and Antonovici worked on his owls, Bishop Valerian Trifa had also been busy. The product of his labor appeared in what seemed to be two innocuous photographs published in the 1971 issue of *Solia*, a journal of Trifa's episcopate.

On page 175, there was a picture of a monument in Spain surrounded by smiling men. The monument had been erected to honor Mota and Marin, two Rumanian Iron Guardists who had been killed fighting for Franco's Nationalists during the Spanish Civil War. Among the proud men photographed in 1970 in front of the Mota and Marin monument was Horia Sima, leader of the 1941 Iron Guard revolt. The caption beneath the picture boasted that the forty-six parishes in Bishop Valerian Trifa's episcopate had made substantial contributions toward building this monument.

In the same issue of *Solia*, on page 172, there was another fascinating photograph Antonovici and Kremer studied very carefully. It was a picture of the Parochial Council of the St. Nicholas Parish in Detroit, a church directly controlled by Bishop Trifa. Among the councilmen they discovered:

Reverend Dumitru Mihaescu. Mihaescu, like Trifa, had been a member of the Iron Guard in Rumania. He, too, was convicted *in absentia* by the Rumanian government in 1941, and spent the war in Fichtenheim until, in 1944, he joined the Rumanian National Army in Germany. He was living in Brazil when Trifa ordered him to America and had him ordained a priest.

Dumitru Lungu. Another Guardist who found exile in Fichtenheim, Lungu today lives just outside Detroit in Windsor, Ontario, and is a major contributor to Iron Guard journals published in America and Spain.

Mircea Banciu. Banciu, who also spent the war in Germany, is in charge of distributing Iron Guard material throughout the United States.

Chirila Ciuntu. Ciuntu is perhaps the most important man in the worldwide resurrection of the Iron Guard. As treasurer of the American legionnaires, he collects the contributions from the American nests and personally delivers these monies to Sima in Spain. In 1941, he was sentenced to death for the crimes committed as an assistant to the Guardist police inspector. After Trifa became bishop, he emigrated from Argentina to Windsor, Ontario, a ten-minute drive from Detroit. Ciuntu, a steel worker, admits, "Sure I see Sima in Madrid. We are friends. I was with him in Germany, with Trifa, too. What do I do in Spain? I buy books, anti-Communist books. We find that Jews are Communists. We find that everywhere we live the Jews are trouble."

Octavian Rosu. Another legionnaire sentenced to life by the Rumanian government, Rosu escaped to Fichtenheim where he helped organize the Rumanian National Army which fought with the Nazis. After the war he remained in close contact with Sima. In 1969, he emigrated from Rome to Detroit at the request of Bishop Trifa.

This photograph of the members of the St. Nicholas Parish in Detroit, however, was just one part of the network that Trifa controlled. This was just one of his Iron Guard nests. From Europe and South America, Trifa ordered eight key Guardists, all veterans of Fichtenheim, to the United States. Though they were without theological training, Trifa, as bishop, had them ordained as priests. These "priests," in turn, now direct other nests, nests in Detroit, Philadelphia, Cleveland, and New York.

Trifa's plans for the Iron Guard, though, have not been confined only to the United States. In the August 1972 edition of *Solia,* the president and the vice president of the Inviera (Resurrection) Parish in Buenos Aires congratulated Bishop Trifa on the twentieth anniversary of his ordainment. The priest in charge of the parish is Mile Lefter, another convicted Guardist who also became a priest without prior theological training. The president and vice president of the Inviera Parochial Council, Mardarie Popinciuc and Petre Misa, were inspectors for the Iron Guardist police and had been sentenced to death in Bucharest in 1941. Trifa keeps in communication with these South American nests through Stelian Stanicel. Stanicel, a former secretary of the Guard's founder, Zela Codreanu, and Secretary General for the Bucharest police department from 1940 to 1941, was also convicted by the Rumanian government for Guardist activity. Now he is a U.S. citizen, working in a travel agency and living in Detroit.

By the time Kremer had collected his eighty-nine exhibits, over thirty convicted Guardists had immigrated to the United States and joined nests under the direct control of Bishop Valerian Trifa. Like Kremer, these men refused to forget. The future, they hoped, would be built on the past. Some tried to fit into American life, becoming steel workers or librarians or travel agents. But all the time they were rootless immigrants hoping to return to Rumania, hoping to return as legionnaires.

For now they could only wait. George Roman, former Parochial Council President of a Trifa church, remembers meetings of his nest at the St. John's Parish in Detroit: "I attend many of these meetings. We repeat oaths of allegiance to Horia Sima. We salute the commander of the nest with Hitlerite salute. There are pictures all around of Codreanu. We distribute all kinds of literature. You know, anti-Semitic stuff. And we get copies of the legionnaire paper from Spain, *Tara si Exilul* [*The Country and the Exile*], to give out at church. We also give out copies of *Drum* [*The Way*], an American Guardist paper. At every meeting we collect money for Sima in Spain. I personally brought $3,000 collected at two meetings to Chirila Ciuntu in Windsor. Mostly, though, we talk and we dream. We talk about how safe we are here in America and how we can't wait till we get the orders to return to Rumania and push the Communists out. That is the day we still dream about—the day our exile is over and the Iron Guard can return to Rumania."

DR. Charles Kremer now had trouble typing letters. He was in his seventies and his eyes were failing, but he refused to quit. He told Antonovici, "We can't stop now. With you I got something terrific. I'm certain the government is going to give in."

So Kremer got friends or friends of friends to type

his letters. He would hand his typists long letters written in a compact, almost undecipherable script and when they questioned a word he would shout, "What's the matter with you? We haven't got forever. If you can't read, you shouldn't offer to help." Each week, however, new letters were sent to the Immigration Service, politicians, and newspapers.

The replies he received in 1972 were much like those he had received in 1962. Ten years of letters had not impressed the government. "I'd read what they sent," said Kremer, "about the extensive inquiries they had done and I knew they were full of crap. It was a cover-up pure and simple. I had given them the names of witnesses. How many had they interviewed? None. And had they questioned Antonovici? No. Charlie Kremer knows when something is rotten and believe me the Immigration Service is rotten."

Still, he sent letters. By now his letters were no longer civil. It had become a bitter, private battle—Charlie Kremer versus the Immigration Service. A letter to INS Associate Commissioner James F. Greene was indicative of the dentist's style:

"Don't you think that my presentation containing eighty-nine exhibits, running into many hundreds of pages, *deserves* a *written answer,* and at least a show of interest on your part? Why don't you delegate a person in either the Washington or New York City office to examine and discuss my file and thus give me an opportunity to compare my file with yours? THIS HAS NEVER BEEN DONE—WHY?

"I cannot help but be frustrated that since April 26, 1952 . . . I have received the same lack of cooperation."

James F. Greene's response also was indicative: ". . . this Service had considered every scrap of information and evidence in this case, and had concluded that there was insufficient evidence. . . ."

And so, Kremer was convinced, the cover-up continued. He had sent Immigration eighty-nine exhibits.

What more did they want? They had never even interviewed any witnesses. Trifa, like Malaxa, would die a free
man in America.

Then on March 23, 1972, Kremer received a letter
from Lowell R. Palmes, assistant director for citizenship,
Detroit. This letter, out of all the hundreds, nearly convinced Kremer to give up.

Palmes's 1972 letter was a response to a request the
dentist had first made five years ago for a copy of Trifa's
testimony at the bishop's "open and public" naturalization
hearing. It had taken the government five years to discover:

"At the time of the naturalization hearing oral testimony was taken, and there was no record made of the
testimony given. The only record in the court was the
order granting citizenship which was signed by the pre-
siding judge."

Sidney Freed, the Detroit district INS examiner, had
simply decided it was not necessary to follow normal
practice and make a transcript of Trifa's testimony. At his
hearing, Trifa denied being in the Iron Guard and making
anti-Semitic speeches. "There was no reason not to believe the Bishop," said Freed.

"When I found out," said Kremer, "that no written
record had been made at the hearing, I absolutely almost
busted a blood vessel. What kind of extensive investigation
did those crooks conduct? I tell you, it was the lowest
moment of my life. It seemed everything Charlie Kremer
did wasn't enough. If Trifa had bought the entire Immigration Service, how was Charlie Kremer to fight that?"

For weeks the dentist sat at home. He stopped sending
letters. He was beginning, he remembers, "to feel like a
seventy-year-old man."

His elixir came unannounced in the mail. A friend in
Detroit mailed Kremer a front-page article from *The Detroit Free Press*. Hilary Ward, the newspaper's religion
editor, had received one of Kremer's letters and copies of
his eighty-nine exhibits. On a hunch Ward drove to Grass
Lakes and interviewed the bishop. He got quite a story:
Trifa, for the first time, admitted membership in the Iron

Guard; however, he denied killing anyone—"neither Christian nor Jew."

"When I saw this article in the Detroit paper, I knew all those years had not been in vain," said the dentist. "I always believed in the old Rumanian proverb, 'Every bird dies by his tongue.' And now I knew Trifa had finally been caught by his."

The article became the dentist's ninetieth exhibit. This was his lucky number. On September 28, 1973—thirty-two years after he had first circled Trifa's name in red—he received a letter from Charles Gordon, general counsel of the Immigration Service. Gordon had received copies of two letters Kremer had sent to Henry Kissinger and the Attorney General. Gordon had read these letters and decided, "This office will conduct a new investigation into the matter, giving full consideration to all material submitted by you."

"I couldn't believe my eyes when I read that letter," said Kremer. "A new investigation! I read and re-read that sentence. It was unbelievable, but I knew all along I would win. You know Charlie Kremer. Once he makes up his mind, he can do anything."

Kremer received the letter in September 1973. Six months later the Service had still not interviewed any of the witnesses. Kremer now decided to get on a train to Washington and confront Gordon.

The dentist had dressed carefully for the meeting, wearing a white shirt, a tie, and a freshly pressed suit. During the train ride he told himself over and over, "Don't lose your temper, Charlie Kremer. Don't lose your temper."

The two men met in the general counsel's office in the Immigration building. Gordon was friendly and Kremer was respectful. Gordon promised the investigation would start soon.

"You got to contact these people right away," Kremer insisted. "They're not young fellows."

"We haven't been asleep," Gordon replied.

"Well," said Dr. Kremer, "I haven't slept for thirty years."

BISHOP Valerian Trifa is angry. He is sitting in the comfortable living room of the Vatra and he is yelling. "It is a plot against me. I am a victim of a Communist plot." He sits there, a short, bald, old man of sixty-one, wounded and fragile, hunched over and lost in the folds of his black vestment. His voice, however, is very intense. He does not attempt to smile; he obviously does not like to be questioned. The words hang like icicles in the air. Yet, he seems to move easily in and out of anger.

"Yes," he says calmly, "I wore the Iron Guard uniform. But I was never a legionnaire. Never. Never."

Asked about his 1941 trial, he erupts into a full shout, "Lies, Communist lies." Asked about Guardist priests, he becomes enraged. "The Communists are spreading those stories."

He sits like a pouting child, refusing to speak. With his large, bald head and dark-rimmed glasses, he, incongruously, resembles the cartoon character, Mr. Magoo. "I will not talk about specific incidents. This is not the time or the place." All he will say is, "I'm not ashamed of my past at all. For those circumstances and in that time I think that I didn't have any other alternative but to do what I thought right for the interests of the Rumanian people."

The "time and place for specifics," however, is approaching. On May 16, 1975, the U.S. Attorney in Detroit filed a complaint instituting proceedings "to revoke and set aside the order of the court admitting Bishop Trifa to citizenship and to cancel his certificate of naturalization on the grounds that the order and certificate were illegally procured . . . by the concealment of material fact and . . . misrepresentation."

Trifa's episcopate will provide their bishop with a legal

defense. In its official statement, the episcopate's "department of public relations" blamed the charges on "Rumanian Communists" who "sought allies among the Jews
and found one dentist in New York by the name of
Charles Kremer."

Trifa's lawyer, John J. Sibisan of Cleveland, promises,
"There will be denial of all charges." His strategy, as
reported in the Detroit papers, will be to argue that the
government knew of Trifa's Iron Guard past when they
granted him citizenship. This argument is grounded in
legal precedent: A 1957 deportation order was overturned
when it was proven the government had known of the
defendant's criminal past when it granted him citizenship.
The man in the 1957 case to whom Trifa is compared—
Mafia Don Albert Anastasia.

Trifa's case, a year after the initial charges, has still
not come to trial. A date has still not been set. Despite
the probability that the case could drag on for ten or
fifteen years, the government seems in no hurry to enter
the courtroom. And then, even if the government wins
and a time-consuming appeal is denied, Trifa can still
remain free in America; the government will have to initiate a separate proceeding for deportation.

On April 26, 1952, Dr. Charles Kremer wrote his first
letter to the Immigration Service. It took Kremer twenty-
five years, thousands of letters, trips to two continents,
and ninety exhibits to convince the government that what
he originally wrote was true.

CONSTANTIN Antonovici lives in fear now that the
charges against Trifa have been made public. Already he
is convinced he has received a warning.

He was walking outside the Cathedral of St. John the
Divine around dinner time on a summer's night when he

was grabbed from behind by a black man. "He never said a word. He didn't want money. He just wanted to hurt me. He punched me and kicked me and then he took my glasses and crushed them into my face. The glass could have gone in my eye and blinded me. Think of it! What good is a blind sculptor?"

Antonovici is certain the black man was hired by the Iron Guard.

He is afraid to leave his studio; the crypt has now become another cell. He receives phone calls, he says, from Guardists who vow they will kill him.

Near his bed he keeps a copy of *The Bolan News,* a paper published in New York by a Guardist sympathizer who works as a doorman. An article in the paper attacks Kremer: "His hate against everyone who tries to defend himself against the Jewish take-over is well known. This is a classic tactic of Jewry."

But the paper's fiercest rage is aimed at Antonovici. His testimony, the paper reports, is "a gesture of Judas." "It's inadmissible for a good Christian to throw so many lies on another Christian."

The sculptor has underlined the last lines of the article: "We shall never forget them, let them be sure. And the punishment they deserve will hit them when they feel most secure."

Ever since his mugging and the article in *The Bolan News,* Antonovici has not been able to create new owls. He still sculpts, but he now works on other projects. "I cannot make my owls anymore," he complains. "I don't know why, but my heart is no longer in it."

IT was not long after the U.S. Attorney filed suit against Trifa that Dr. Kremer, now seventy-eight, started gathering exhibits for a new case.

During a 1971 visit to Bucharest to obtain a transcript of the Rumanian government's case against Trifa, Kremer had been involved in an auto accident. The car the dentist was riding in had been struck by another auto which ran a red light. Kremer's door flew open and he tumbled to the street, permanently injuring his back and leg. The driver of the car which had struck Kremer's was Valentin Ceausescu, son of the President of Rumania.

Now, four years after the injury, Kremer began a campaign to recover "$55,000 in medical care and lost income caused by the accident" from the Rumanian government.

Once more the dentist started dictating letters, letters to the President, the Cabinet, senators, congressmen, his entire list. When the State Department did not reply to two letters, Kremer decided to inform the U.S. government just who they were avoiding. He wrote to Henry Kissinger:

"I do not consider this an appropriate help for our citizens in need.

"I am an experienced victim of such handling by the American establishment's bureaucracy. . . .

"I am not only tired, but thoroughly disgusted and purely revolted at the manner in which an American citizen's pleas. . . ."

Kremer's letters did not help. The Rumanian Embassy said the case was closed and the claims were "unfounded." The State Department explained that it "would not be useful to pursue the matter further."

But Charlie Kremer, the "experienced victim," refuses to give up. So far he has collected eighteen exhibits. So far he has only reached the letter S.

"They think they can tell Charlie Kremer his case is unfounded," shouts the dentist, still forceful at seventy-eight. "I sent them some terrific stuff—x-rays, letters from doctors—and they refused to look at them. It's another Trifa. It's just one more cover-up. They think they can get away with this, but Charlie Kremer won't let them. I did what nobody else could do. Charlie Kremer got Trifa when everyone said forget it. Charlie Kremer's going to win this case, too. Once Charlie Kremer makes up his mind, nothing can stop him."

A FEW days after Tony DeVito heard about the U.S. Attorney in Detroit filing charges against Trifa, he spoke with his friend Vince Schiano, the other member of the Immigration team which brought Hermine Braunsteiner Ryan to trial.

"What do you think, Vince? You think the Trifa case will come to trial?"

"Tony, Tony," moaned Schiano. "I told you once before you're no virgin. When are you going to grow up?"

"Well, you gotta give that old dentist credit. I tell you, he's a fighter."

"Sure, Tony. But let me tell you a story. You remember I worked on the Malaxa case, that other Iron Guard guy?"

"Sure."

"Well, there was no question in my mind that the fix was put on. I was the prosecutor. I had more than enough evidence to win. Anyway, one day I'm just sitting in my office and this Rumanian guy comes in. He comes in and he's carrying a brown shoebox. He just walks in and says, 'You know, Mr. Malaxa has this spiritual problem and he wants to resolve it. He put into my keeping $200,000 which is supposed to take care of a lot of things. What should I do with it, Mr. Schiano?'

"I couldn't believe it, Tony. This guy was offering me $200,000 and it was right there in this shoebox in front of me. I told him to bank it, collect some interest, maybe. I'm not his financial advisor. That's his problem.

"What I'm trying to say, Tony, is that Malaxa got off clean. Who knows what it cost him? You'll see Trifa will get off, too. The same money that paid for Malaxa will pay for his friend Trifa. Mark my words, Tony. Trifa will never spend a day in jail."

"Yeah," said DeVito, "I guess I know Immigration as well as you do. I guess you're one hundred percent right."

The two friends were silent. There didn't seem to be much more to say. There was a long pause before DeVito spoke. "Still," he said, "you've got to give that dentist credit. He's a hell of a fighter."

3

The Good Life

THE Ryan trial had made Tony DeVito a celebrity. He was a bit uncomfortable with this public role, but he was not reluctant.

Tonight he had taken an empty Sunday evening train in from Long Island to attend a meeting of the Jewish War Veterans in a midtown Manhattan Holiday Inn. He chose a seat in the middle of the second row of wooden chairs in the electric green room and sat silently, clutching a black Samsonite attaché case. He wore a dark, unstylish suit and his gunmetal hair was brushed straight back as was the fashion a generation ago. His clothes, his grim, intense expression and even his attaché case helped give him a dull, bureaucratic air as if he should instead be sitting in a room lined with desks. For the others in the meeting hall the evening was another monthly reunion; the veterans and their wives happily milled about shaking hands, trading gossip, kissing cheeks, and hoping their extravagant concessions to style had disguised the latest indiscretions of middle age.

DeVito, though, was all business. He had attended enough of these meetings to appreciate their tone and style: Each time he went to an evening sponsored by a Jewish organization he left angry.

"Sure, they make a big deal about Nazis in America," he would tell his wife, "but it's just a crock. They should organize. They should force Washington to do something. They go on about how it's a disgrace and then that's the last you ever hear of them. And when you finally come across some guy who's all steamed up, all he wants to know about is the one Nazi he's after. They don't give a damn about the total picture. You think Kremer gives a damn about Soobzokov? Fat chance. If you told him Hitler was across the street, he'd still be asking what's new in the Trifa case."

DeVito could never understand why anyone was not shocked into action by the revelation that 59 Nazis were hiding in America. But for Jews to ignore this reality, he felt, was inexcusable. He would leave these meetings with vague promises of support and on the train ride back to Long Island he would sit with his attaché case across his legs, his mind fixed on one image: the Jewish collaborator being stoned in Dachau. These disinterested Jews were also collaborators. The years of inaction, the stolen files, and the cover-ups had agitated DeVito until he perceived every situation as a subtle struggle between two sides— the collaborators and the hunters. For DeVito, this distinction was both necessary and sufficient.

Tonight he sat silently for most of the meeting, the attaché case resting across his lap as though it should have been a friendly cat. It wasn't until the moderator, a commander of the Jewish War Veterans, mentioned one name that DeVito abruptly rose to his feet. A week ago DeVito had received a phone call promising that this certain person would be discussed at a meeting of the Jewish War Veterans. Would DeVito be interested in attending? DeVito was very interested. He recognized the name immediately; it was the first on his list of 59. The name was Andrija Artukovic.

"Mr. Chairman, I wonder if I might say a couple of words about Artukovic," DeVito interrupted, talking in a soft, almost shy voice. Clearly, he did not enjoy speaking to an audience.

"Certainly, Mr. DeVito." And then the chairman turned to the crowd. "For those of you who don't know," he said, "Mr. DeVito is the man who helped bring Hermine Braunsteiner Ryan to trial."

There was some enthusiastic applause and DeVito, embarrassed, stared down at his attaché case. The applause, though, seemed to give him confidence and when he spoke his voice was louder and more forceful.

"Let me tell you something about Artukovic," he began. "Artukovic is a murderer. He's responsible for the deaths of thousands of Jews in Croatia during the war. There's no doubt about that. Yet Immigration says they can't deport him to Yugoslavia because he'd be a political prisoner.

"Well, let me just tell you that's a crock. The whole affair stinks." After each burst of words DeVito ferociously jabbed his index finger in the air; he appeared and sounded like a man locked in a hot, barroom argument.

"Let me just tell you that there was a case a while back where a Yugoslav seaman jumped ship and tried to get asylum in the United States. Immigration had no problem sending that guy back to Yugoslavia one, two, three.

"But that guy was just a poor seaman. Artukovic, on the other hand, is a very wealthy man with a lot of important friends. He's a very, very rich murderer. You can just imagine how he got his money. And you can imagine how he spends it.

"Look, this whole thing stinks. Since 1951, the Immigration Service has known Artukovic's been hiding in California. Yet, they let him stay. He's a war criminal. There's no doubt about that. And now he just sits in sunny California counting his money and living the good life."

NOT many people go to Mary's Cafe anymore. The coffee shop is—quite literally—off the beaten path. Lively, neon places offering "Beer, Beans and Booze" or "Executive Luncheons" have crowded along this strip of the Pacific Coast Highway south of Long Beach, California, and have elbowed Mary's into the tepid, sandy background.

In this fury of southern California suburban modernism and commercial drama, Mary's remains a bit of an anachronism. It is a homey, family restaurant with hand-lettered signs, a truck-stop left over from the days when "going to the beach" was a big trip.

In those days Los Angeles seemed a hectic world away from the local marshes and the empty, fine sand beaches leading to expansive, glitter-blue stretches of the Pacific. Back then, Seal Beach, Surfside, and Huntington Harbor were mostly summer communities dotted with wooden beach shacks where middle-class Los Angelinos spent two quiet weeks trying to get away from it all.

But all that was years ago, years before the Freeway and the Coast Highway turned a strip of southern California country into still another Total Electric beachfront suburban commuter paradise, just an air-conditioned rush-hour ride away from the Big City. Now the marshes have been filled in and transformed by developers into luxury inlets for hulking cabin cruisers and antiseptic white Chris-Crafts moored giant steps away from the front doors of ranch homes with central air-conditioning and electronic garage doors. And the ratty bungalows by the sea have, by the magic of social mobility, become cottages fit for executives. Twenty years ago a three-bedroom shack in Surfside sold for $5,000 and buyers were scarce; today, beachfront cottages cannot be bought for less than

$100,000 and as soon as one is advertised, Mercedeses flock to the seller's door.

But Mary's Cafe was here before all that. It is a holdout from the time when locals worked rather than basked in the sun. A lot of people who have been around since the old days, out of loyalty or even a certain old-boy snobbery, still frequent the cafe; in southern California, a land where nearly everyone started following the sun from somewhere else, even a ten-year residency gives a family the same sort of possessiveness and position which in other parts of America can only be acquired by successive, landed generations.

Ed Sulka, who first moved into a Surfside shack just a golf ball's drive away from the ocean in 1947, is one of the "old boys" who still lunches at Mary's. He was finishing his apple pie in the back booth when his son nudged him. "Dad, isn't that Andrew who just came in?"

Sulka looked at the deeply tanned, stocky man who stood at the door.

"It sure as hell is," said Sulka and then quickly tried to bury himself in his pie. Between rapid mouthfuls he told his son, "Hope he don't see me. He's gonna want to kiss me like he keeps on telling me they do in the old country. He's gonna want to kiss me in front of all these people. Hell!"

"Aw, Dad, why do you go and say that? You know you're happy to see him. Andrew is a super guy."

"I know, I know. But I sure as hell hate to be kissed, that's all."

But there was no avoiding it. Andrew saw the two men in the back booth and rushed over.

"Eddie, good to see you," Andrew said to the son who rose and now stood at least a head taller than he. "I heard all about you and that baseball from your father." The two men shook hands.

And then Andrew turned toward the father. Both men were about the same age, in their late sixties, and both were models of sun-preserved southern California good health, dark, ruddy tans contrasting handsomely with thick gray and sun-white hair. Sulka still had a cowboy's body, long and, though a bit filled out in the gut, noticeably hard and lean. Andrew was shorter and broad like an aged linebacker.

"Ed," said Andrew to Sulka, "so good to see you. It's been months."

Andrew reached out and enthusiastically hugged the taller man with his thick forearms and planted a loud kiss on his cheek.

"See," said Sulka to his son while still trapped in the embrace, "I told you he would kiss me."

Both Andrew and Sulka laughed. Despite his embarrassment over the kiss, Sulka was happy to see Andrew. The two men went back a long way together. Over twenty years ago when both men were trying to start new lives in Southern California, they had been next-door neighbors. Back then they drove to work together, their kids played together, their wives borrowed eggs and sugar. And back then Ed Sulka was one of the first people to stand up for his friend and neighbor when it was revealed that Andrew's real name was Andrija and that as Andrija Artukovic he had been responsible for thousands of deaths during World War II.

1945 wasn't a very good year for cowboys in Cortez, Colorado. Ed Sulka had been born, raised, and married on Colorado cattle ranches, but now—for the first time—he was out of work.

"Things got so bad," remembers Sulka, "until I had no choice. I packed the wife and Ed, Jr., into the old Ford and went to the land of milk and honey."

Life was better in Los Angeles, but not much. Sulka worked for $18 a week in a grocery. He swept up, worked the check-out counter, and ran deliveries. He didn't mind the work as much as he minded city life. "You couldn't breathe in Los Angeles. It was all one big jumble of smog and noise. I wanted Ed, Jr., to have a childhood like mine. I wanted him to grow up in the outdoors."

So Sulka packed his family and their possessions into the Ford and once more followed the sun. They drove south from Los Angeles, past the suburban centers of San Pedro and Long Beach, until the traffic thinned and the unpaved road which ran along the coast led them to the oceanfront town of Seal Beach. Here the land was still naked and wild. There were inlets of dark green marshes smelling of swamp where, early in the morning when the fishing was best, so many birds filled the hazy dawn with exotic cawing and chatter that Sulka, the man from the Rockies, "felt as if I were lost in a jungle." In the evenings, Sulka would take his son and stand on an empty beach and look out into what seemed to be the limitless openness of the Pacific, iridescent from the pink-red sunset: father and son grounded to the very edge of America, an entire country behind them.

It was here that Sulka decided to settle down, to create roots and start a new life. A local paper advertised vacancies in a little row of white-painted wooden houses called Surfside. For $50 a month the Sulkas rented a two-story bungalow with a staircase only as wide as the cowboy's shoulders which led to three box-like bedrooms. In the back was a gray-fenced yard which became crowded when a picnic table and two benches were added. Beyond the yard was the dirt road; north, the road led to Los Angeles; south, it led to Tijuana. In front of the bungalow was the Pacific.

The man who rented Sulka bungalow B-63 in Surfside also offered him another opportunity. He owned a small grocery and luncheonette right in the midst of all these beach shacks; would Sulka be interested in running it? For almost two years, Sulka and his wife ran the Surfside commissary, but it was a losing proposition: Sulka couldn't make money selling bread or ice cream cones when there were so few customers.

When the owner was down from Los Angeles for a weekend of sun and fishing, Sulka explained why he was quitting the commissary. The man was understanding; he even offered Sulka another job. His Surfside property was just a hobby and an investment. His real business, he told Sulka, was a large construction firm in the city. It just so happened that his truck foreman had quit; would Sulka be interested?

"I wouldn't have to move back to Los Angeles. I mean I could commute to work, couldn't I?"

"Sure, Ed. It's a long drive, but that's your problem."

"Then I'll take it. It's a deal."

The two men shook hands.

Then the other man turned to Sulka and said, "One thing, though. I'd appreciate it if you could do me one favor, Ed."

"Sure thing," said Sulka.

"Well, you see my brother is coming in from Europe next week. Now that the Communists are running Yugoslavia the country's no longer safe. He's coming in with his wife and family and I'll be giving them the bungalow next door to yours, B-62. I'd appreciate it if you could sort of look out for him. It's going to be difficult. He's going to be setting up a new life in a new country and all . . ."

"Don't worry. I'll be glad to give him a hand. I know what it's like to be a stranger out here myself."

"Thank you. I appreciate that. And there's one other thing. He's going to be working as a bookkeeper for us in Los Angeles. I wonder if he could ride up with you in the mornings?"

"No problem. I could use the company. By the way, what's his name?"

"Andrew. And of course his last name is the same as mine—Andrew Artukovic."

In the summer of 1948, Ed Sulka and Andrew Artukovic became neighbors. Each morning at 6:30 the two men climbed into Sulka's Ford and began the two-hour drive up Main Street to the P & J Artukovic Construction Company in Los Angeles. The two men didn't talk much at first; Artukovic was uncertain about his English and Sulka was never one for making conversation. "For a while," Sulka remembers, "he was just very polite. 'Good morning, Mr. Sulka, how is Mrs. Sulka today,' and all that. I'd tell him to call me 'Ed,' but he'd just keep on with this Mr. Sulka business. He was a hell of a gentleman."

After about a year, familiarity made a more easy friendship possible. "He would go on, sometimes for the whole ride, about how lucky I was to live in America. He'd tell me people in this country don't realize how the Communists are trying to take over the world. He'd go on about the Communists and I'd just let him talk. Oh, he was very bright. But, I just didn't understand half the things he was talking about. I'd rather look at the sports page than read any of the bad news."

Sometimes, though, the two men would talk about the future, the plans they had for their sons. Sulka knew what he wanted for Ed, Jr.: "Ed was always an athlete. From the day I gave him his first bat and ball I wanted him to play in the majors." And Artukovic had plans for his boy, Radaslav: "Rad, that's what we called him," explained Sulka, "was a quiet boy, but he was as smart as the dickens. His father told me he hoped the boy would become a lawyer the way he had been in Yugoslavia." Both men hoped they could create comfortable lives in southern California, new, safe lives which would allow their sons to realize their fathers' dreams.

Proximity also overcame reticence and helped to bind the two families. "One of the first things I bought after I had saved up a little money was an encyclopedia. I wanted Ed, Jr., to have all the things I never had when I was a kid in Colorado. But I should have known—Eddie wouldn't even look at it. He was always out on the beach playing ball. Andrew's kids, though, were always coming over to look at it. I tell you, they were the smartest things.

His two little girls were just in the first grade and they were reading like college professors. They came over and borrowed all the volumes, A to Z. They were always so polite. I never saw anything like those kids."

Ed, Jr., was nearly four years older than Rad, but the two boys were constant companions. A basketball hoop hung over the garage of Artukovic's bungalow and they would play one-on-one for hours. It was not much of a contest. Ed was a natural, the moves and rhythms of sport came instinctively. Rad was more awkward, yet he played with a sincere interest and even a conscientiousness. Knowledge and skill at games, Rad perhaps felt, would make him less of a foreigner.

"Rad idolized Eddie," said Sulka. "Little Rad would always follow Eddie who was about twice his size and try to get him to teach him how to take a lay-up or throw a curve. I set up the first little league in Seal Beach so my Eddie would have a chance to get used to some real competition. And who do you think was among the first kids to sign up? Little Rad. He wanted to be a ballplayer like Eddie something awful."

On Sundays, the Artukovics and their four children would take the bus to the Catholic church in Westminster. In those days, most of the parishioners were Mexicans who worked as pickers in the nearby strawberry fields. Until 1943, the Blessed Sacrament Church of Westminster had served as a mission, a stopping place for Columban priests returning from proselytizing trips through the Orient. The church which the Artukovics now attended still retained much of this mission quality: Set along a palm-lined drive, it was a large, wheat-colored stucco structure, with pastel frescoes and graceful, curving Spanish lines rising toward a high bell tower. Under Father Robert Ross, Westminster became an active, community-oriented parish. Most priests who remember Ross grasp at the same word to describe him: "dynamic." He was a tall, handsomely gray-haired man who brought a stern but impressive presence to the pulpit.

"Father Ross had the sort of personality which reached

out and grabbed people," recalled Father David Mc-Gowan, who has replaced Ross as chaplain to the Westminster Knights of Columbus. "He saw all issues as black or white, right or wrong and he was a priest who thought it was his duty to speak out on what he believed."

One of Father Ross's causes was integration. He was an active and vocal supporter of Gonzalo Mendez, a Mexican-American asparagus farmer who sued to allow his children to attend the same Westminster schools as white children. Ross's sermons criticized the local superintendent of schools who argued that Mexicans were "inferior to the white race in matters of personal hygiene, in their ability, in their economic outlook, their clothing, and ability to take part in school activities." The March 1945 Mendez decision became a landmark: It ruled that segregation of Mexican children violated the Fourteenth Amendment, the first time segregation was denounced in a federal court.

Ross was also vehement in his opposition to Communism. He saw Marxism as an evil determined to destroy all he believed in, a threat aimed directly at the Church. Andrew Artukovic and his family, devout Catholics who —the way Ross heard and believed the story—were refugees from the Communist Yugoslav government of Tito, were quickly adopted by Ross. The priest told parishioners that he "did not know what the world was coming to when fine, educated Catholics like the Artukovics were forced to run for their lives." Father Ross became one of the Artukovics' closest friends in southern California. Often after Sunday services Father Ross would return to Surfside as a luncheon guest at the Artukovic bungalow. And, just as Father Ross stood by Gonzalo Mendez as he fought for integration in the courts of California, so would the priest support Andrew Artukovic during his eight-year legal battle.

This was the quiet southern California life that both Sulka and Artukovic settled into. In this small community of sun, beaches, and California opportunity, both men hoped their running had come to an end. They both hoped to slide into a secure, sun-tanned middle age as they watched their children grow.

For three years Artukovic managed, on the surface at least, to ignore the past. He concentrated on the future: his job as a bookkeeper, practicing his English, constructing kitchen cabinets for his bungalow, and even joining the local civil defense program. Then, his new life fell apart. At the time, it seemed sudden, startling both Ed Sulka and Father Ross. But there had been hints, mysterious intimations that must have provoked a great fear in Artukovic and his wife: They had not run far enough.

In the first week of May 1951, the local Long Beach newspaper carried two small items in its police blotter. The first story concerned a burglary at the P & J Construction Company. Detective Sergeant P. W. O'Neil discovered a hole approximately two feet square burned into the door of one of the firm's safes by an acetylene torch. According to a company spokesman, the safe contained only "papers and documents," but nothing appeared to be missing. Two days later another item in the police blotter reported that the county police had been alerted after "strangers" were "observed watching" the construction company offices.

It took just five days for these two small items to reach the front page. On May 8, 1951, two deputy U.S. marshals walked into the P & J Artukovic Construction Company and demanded to see Andrija Artukovic. They were directed to the desk of Andrew. "You're under arrest," they announced to the bookkeeper. "The charge is murder."

That evening the Long Beach paper had a banner headline: "Reds Seek Surfside Man As Criminal." Reporters gathered outside the Artukovic bungalow and were lectured by an angry Father Ross, "If he doesn't want to talk to you, why don't you leave him alone." One enterprising journalist knocked on the door of the house next to Artukovic's and interviewed a bewildered Ed Sulka: "Everything I know about him is good. He has been riding to work with me for about three years. He doesn't speak very good English and seldom said much on the way to work."

The next day Artukovic called Sulka to tell him he wouldn't be riding to work that morning. Instead, Artukovic, with Father Ross at his side, stood in front of his bungalow and announced to the crowd of reporters, "I am innocent, absolutely innocent." He then quickly returned to the safety of his little house.

It was after the first newspaper story, Sulka remembers, that "Andrew stopped coming to work. I'd have to set out each morning by myself and for a good part of the drive I would be thinking how it must have been a mistake. It just didn't seem possible that Andrew or Andrija or whatever they were calling him had been a Nazi and a murderer. It just didn't seem possible at all."

THE task seemed impossible. Yet Andrija Artukovic made certain it was performed swiftly and efficiently. There were no mistakes. Within one year after becoming Croatia's Minister of the Interior, Andrija Artukovic authorized and then supervised the arrest and internment of the country's thirty thousand Jews. Ninety percent of those arrested would not survive.

Proud of this accomplishment, Minister of the Interior Artukovic stepped before the Sabor, the Croatian parliament, on February 26, 1942, and boasted to the delegates how he was helping to write "a new, and most glorious page of . . . history." It was also a speech explaining his official policy—the policy and rationale for genocide.

"Immediately following the birth of the former Yugoslavia," Artukovic told the Sabor, "all enemies of the

Croat people—the Jews, Communists, and Freemasons—
united to destroy the Croatian people and all their national
characteristics.

"In the life of the former Yugoslavia, the Jews worked
for and prepared the world revolution. . . . The Jews, as
one of the most dangerous international organizations,
tried to achieve world Jewry . . . in order that the Jews
might gain full mastery over all goods of the world and
all the power in the world. To the Jews, other people
served as a means to their dirty profits and their insatiable
materialistic and ravenous control of the world.

"The Jews wanted to achieve these aims not only
through international Jewry as such, but also through the
Communists. Communism is the child of Jewry and one
of the principal levers for the world mastery of the
Jews. . . .

"Through various organizations the Judeo-Communists
have tried to bring about the disintegration of the Croatian
national body, to kill belief in its youth and the love of
family and homeland. . . .

"The Croatian people, having re-established their independent state of Croatia, could not do otherwise but to
clean off the poisonous damagers and insatiable parasites
—Jews, Communists, and Freemasons—from the national
and state body."

Minister of the Interior Artukovic's speech was interrupted by applause and shouts of bravo. He waited until
the assembly quieted before he concluded:

"The independent state of Croatia, as an Ustashi state,
finding itself in a state of self-defense against these insatiable and poisonous parasites, settled the so-called Jewish
question with a decisive and healthy grasp."

The Sabor erupted into sustained applause. At that
moment it would have been very easy for Artukovic to believe that his years on the run, the years in exile in Italy
and France, were finally and permanently over. At that
moment, as he received an ovation for supervising the
internment of thirty thousand Jews, it would have been

easy to believe that the Ustashi and their "call to blood" would settle all his future problems "with a decisive and healthy grasp."

ARTUKOVIC'S 1941 speech was, in many ways, a direct result of another speech made fourteen years earlier to the Sabor—a speech which ended in murder. In 1928, the year of this assassination, the Sabor governed a liberal, centralized federation of six traditional republics. The historic provinces of Croatia-Slavonia, Dalmatia, Bosnia-Herzegovina, and Montenegro had been pulled together by Crown Prince Alexander Karageorgevic at the end of World War I into a new country called "Yugoslavia." It was a fragile union; centuries of nationalism and religious antagonism could not be erased by constitutional decree.

The most vociferous objections to this new union came from the Croats. Leaders of this Balkan tribe often acted as if they were more eager to destroy the Serbs than to enter into a centralized kingdom. In the 1920s, Croats found philosophical support for their almost instinctive commitment to Serbian genocide in the popular Peasant Party and the Party of the Right. The platform of the Party of the Right was succinctly articulated by its founder, Ante Starcevic: The Serbs and all other non-Catholics were "a breed fit only for the slaughterhouse."

For years such slogans suppressed deeds; promises that would have to be confronted in the future. Then in 1928, a Croatian leader, Stefan Radic, was shot on the floor of the Sabor by a Serbian nationalist. It is from such events where murder and drama are united that history is rewritten: Martyrs are born as real men die, movements follow, and governments crumble.

The result of this assassination was another secret Croatian society—the Croat Revolutionary Organization. Like all other Croat groups since the nineteenth century, it urged the destruction of any unified, centralized kingdom, and hoped instead for a separate Croat state, a state which would not tolerate non-Catholics. Yet, unlike all the other Croat groups, the Croat Revolutionary Organization— which came to be known as the Ustashi (Insurrection)— would fulfill its promises with a bloody vengeance and dedication.

The head of the Ustashi, its *poglavnik,* was Ante Pavelic, a veteran of many Croat right-wing movements. Pavelic molded a political movement demanding fanatic excess and, in return, offering expiation for these passions through mysticism, Croatian nationalism, and Catholicism. Upon joining the Ustashi, the novitiate was immediately indoctrinated with its mystery and authority. The initiation rite required that one swear before a crucifix framed by a dagger and a revolver an oath promising total devotion: "I swear before God and all that I hold sacred that I will observe the laws of this society and will execute without condition all that I am ordered to do by the *poglavnik.* I will scrupulously preserve all secrets entrusted to me, and I will betray nothing, no matter what it might be. I swear to fight in the Ustashi army for a free, independent Croat state under the absolute control of the *poglavnik.* Failing in my oath, I shall accept death as the penalty. God help me, amen."

The choice of the three symbols—the crucifix, the dagger, and the revolver—was not a casual one. The Ustashi "call to blood" that Pavelic was demanding of his followers would be a religious calling. The intensity of Croatian Catholicism would now be transferred, Pavelic hoped, to a political movement. The devotion, duty, and bloodletting which the Ustashi promised, would become a holy war to create a Croatian state, a state which would be both separate and Catholic. As Ustashi member Dr. Mile Budak, later to become the Croatian Minister of Education, said, "The movement of the Ustashi is based on religion. For the minorities we have three million bullets. We shall kill one part of the Serbs. We shall transport another, and the rest of them will be forced to embrace the Roman Catholic religion; thus, our new Croatia will become one hundred percent Catholic. . . ."

The Ustashi was less than a year old when Andrija Artukovic, then a twenty-nine-year-old lawyer, swore his oath of allegiance before the crucifix, the revolver, and the dagger. He seemed a natural Ustashi recruit. The eldest son of a family of Croat farmers living in Bosnia-Herzegovina, Artukovic was raised to be a devout Catholic and a fierce supporter of an independent Croatia. And as a lawyer practicing in the Croatian town of Gospic, Artukovic had been active in other Croatian separatist parties.

It was in the Ustashi, though, that Artukovic was able to translate his political and philosophical training into action. For over a decade he was totally involved in Ustashi politics, a politics of sporadic terror and violence. Artukovic participated in and helped pilot a campaign of attempted revolts and assassinations that kept him on the run across Europe for nearly a decade. It was in this period of exile and violence that Croatia's bloody future was planned. Terrorists, but in actuality merely powerless exiles, the Ustashi only found comfort in the future, a future where the Ustashi—Catholics and Croatians—would be the only survivors.

The first steps toward the realization of this future were taken in 1929, when Artukovic and Pavelic were forced to flee Yugoslavia because of their inflammatory political statements. The two leaders established themselves in Hungary where they organized Ustashi newspapers and, more importantly, training camps for the soldiers they hoped would liberate Croatia. By 1931, other Ustashi camps had spread to Italy. Recruits were taught that violence was the only way to power.

But, in 1932, violence failed. Artukovic led a band of Ustashi terrorists into the Lika district of Croatia where they fire-bombed a police station, a signal, they hoped, for a "spontaneous" revolt. There were only deaths, no revolt. Artukovic once more had to flee Croatia. During the next two years he spent time in England, Austria, and France before settling in Italy to direct the Ustashi training camp in Bovigno.

It was at the Bovigno camp that plans were made for a daring assassination, an act the Ustashi hoped would finally give them control of Croatia. The assassination was successful, but the hope failed. In 1934, while King Alexander of Yugoslavia was meeting with the French Foreign Minister Louis Barthou in Marseilles, a band of Ustashi soldiers attacked. Both the king and the foreign minister were killed. But it was no victory for the Ustashi. Again, the mass, spontaneous revolt did not follow.

Pavelic and another Ustashi leader were condemned to death by the Yugoslav government, but they escaped to Italy where Mussolini offered political asylum. Artukovic was not so lucky. He was caught in France and extradited to Yugoslavia, spending a year in a Belgrade jail awaiting trial. This was Artukovic's first trial and the judge reached the same verdict as would other judges reviewing Artukovic's life for the next forty years—the evidence was damning, but insufficient to find Artukovic guilty.

He was released and returned to Zagreb, the capital of Croatia, where he received a hero's welcome. Zagreb, however, was an uncomfortable place for conspicuous Croatian heroes; they could too easily become dead martyrs. In 1936, Artukovic fled once more to Hungary. He remained there for five years, leaving only to make the arrangements which would ultimately bring the Ustashi to power. After years of slogans, random violence, and failed revolts, the Ustashi realized the only way to power was through Adolf Hitler and the Third Reich.

Andrija Artukovic was a guest of the German government at the Hotel Kaiserhof in Berlin when Enterprise 25 took place. Enterprise 25, the code name for Hitler's order to his high command to destroy Yugoslavia "both militarily and as a state," began minutes before 7 A.M. on April 6, 1941. On that morning Luftwaffe planes bombed Belgrade while German troops, along with their Italian, Bulgarian, and Hungarian allies, crossed Yugoslav borders. Within four days, German forces occupied Zagreb and were pushing south. A telegram sent by Pavelic in Rome to Hitler rejoiced, "At the moment of the entry of the glorious and invincible German troops into my homeland, I take the liberty, Fuehrer, of conveying to you my gratitude and devotion. Independent Croatia will tie her future to the New Order in Europe which you, Fuehrer, and the Duce have created." On April 17, 1941, the Yugoslav army surrendered. The union which one world war had created was now destroyed by another.

The Nazis supervised the partitioning of the country. The Italians were given most of the Dalmatian Coast. Hungary and Bulgaria grabbed other pieces of the spoils, while the Nazis kept Old Serbia, with its capital of Zagreb, for their own rule. Croatia, though, became an independent state—a Ustashi state, designed and ultimately controlled by the Nazis.

Five days after the proclamation of the "independent" state of Croatia, Pavelic and Artukovic, accompanied by German and Italian troops, led a contingent of two hundred armed and uniformed Ustashi soldiers through the streets of Zagreb. They had returned, finally triumphant, to take control. Immediately a Nazi-sponsored cabinet was announced: Pavelic as chief of state and, as his number-two man, the Interior Minister Andrija Artukovic. The decade of exile was finally over. For years, power had been the obsession. Now, an independent Croatia realized, a new, more terrible obsession would take its place—the complete and permanent institutionalization of this power. The ferocious brutality that powerless exile had masked, Ustashi rule would quickly expose. During this first summer alone, an estimated 180,000 Serbs, Jews, and gypsies would be slaughtered.

The man directing this genocide was Andrija Artukovic. It was Artukovic who on April 30, 1941, signed "the

decrees of racial affiliation" which defined the term "Jew."
Artukovic's Croatian adaptation of the Nazi racial law
was even more stringent than its model. Another series of
anti-Jewish laws, all based on the Nazi Nuremberg Decrees, quickly followed: the nationalization of Jewish
property and business (No. CL-348-Z, June 1941); the
prohibition of intermarriage (No. CXLVII-333-Z, June 4,
1941); the prohibition of employing female Aryan servants under forty-five (No. 103-Z); the establishment of
racial origin for members of the state bureaucracy and
the professions (No. 342-Z, June 5, 1941); and the racial
identity law which required that "persons of the Jewish
race over the age of fourteen must wear signs identifying
themselves as Jews in the form of a round, tin plate when
outside their homes . . . this sign must be worn so that it
can be seen on the left side of the breast" (No. 336-Z,
June 4, 1941). Each of these decrees was signed by Interior Minister Andrija Artukovic.

But legislation was not a sufficient solution to the
"Jewish question." The "decisive and healthy grasp" which
Artukovic boasted about to the Sabor came in the form
of decree CCIX-1779-ZZ. This law, signed by Artukovic,
legalized the establishment of twenty concentration camps.
The camps were directly controlled by Artukovic; it was
the intelligence service, security service, and Ustashi police units specifically under the command of the minister
of the interior which organized the mass arrests and supervised the exterminations.

Jasenovac, a former brickyard, was transformed under
the personal direction of Artukovic into the largest Croatian extermination camp. Artukovic, working with the
assistance of Adolf Eichmann, supervised the conversion
of the brick kilns into ovens where thousands of Serbs
and Jews were burned alive. Death at these camps, though,
was not just by anonymous fire. TheUstashi, more so
than even the Gestapo, demanded a more personal involvement in their evil.

The Ustashi murderers killed their victims with an
atavistic passion: throat slashings, eye gougings, tongue

extractions, axe decapitations, and disembowelments—all were common ways of death for "enemies of the state." The Ustashi seemed to lust after barbarism, personally challenging each other to respond more wildly to Pavelic's "call to blood." At Jasenovac, contests were conducted to see which Ustashi could execute the fastest with his *graviso,* a long, curve-bladed knife. Petar Brzica was the champion: His *graviso* cut through 1,300 throats in a single night.

For nearly four years the killings continued. Artukovic's executioners hunted in the towns and cities of Croatia for those he had labeled "the poisonous damagers and insatiable parasites." His men were very effective: Over 300,000 Yugoslavs were victims of the Ustashi. And, despite all the killings, Artukovic personally demanded more excess. It was Artukovic, according to Yugoslav documents, who ordered Chief of Police Franjo Truhar: "Kill all the Serbs and Jews without exception." It was Artukovic who warned the mayor of Cerin: "If you can't kill Serbs or Jews you are an enemy of the state." It was Artukovic who scolded Simun Buntic for killing only two Serbs: "You should not have come to me at all if you have not killed two hundred Serbs."

But as the Reich crumbled, so did the independent state of Croatia. On May 4, 1945, the German troops pulled out of Croatia and the Ustashi followed. For Pavelic and Artukovic, the years on the run began once more. They changed into civilian clothes and, under the protection of the retreating Nazis, managed to reach Austria.

The Church, which had supported them in power, now supported them in defeat. Pavelic and Artukovic moved through a network of Austrian monasteries, disguised as Father Benarez and Father Gomez. Pavelic, always cautious, clipped his distinguishing bushy eyebrows, grew a beard, and wore false glasses. Using a passport in the name of Dal Aranyos, a priest, he sailed from Rome in 1948 to Buenos Aires. These disguises and precautions were necessary: Both Pavelic and Artukovic were in-

cluded in the first official "wanted" list issued by the United
Nations War Crimes Commission in 1945.

Artukovic waited in a convent at Bad-Ischl, near Linz,
for his opportunity to escape from Europe. Years later
under questioning from Immigration Service officials, he
would offer a laconic description—no hints of either adventure or fear—of the rest of his journey to America:
"Somehow I made my way into Austria. There the English
occupation troops caught me and arrested me. They put
me in a camp near Spital Drau. However, after two
months' interrogation they released me. Subsequently, I
continued to live in Austria until November 1946.

"I then crossed into Switzerland where, for reasons of
my own personal security, I assumed the false name of
Alois Anich.

"I stayed in Switzerland until July 1947. Then with
the knowledge of the Swiss Ministry of Justice, I obtained
personal documents for myself and my family which en-
abled us to travel to Ireland.

"Using the name Anich, we stayed there until July 15,
1948. When our Swiss documents expired, the Irish issued new papers and under Irish papers we obtained a
visa for entry into the United States of America.

"We arrived on a temporary visitor's visa, landing in
New York on July 16, 1948. Two days later with my
whole family, I arrived in Los Angeles, where I met with
my relatives and my brother whom I had not seen for a
full eighteen years."

It must have been a joyous reunion. For four years
Artukovic, the Interior Minister, had been the hunter,
pursuing his victims and issuing the laws which condemned hundreds of thousands. Now, he was hunted. In
Surfside, California, however, the succession of new countries, new aliases, new impermanences, new escapes finally
must have seemed over. Here was a remote hide-out, truly
at land's end, cut off from the world of real events. Here
was a land where everyone came from somewhere else
to start new lives. Artukovic, too, hoped to begin a new
life in a beachfront bungalow. He would disguise his

past so he could survive in the present. The dreams of power, of possibility, would—out of necessity—become vague, passive memories. His new life centered on survival.

For Pavelic, escape was not possible. He was shot while walking down a Buenos Aires street by persons unknown and later died of his wounds in Spain. Another Ustashi, Gestapo Chief Eugene Kvatevrik, was also assassinated in Argentina.

Artukovic was luckier. He felt secure enough to list his name and phone number in the Long Beach telephone directory—PL 5–1147. He established a new life and made new friends. His children played on the beach. His wife found a job in a local hospital. His future, by default, would no longer be measured by his accomplishments, but by those of his children. The Interior Minister was now a bookkeeper. His daughter, Zorica, would win the Orange County High School essay contest. Her theme—"The Four Freedoms."

Then, suddenly, his past was publicly unraveled. The California headlines announced, "Reds Seek Surfside Man," and in 1951, Artukovic was forced to stand trial for extradition to Yugoslavia as a war criminal.

No assassination squads had been sent to stalk Artukovic. Vengeance in Peronist Argentina was, by need, pragmatic and anonymous. In America, it must have been confidently decided, justice would cooperate with revenge: The courts of California, it must have been believed, would target Nazis as swiftly and as efficiently as an assassin's bullet.

BEYOND the palm-lined drive, past the uniformed doorman, up high above the city in a spacious, pink-walled suite of the Beverly Hilton Hotel, Andrija Artukovic prepared to re-enter the world of real and large events. The Yugoslav request for his extradition as a "murderer of peaceful and innocent men, women, and children" had transported Artukovic out of his small, stable, suburban life. He was no longer the commuting bookkeeper living in a bungalow. Once more, Andrija Artukovic was in the headlines.

In the suite at the Beverly Hilton Hotel, Artukovic and his lawyers prepared for his first formal press conference. Just days before they had lost their first attempt to quash extradition; however, it was, as lawyers are accustomed to say, a promising defeat.

Artukovic's initial maneuver was to admit to the Immigration Service that he had entered the country under the alias of Alois Anich and then to petition that he be allowed to register under his own name as a displaced person. It was a legal gesture which must have amused Artukovic: The Displaced Persons Act was designed to allow victims of Nazi political and religious persecution to enter the United States.

On October 14, 1951, after conducting hearings, the Immigration Service denied Artukovic's request. But, these hearings were promising because they revealed an important clue, a clue about an alliance which would influence the future of Artukovic's life in America. The clue lay in the identity of certain character witnesses who testified in Artukovic's behalf: These witnesses were agents of the FBI.

Only ten years ago, the FBI had opened a "secret, classified" file on Artukovic's brother, John, then a struggling Pittsburgh contractor. The FBI and the OSS were concerned about John's connections with fascist and Ustashi agents in the United States, and his prominent membership in various Croatian independence committees. But now in 1951, the FBI and both Artukovics were allies in a new war—a cold war against Communism. Conceivably, the alliance might even have first begun toward the end of World War II. As Tito's partisans advanced, the OSS operations in Yugoslavia, under the direction of Pitts-

burgh investment banker Joseph Scribner, then assistant
chief of the OSS Special Operations Branch in Washington, were beginning to be motivated more by a fear of the
Communists than of Hitler. Yugoslavs hired and trained
by the OSS were abruptly discharged because of suspected
political sympathics for Tito. And once the war was over
and dismissed as history, FBI and CIA agents were eager
to recruit old enemies as new friends.

John Artukovic seemed to prosper just as—perhaps
coincidentally—he and his brother acquired these new,
Cold War friends. He moved from Pittsburgh to Los Angeles and became a successful contractor. His work consisted primarily of municipal and county contracts; for
example, a $1,089,935 Los Angeles county flood control
project and a $891,614 contract for laying the joint out-
flow sewers from Bellflower to Whittier. According to
some sources, the Artukovic Construction Company also
did work for the Seal Beach Naval Station, just down the
beach from Andrija's bungalow. The Department of Defense, however, denies this. It also remains undetermined
whether John's new friends in government helped his
company obtain these lucrative municipal contracts. Yet,
it is certain that the discreet phone calls the FBI or the
CIA could have initiated to discourage these contracts
were never made. The Artukovic Construction Company
grew to be one of the largest in the Los Angeles area, employing nearly seven hundred workers. And, John Artukovic's wealth began to be measured in millions.

As Andrija Artukovic prepared to meet the press in
the Beverly Hilton Hotel suite, he knew a trial on the
Yugoslav charges was inevitable, but he was confident.
His brother was later to explain to reporters, "Immigration
knows all about Andrija in Washington." Artukovic's
strategy, therefore, would be to fight back, to deny everything to the press. He would portray himself as a victim of
Tito, a refugee from Communism. In southern California,
as in most of America in the 1950s, that would be an
effective defense.

The reporters who went to the hotel suite that afternoon

looking for hot copy must have been disappointed. There
was nothing extraordinary about Artukovic, no hint of
a personality capable of tremendous evil. Artukovic, now
fifty-two, seemed like just another suntanned, robust Cali-
fornian: the sort of chunky but thick-muscled man who
stayed squatly fit into middle age by playing handball in
the sun each week. He was dressed neatly in a blue suit,
a white pocket handerchief in the breast pocket, a white
shirt, and a tightly knotted silk tie. His clothes echoed
his attitude: correct and civil. Though silver gray, his hair
was still thick and cut short, framing a face without pre-
tensions. When necessary he could smile a wide, guileless
smile, but smiles were rare. He had an open, broad-
featured, round, peasant's face, a blank face that did not
betray any intimacy with adventure or cunning. With his
sagging jaw and heavy, illformed lips, Artukovic looked
merely weary. He was uncomfortable in his best Sunday
suit and, uncertain of his English, he was nervous before
the crowd of reporters. In America he had become a man
unprepared for public situations. Andrija Artukovic
seemed, at a glance, more believable in his new role of a
suburban bookkeeper, than as a government official responsible for 300,000 deaths.

"At no time, in any of the positions I held, did I have
jurisdiction over the secret police and I never signed any
death warrants. Neither did I execute any warrants of arrest," Artukovic immediately announced to the reporters.
He spoke sitting at a small table with his hands clasped;
as he continued, his clasping hands became clenched fists.

The charges against him, Artukovic explained in a
steady, accented voice, were "politically motivated." Tito,
he insisted, was a "Communist and a Serb" who wanted
to extradite him for "political crimes." Artukovic offered
this explanation in an easy, guttural monotone. It would
have been difficult for any reporter to realize the bookkeeper was deliberately lying; yet, Artukovic was well
aware that Tito, like himself, was a Croat.

Artukovic admitted he had served in the Croatian cabinet—that would have been foolish to deny—but, he said
his was a position without power. As Interior Minister,

he explained, he was only "in some authority over transportation."

It was a careful and controlled performance. Artukovic, somber and indignant, constructed his invention of events to culminate in one last, morally redeeming anecdote. As he told this final story, his voice became even softer; it was the bereaved tone of a man wronged.

"It was in March or April 1942," Artukovic began, "that I learned at the last minute that a whole trainload of Jews was to be transported to Germany. On my own responsibility, and at my own risk, I ordered the train stopped. All were sent back." It was an action, Artukovic claimed, which infuriated the Nazis: "The German ambassador wouldn't even speak to me."

The press conference ended with this invented bit of history and no questions were allowed. As the reporters left the hotel suite, both Artukovic and his lawyers were pleased with the performance. Artukovic had denied all charges. At the hearing on extradition just weeks away, he would maintain this attitude. He was no longer Artukovic the Ustashi leader; he had become, in southern California, Artukovic the anti-Communist. It was a role, he could be certain, that would appeal to his new friends both in and out of government. Artukovic must have been confident that, like the Jewish problem he had settled ten years earlier, his extradition hearing would be resolved in one "decisive and healthy grasp."

On the hot ride back to Surfside, Andrija Artukovic could not have realized that his next eight years would be spent in and out of courtrooms.

THE headlines that fall day in 1951 were all about Yugoslavia, about new wars and about old wars. In Washington, Secretary of State Dean Acheson sternly warned the Russians that any attack on Yugoslavia "would strain

to the breaking point the fabric of peace." And in Los
Angeles, the Yugoslav consul, acting on authority of
Ambassador Vladimir Popovic, signed a complaint for
"common murder" against Andrija Artukovic. The complaint accused Artukovic of 1,239 specific murders including 58 children, 47 Serbian Orthodox priests, 48
rabbis and cantors, and—in columns stretching for thirteen pages—listed "peaceful and innocent" female victims.

Two deputy U.S. marshals arrested Artukovic and he
was jailed without bond. Before going to jail, he told reporters, "It is all lies. I am absolutely innocent." He
remained in jail for two weeks. Those fourteen days were
the only period Artukovic would spend in an American
or foreign jail for the rest of his life.

While Artukovic waited in jail, his lawyers prepared
for the first extradition hearing involving a Nazi war
criminal arrested in the United States. It would be an
eight-year courtroom debate where the initial urgency of
Artukovic's guilt or innocence turned quickly superfluous;
a willing court would allow the mechanism of American
justice to carp studiously over other issues. The columns
of names, thirteen pages long, would soon be forgotten.

During the next eight years, Artukovic was eased into
the background, a detached, almost disinterested middle-
aged man sitting mute in the courtroom as if unconcerned
and uninvolved. Justice—or even vengeance—his lawyers
hoped to contend, was not the issue; Artukovic's extradition was a question of law. The central actors became,
instead, a team of three defense attorneys. Each was a
specialist in immigration law and each contributed a
posture to the homogenized personality the defense hoped
to present and—by extension—confer on their client, Andrija Artukovic.

Attorney Robert Reynolds was brought into the case
from Washington. He would offer a sternly moralistic
touch to the drama, raising fretful questions in his lilting,
down-home voice about the injustice being done to Artukovic, the victim of Communist chicanery. Simply

through Reynolds's red-cheeked, even folksy presence, Artukovic himself became more American, another old boy among his cronies. During the next eight years Reynolds would argue: "This is just a Communist plot against him. He always fought them. They were opposed to what he represented . . . Those poor fellows [Ustashi] in power at the time couldn't do anything. The Nazis marched in with their armies and those poor fellows had to do what they were told."

In an interview just before his death in 1974, Reynolds explained his participation in the case to a curious journalist, declaring flatly, "Nuremberg was a mistake because it was the winners saying who was guilty." Reynolds then challenged the claim that nearly thirty thousand Croatian Jews had been killed. Yugoslavia, he said, never had a large Jewish population "because it was quite a poor country and it didn't attract businessmen—and the Jewish people are businessmen, *good* businessmen."

The other participants in Artukovic's defense were California lawyers. Edward J. O'Connor (now a Superior Court judge in Los Angeles) had previously served on INS alien hearing boards during World War II and had been an attorney with the Department of Justice from 1933 to 1939. O'Connor, though, was chosen not just for his connections or experience, but also for the image of scholarly erudition he projected. There were questions of international law involved in this case and O'Connor's job was to elevate these issues to idealized judicial arguments, unconnected in any way to World War II or concentration camps or tortured victims. He would contend, proudly, "The United States isn't going to go along with any blank statements they [the Yugoslav government] make!"

Vincent Arnerich, the third member of the defense, was a skilled lawyer with a conservative reputation. And, as he explained to a reporter, "Andrew" and he were of "the same ancestry—I was born in the United States, but my parents were from the old country." Part of Arnerich's task was to portray himself and Artukovic as refugees who found freedom in America, both men sheltered by an America ready to repulse the advancing Red Menace.

This legal team's first step was to demonstrate that they were prepared to fight a dramatic courtroom battle. They quickly filed an affidavit declaring their client—who presumably had given each of his attorneys sufficient retainers —a pauper. The strategy to disguise Artukovic in poor man's clothing, though, was actually part of an attempt to pressure the two governments involved. It was a bluff aimed at both the United States and Yugoslavia. If Artukovic were a pauper, then the U.S. government would have to pay the expenses for witnesses the defense now promised to call from across America and from Spain, France, Portugal, England, and Yugoslavia. One of the potential witnesses mentioned was Archbishop Stepinac. This was the part of the threat conceived to embarrass Yugoslavia: The archbishop was in a Yugoslav prison for his collaboration with the Ustashi.

But, no witnesses were called. The defense team was eager to avoid any issue dealing directly with Artukovic's guilt or innocence. Instead, they searched for ways to invalidate the legality of extradition. O'Connor and Reynolds filed a habeas corpus motion on two grounds: The charges against Artukovic were "of a political character" and, therefore, were not an extraditable offense; and, more sweeping in effect, the 1902 treaty between the United States and the Kingdom of Serbia under which the Yugoslavs were trying to extradite Artukovic was invalid: Serbia no longer existed.

The arguments were made before Judge Pierson Hall. Years later, Drew Pearson would describe Hall as a "politically minded Democrat"; in California in the 1950s it was good, ambitious politics, Pearson contended, to be anti-Communist.

Hall listened to the habeas corpus motion and then ordered attorneys for both sides to file briefs arguing the validity of the treaty. "I've been impressed by the sincerity and honesty of the defendant," the judge continued and then set bail for Artukovic at $50,000.

Ronald Walker, the attorney representing Yugoslavia, objected. He read a telegram from the Yugoslav ambassador in Washington: The ambassador was "insulted" that the right to extradition was challenged.

"Just a minute," Judge Hall yelled across the courtroom. "I understand," he observed, casting aside both judicial restraint and impartiality, "that the Yugoslav government has been insulting this country. . . ."

And so Artukovic's first day in court ended. He left after paying the $5,000 bond, surrounded by his family, once more a free man.

For the next nine months Judge Hall pondered whether the "integral and political changes to the 1902 Kingdom of Serbs, Croats, and Slovenes affected the validity of any treaty." On July 14, 1952, Judge Hall ruled that the treaty was invalidated: No extradition agreement existed between the United States and the Federal Peoples Republic of Yugoslavia.

Artukovic had again escaped. Outside the courtroom, he was jubilant, smiling and waving at the press. The decision, he proclaimed, was "a triumph not just for me, but for American justice. I am thanking God for it." And slipping into his role of a professional anti-Communist, he added, "You cannot imagine what this will mean to oppressed people outside this country. It is a triumph for them, too."

Artukovic's triumph, however, was short-lived. Two years later in 1954, following appeals by the Yugoslav government, the Ninth Circuit Court and ultimately the Supreme Court reversed Judge Hall's decision: "The extradition treaty executed by and between the United States and Serbia in 1902 is a present, valid and effective treaty. . . ."

The case once more returned to the courtroom of Judge Hall. The Yugoslav government again prepared to submit evidence concerning the 1,239 murders for which Artukovic was originally charged. But evidence was never submitted. Artukovic's defense raised another legal issue—Article VI.

Article VI of the 1902 extradition treaty stated that "a fugitive criminal shall not be surrendered if the offense . . . be of a political character." Artukovic's lawyers contended that their client's participation in the 1,239 murders "in as much as they refer to him as a minister in a government were political in character." "Andrija Artukovic," Robert Reynolds said with careful and sincere gravity, "is a political refugee."

Judge Hall again agreed. Artukovic returned to Surfside a free man. Once again, he had escaped. A Long Beach newspaper ran the headline, "Artukovic Wins Plea in Extradition Battle." Below the headline was a picture of Artukovic taken that day. He was not just smiling. His mouth was opened wide, but his teeth were tightly clenched. To many, it could have easily seemed the disfigured grin of a man determined not to laugh.

The Yugoslavs, though, refused to end their legal pursuit. For three years the case worked its way through circuit courts until it reached the Supreme Court. In September 1957, a seven to two vote ruled that Artukovic would finally have to stand trial. The Supreme Court decision ruled the charges were not political: "The offense of murder even though committed solely or predominantly with the intent to destroy, in whole or part, a national, ethnic, racial or religious group, is none the less murder."

When the new trial was announced, a reporter observed that "Artukovic's shoulders began to twitch slightly. His sharp, seamed face became a mask." Artukovic, though, composed himself to say, "Never did I think such a thing could happen in this wonderful country. I have been persecuted and jailed by the Germans, the Serbians, the Yugoslavs, and others. That was in Europe, however. One cannot imagine that one would be exposed to this in this country."

As he left the courtroom that day, Andrija Artukovic

might have believed that there was nowhere else to run, that he was finally trapped. After the six years of legal debates he would now have to stand trial for extradition on the charge that he murdered 1,239 "innocent and peaceful men, women, and children."

"IT was a setup from the start," remembers George Danielson. "In the late 1950s we still had very hot anti-Communist feelings in this country and the issue became a simple one: Artukovic was a symbol of anti-Communism."

In the spring of 1958, when Andrija Artukovic's extradition hearing opened in Room 10 of the federal courthouse in Los Angeles, George Danielson was the attorney for the Yugoslav government. Eighteen years later he is a congressman from southern California. When talking about the extradition hearing, he tries to maintain his customary thin, almost aloof tone. His expression is neutral, but clearly he is controlling himself, trying to put a deep anger into the sort of steady, unflustered, responsible sentences that are expected from a congressman.

"O'Connor made a lot of the same arguments in this case as he had in the two habeas corpus hearings," Danielson explains. "They made Artukovic's defense a three-part proposition. First off, they said that Artukovic didn't murder anyone. They wanted people to believe Artukovic didn't even have the authority to murder anyone. Their second line of defense was that these were political crimes, murders committed while a war was being fought and no one individual could be blamed. And then, if all else failed, they came up with the old standby argument: The charges were political and therefore unextraditable.

"I fought them tooth and nail," Danielson insists. He

is a small, tight man with smooth, gray hair and even features. His face is a subtle backdrop for dark, forceful eyes. It is easy to imagine him as a fighter. Even now, as he talks, his eyes widen as though inflated, and his hands are gesticulating. He can no longer sit still; he is unable to deal passively with the memory of the trial. He leans forward, then back, until finally he must jump up.

"There was just nothing political about Artukovic's crimes," he shouts. "These weren't war crimes, but simple, common murders. I went through all the lists of people Artukovic had murdered and I weeded out those who were even remotely involved in the war. I selected those people in concentration camps, people out of the armed struggle. The people I was trying him for murdering were nothing but women, children, and clergymen. None of these people were fighting in any war. At the time I called Artukovic a cold-blooded, merciless butcher and I meant it." Danielson, in frustration, begins pacing across the room, pacing out his anger.

"But I was really up against it," he says, returning to his seat, once more controlled. "They brought up all kinds of interpretations of history, how Serbs and Croats had been killing each other for years and this war was no different. I hit them with 130 exhibits, eyewitness testimony to the Ustashi murders. The problem was we didn't bring into court any live witnesses. Perhaps that was my big mistake. This was only an extradition trial, though. We thought we would save the eyewitnesses for the actual murder trial. Artukovic's lawyers didn't wait. They brought in all kinds of witnesses. They flew them in from around the country, from Europe, and from South America. Where they got that kind of money, I just don't know. Maybe his brother footed the bills. One thing is certain, though: A lot of money was spent to keep Artukovic a free man, a lot of money that just seemed to come from nowhere."

Danielson's gravest tactical error, however, might have been his reluctance to challenge Artukovic's witnesses. Besides being expensive to transport to Los Angeles, the witnesses had other common bonds: Each was either a sworn Ustashi, a Ustashi sympathizer, or a fugitive wanted for war crimes in Yugoslavia. Consider Artukovic's character references: Rene Herman, who under questioning described Artukovic as "a benevolent administrator"; Herman was a sworn Ustashi, the personal secretary to the son of a Pavelic cabinet minister. Tomica Mesic, who lectured the court that "the murders were actually committed by the Communists"; he was a contributor to Ustashi newspapers. Reverend Stephen Lackovic, who called Artukovic "a great citizen who could never kill a human soul"; the reverend, having sworn the Ustashi oath, served as a Ustashi army chaplain. Reverend Charles Kamber, who came from Buenos Aires to testify that "no one person could be held accountable"; Kamber had served as a Ustashi prefect of police, swearing the Ustashi oath and wearing the uniform. Yet, each of the witnesses' testimonies went unchallenged; the court was left to believe the witness acted as an impartial observer.

Through the entire hearings, Artukovic remained silently seated next to his attorneys. He did not testify. He remained unquestioned, unchallenged, nodding in mute agreement as the witnesses insisted he was blameless.

"It wouldn't have mattered if I had put the witnesses through the wringer or not. What you got to understand is that they never wanted to find Artukovic guilty," complains Danielson. "The case was being heard before U.S. Commissioner Theodore Hocke and he was looking for any way he could not to grant extradition.

"Look," says Danielson, now removing his glasses and pointing with them as if they were a weapon, "let me say this about Hocke. He was no judge. He never practiced law. He was a deputy clerk of the court who got his appointment through the Rotary Club. Ted Hocke didn't know shit from shinola about international law. He could never understand the issues in the Artukovic case," says Danielson, once more jumping from his leather chair. But there is nothing Danielson can do; he can only sit down, embarrassed and frustrated by his rage.

It took Hocke six months to reach the verdict Danielson had been expecting since the hearing began. On Thursday, January 15, 1959, Hocke announced his decision: Andrija Artukovic could not be extradited. Hocke ruled there was insufficient evidence and, further, that the crimes for which Artukovic had been charged were of a "political nature."

"I hope I never live to see the day," Hocke told the packed courtroom, "when a person will be held to answer for a crime in either California or United States courts upon such evidence as was presented in this case on behalf of the complainant."

It had taken eight years since the original request for extradition, but now Artukovic was finally—and perhaps permanently—a free man. Two of his crew-cut Croatian friends lifted a smiling Artukovic to their shoulders in the hallway outside Room 10. Artukovic waved to the crowd, confident that he had at last escaped.

Danielson still remembers the day the decision was announced. "I felt back then that justice wasn't served and I still feel that way today. Hocke never really confronted whether Artukovic was a murderer. He just said there was no evidence and the charges were political. Hocke was 180 degrees off. It was that simple.

"Why, just a couple of years ago," Danielson continues, "I was sitting in a Long Beach restaurant with my wife and in walks Artukovic. He sees me sitting there and, what do you know, he walks right up to my table. He says, 'You look fine, Mr. Danielson.' I couldn't answer him. I couldn't eat my meal. I just told my wife we had to leave the restaurant. It upset me that much! It's almost unbelievable. Imagine, a Nazi murderer can walk around free in California."

Danielson is quiet for a moment. Just telling the story of meeting Artukovic in the restaurant has upset him. Finally, he begins in his normal, controlled voice. "You know what I would like? I would like Yugoslavia to appeal the case. I would sure like to go against Artukovic before a judge who knows something about international law."

But appealing the decision will be rather difficult. There are, it seems, complications. In the fifteen years since the extradition hearing, the transcripts of all the court proceedings have mysteriously vanished from the federal archives in the Los Angeles suburb of Bell. The 130 Yugoslav exhibits and affidavits are gone. No one knows who stole the transcripts. Or even how the crime was committed. All that remains is a large manila folder marked "Artukovic" with the word "missing" written in capital letters next to the case number. Inside, the folder is empty. Like the entire Artukovic affair, all that remains is suspicions.

REPRESENTATIVE James B. Utt of Orange County, California, liked to consider himself something of a detective. He discovered clues everywhere he looked, hints of the same great evil. His logic always deduced the same conclusion—a Communist plot was in the works.

It was only by accident that in 1960 he discovered the gift box plot. Someone, benevolently, had given the congressman a present. But Utt saw something more. At a meeting of the San Diego County Federation of Republican Women Voters, Utt confided his discovery to the startled and enraged women. High above his head he held a small, Italian-made carved box. The lid of the box showed an eagle proudly perched beneath a pennant and a star. This box was his evidence. He announced to the assembled ladies, "This is a clever way to advance the idea that the Communist sickle is hovering over the American eagle." Triumphant, Utt the detective accepted the Republican women's applause; he had—singlehandedly—foiled another Communist plot.

A few days later, though, Erwin Christensen, author of *The Index of American Design,* saw less to the plot than met Utt's eye. Christensen identified the design as a copy of one conceived by John Bellamy, a nineteenth-century American woodcarver who originated the eagle brandishing the pennant as a decoration for U.S. Navy ships. An identical design, Christensen explained, is found on a textbook used in a local San Diego school. The textbook is entitled *A History of a Free People.*

Utt, a bit less aggressive, still remained dubious. "Well, several people looked at it," he said, "and came to the same conclusion. It may be a completely American design, but in the light of things I thought it was propaganda."

The gift box plot, however, was only a minor deduction when compared to Utt's greatest discovery: Operation Water Moccasin. Operation Water Moccasin had been announced in the press as a training exercise for U.S. troops and Green Berets stationed at Fort Bragg in North Carolina. Some foreign observers, the Pentagon stated, would also be present.

This was enough of a clue to set Utt's deductive mind hurtling toward the logical conclusion: Water Moccasin was "a United Nations plot to take over the country." He envisioned "barefoot Africans" and "hordes of Mongolians" overrunning the United States.

Sometime before his ominous pronouncements about Operation Water Moccasin and just after his discovery of "a plot to centralize the Girl Scouts," Representative James B. Utt became involved in the case of Andrija Artukovic.

Five days after U.S. Commissioner Hocke denied the extradition motion, Utt introduced a private bill in the House of Representatives. Concurrent Resolution Number 378 called for a "resolution expressing the sense of the Congress with respect to the granting of political asylum to Andrija Artukovic and his family." The bill was eventually defeated by the Judiciary Committee; however, its defeat was not as significant as its introduction. The introduction of the bill gave Artukovic what he needed almost as vitally as citizenship—time. As long as a private bill awaits action by Congress, an alien cannot be deported. And Artukovic, even though his extradition to Yugoslavia had been denied, still had to fear deportation by the U.S. Immigration authorities. He had entered the country eleven years ago on a long-expired visitor's visa. And he had entered under an alias.

During the years while Artukovic's lawyers fought against his extradition and deportation in court, Artukovic's influential friends—both in and out of government—were also busy working to insure that he remain a free man. Since 1953, whenever Artukovic appeared threatened by legal troubles, a private bill for his citizenship was quickly introduced in the House, a bill which would allow Artukovic's lawyers more time to seek a reversal. Utt was not the only congressman who introduced bills in Artukovic's behalf. Representative Frances Bolton of Ohio, a member of the Foreign Affairs Committee, also pleaded Artukovic's case for citizenship. Utt, however, remained the coordinator for Congressional support. And, even when the newspapers discovered his wife on his Congressional payroll, Utt's political career flourished. His campaigns, according to an Orange County newspaper, were always "well financed."

Artukovic also found friends and supporters in the Catholic Church. Reverend Robert Ross, one of the first guests at Artukovic's Surfside home, remained a friend throughout the eight years of legal difficulties. To Ross, Artukovic was another Christian martyr: "Andrija has been hounded not for crime, but for his faith." The reverend petitioned Cardinal Spellman and Cardinal Manning to intervene and both wrote "confidential" letters on Artukovic's behalf which became part of the permanent Immigration and Naturalization Service case file. Ross also toured Orange County, speaking at rallies for his friend. Under the letterhead of the St. Columban Church,

Reverend Ross sent a mailing: "Mr. Artukovic is a good Catholic, a Knight of Columbus; he has a sterling Catholic wife and fine children. At this time funds to the amount of $10,000 are needed to fight the extradition proceeding. A benefit dance will be held at Blessed Sacrament Hall in Westminster . . . Donation is $5 per person." And to the press Reverend Ross announced, "If Andrija could be put on a radio entering Croatia, he could arouse the country. Tito is not safe as long as Andrija lives."

In just ten years in America, Artukovic had succeeded in reestablishing the traditional coalition which had always supported the Ustashi in Croatia: the ultraright and the Catholic Church. The Knights of Columbus, a nationwide Catholic society with over a million members, also joined his defense. At its fifty-fourth State Council in 1956, the Knights "urged the U.S. government to reject any appeal for the extradition of Dr. Andrija Artukovac (sic) and his family to Jugoslavia." According to the Knights, "that country wants Dr. Artukovac and his family for purely political reasons." And, there were rumors—neither confirmed nor denied—of substantial contributions from the Knights of Columbus to Artukovic's defense fund.

As the extradition case moved through the courts, Artukovic became personally active. The mute Surfside bookkeeper of the courtroom, the man who never testified under oath in his own defense, became an enthusiastic orator when not threatened by perjury. At the Catholic Maritime Club in Long Beach he told a shocked assembly of three hundred, "Tito has suppressed, imprisoned, tortured, and killed the Roman Catholic clergy of Croatia by the hundreds." At a rally of the Southern California Croatians, 125 people cheered Artukovic and pledged $3,500 toward his legal expenses. And Artukovic addressed the Arthur L. Peterson American Legion Post. His topic—Communism in Yugoslavia.

But while Artukovic aggressively recruited American right-wing and Catholic support, he also found eager help from another source—the Ustashi. Andrija Artukovic was not the only Ustashi member to escape to the United

States. In Chicago, *Danica* [*The Morning Star*], "an American newspaper in the Croatian language championing the right of the Croatian people to the re-establishment of their own national state," became the American organ for the Ustashi exiles. The paper asked its readers to "be patient for the Ustashi will march again under a Croatian flag." Each issue was filled with messages from Ustashi cells in Argentina or Spain or Canada. There were ads for recordings of Pavelic's speeches and Ustashi marching songs, songs such as the "Ode to the Poglavnik," a chorus of which sings:

"And against the Jews, who are
The possessors of all money,
Who wanted to sell our souls,
Who intertwined our good name
And who are traitors."

The paper also appealed for funds, money to be sent directly to "Leader Andrija Artukovic, B-62, Surfside Colony, Surfside, California."

While his lobbyists worked discreetly across the country, Artukovic spoke with a reporter in his Surfside bungalow. He was upset. He complained he had received "threatening letters." His children, he said, have asked "will we have to go to court again?" and "they hear things" at school. His wife, however, was determined to remain in California. "It's so beautiful here," she said. "The children love the beach."

Andrija Artukovic was also eager to stay in Surfside. He was not fearful of either extradition or deportation. "I put my faith in God," he told the reporter.

His faith was rewarded. And so were the activities of his Congressional, Church, and Ustashi supporters. On May 26, 1959, Michael Leone, the INS special hearing officer, decided Section 243(h) of the Immigration and Nationality Act was applicable to Artukovic. Artukovic, he ruled, could not be deported without fear for his being politically persecuted. Leone's ruling was conditional; it could be reviewed any time. But Artukovic, the man who signed racial codes and laws establishing concentration camps which exterminated hundreds of thousands of Jews and Serbs, was now transferred to a new list by the Immigration Service. The list was headed, "Aliens Granted Political Asylum."

Artukovic could now spend the rest of his life in Surfside, walking the beach, watching his children grow. His name would no longer be in the headlines. He could become, once more, an anonymous suntanned bookkeeper. World War II and Croatia and the 300,000 dead were the memories of another generation.

"I fear no vendetta," said Artukovic. "They [the Communists] wouldn't dare! It is not so easy here as in South America and Europe."

ARTUKOVIC might have remained forgotten if it had not been for a trial in Jerusalem—the trial of Adolf Eichmann.

On May 20, 1961, in the sixth week of the trial, Alex Arnon, the wartime secretary to the Jewish community in the Croatian capital of Zagreb, came to the stand. He was called to testify against Eichmann, but he also mentioned one other name.

"Eichmann's death squad came into Yugoslavia just two days after the German invasion," Arnon said. And this "death squad," he continued, was assisted by a man "recognized by the Nazis as a leader in the anti-Jewish pogroms of 1941—Andrija Artukovic. Working together they seized all the Jews and placed everyone under arrest."

Arnon told the courtroom that over thirty thousand Croatian Jews died in the Croatian concentration camps. Jews in Zagreb, he remembered, had pleaded directly to Interior Minister Artukovic to save the lives of fifty children scheduled to be deported to the camps.

When Arnon finished his testimony, Judge Benjamin Halevi turned to him and asked, "Where is this Artukovic now?"

"Either in New York or California," Arnon answered and then left the stand.

Across the world in California, Arnon's testimony became headlines, headlines once again shouting the name of Andrija Artukovic. Reporters who gathered outside the Surfside house interviewed a furious Artukovic. Perhaps his mood was turned by fear as much as anger: As long as people remembered, his safety became uncertain. Pavelic and others had been tracked down and shot. Only he had escaped. Artukovic was now sixty-two. He had been in California for thirteen years. He was too old to run.

Artukovic shouted at the reporters, "I deny these lies. I'm tired of all these years of lying about me. I never met Eichmann and I honestly say that until this trial came up I never heard his name. I categorically deny that I was responsible for a single death."

But his denial was not sufficient. Already it was too late. It was not long after the testimony in Jerusalem that Operation Fall Key was set in motion.

THE beachfront southern California communities surrounding Long Beach seem to attract retirees. The mild, steady weather, the clear air, and the proximity of the hard blue ocean help to make life seem easier and more comfortable. The business of growing old has been institutionalized into the local economy. Here, the newspapers even editorialize against "Hurry Sickness" and many of the stores and restaurants advertise "special discounts to senior citizens." In Long Beach, there are certain cafeterias, like Jane's, where old people line up each noon, money in hand; they move up the line, picking and choosing foods, while porters carry their trays. After lunch, many of the retirees return to the ocean and a bench in the sun.

Andrija Artukovic fitted well into this random, unfettered life of early retirement. Money, mysteriously, had never been his problem. At sixty-five, he still participated in Church and Knights of Columbus activities. He would walk the beach nearly every evening at dusk. A neighbor noticed that he "would look out into the Pacific like he was praying." When asked, Artukovic was eager to talk about politics, about the balance of power and about the missile gap.

To a casual observer, Artukovic's days seemed little different than those of the other suntanned California retirees. But someone was watching Artukovic closely, watching for a pattern, a difference. Someone was following Artukovic each day and taking notes.

The man following Artukovic "looked like your average businessman, he wore a suit and tie and spoke without an accent." He also filled a "fat dossier" on Artukovic, a dossier which revealed a pattern which structured Artukovic's life: Once a week, in the evening, Artukovic drove to Huntington Beach to play cards with friends. On the way back to Surfside, Artukovic would sometimes stop at a Seal Beach bar for a nightcap.

The man with the dossier also noted something else: "On the rare occasion when Artukovic stopped in for a couple of drinks, he had been accompanied by one large man who drank only Coca-Cola, talked to no one, and watched everybody."

The man with the dossier thought about the presence of Artukovic's bodyguard for a day or two, but then decided it was a problem that could be overcome. On a winter's evening in 1966, he called a meeting in a kitchen of a San Pedro house to announce his plan for Operation Fall Key—a plan to kidnap Andrija Artukovic and transport him to Yugoslavia to stand trial.

It was a plan that would have remained secret if not for

George Robeson, a *Long Beach Press-Telegram* columnist, and a conversation he had with a smuggler and some-time CIA operative, a man Robeson identifies only as "K."

Robeson, like most of his neighbors, came to California from somewhere else. He came from Brooklyn and wound up in California because of the Air Force. When his tour of duty was over, he stayed. "There seemed to be no reason to leave. What more could you ask out of life than the sun and the ocean," he says. But Robeson, somehow, does not seem to mesh easily into the relaxed, almost detached southern California life that surrounds him. He is an active, tense man, a journalist always following up one more lead. He charges into his office like a character out of a B movie, talking tough out of the corner of his mouth and knocking out a story on his typewriter, before heading off for a few quick ones with the boys. He is lean and his thick, dark hair is cut long and shaggy; it is the look of an athlete—his doubleknits suggest a golfer—trying to look hip. Comfortable with both impertinence and cynicism, Robeson is the sort of man who scolds his secretary, "Aw come on, Chickie, do it right." But his tough-guy style has made all types of friends for Robeson over the years in Long Beach, contacts on the docks and in the police. These men are the sources for his columns.

"K met with the man with the dossier," says Robeson in his flat, Brooklyn accent, "in the kitchen of a San Pedro home. The man had a simple deal for K. He told him, 'My people are prepared to pay a great deal of money for Artukovic.'

"K never asked," says Robeson, "who was providing the money. He didn't have to ask. It was clear as glass to him. The man said he wanted to take Artukovic home to trial. It was clear to K that the man meant Yugoslavia.

"The plan they agreed upon," continues Robeson, "was swift and safe. They used the code name 'Fall Key,' Fall being the German word for file and Key was the first three letters of a car parked outside the San Pedro house on the night of the first meeting. The plan was to stop

Artukovic's car on his way home from his weekly card game. Someone would take care of the bodyguard. K's job was to get Artukovic—alive. He was to give him a stiff shot of Nembutal and then gag him, tie him, and shove him in a crate. The crate was to be loaded into a panel truck. The truck would then head out to the Long Beach docks. It just so happened that the night they planned to grab Artukovic, two Yugoslav freighters were in port. One was at the grain elevator. The other was at Pier A. That's a fact. I checked the port records myself for that night. Perhaps K had also checked out the boats and that's why he was certain it was a Yugoslav operation.

"But the deal fell apart. K first upped his price to $50,000. That would be no problem, he was told. But K still wasn't buying. More people were brought into the plot. K panicked. Too many people now knew about the kidnap plan. K was afraid word would get back to Artukovic. It just wasn't worth the risk."

Writing in his column two years after he first heard of Operation Fall Key, Robeson observed, "As nearly as can be determined, the plan either died a natural death or fell into a state of suspended animation.

"But somewhere," the column concluded, "there is a man who kept a file and offered a great deal of somebody's money for a political kidnapping and found a lot of takers in Long Beach."

And, once more, Andrija Artukovic escaped. He did not even miss one card game.

ANDRIJA Artukovic was sixty-nine years old when Reverend Ross died on Catalina Island. By that time Artukovic no longer needed his support.

Artukovic's family had grown. His son, Rad, was off in college. One daughter worked in a smorgasbord restaurant in Long Beach. Another had married and moved to Arizona. His wife, nearly fifteen years his junior, still worked as a data processor at St. Mary's Hospital.

Artukovic remained free, still officially "granted political asylum." In 1973, Sol Marks, district director of the INS in New York, stated, "This case is under active investigation . . . consideration is now being given at our central office in Washington, D.C., as to whether the provision of Section 243(h) . . . can now be denied and deportation instituted."

The central office "consideration" consisted of asking the State Department to review the case; INS claimed it was the State Department's responsibility to determine whether Artukovic would suffer "political persecution" if deported to Yugoslavia. The State Department, however, was in no rush to make a decision. Artukovic had now spent twenty-five years in America. He was seventy-four years old. The State Department delayed thirteen months before announcing its determination.

On April 15, 1974, Fred Smith, the deputy administrator of the State Department's Bureau of Counselor Affairs, concluded, "There was no reason at present to alter the finding and recommendation made by the special inquiry officer in 1959." If Artukovic were to be deported to Yugoslavia, Smith explained, "the fellow could not get a fair shake."

The official government policy seemed to be to wait for Artukovic to die. A natural death would solve an embarrassing situation, a situation that had dragged on unnaturally for over a quarter of a century. Officially, however, the case remains "active," under "present review."

But there is little activity. Joseph Surreck of the Los Angeles INS office describes the likelihood of deporting Artukovic as "almost nil." As Artukovic himself would wish, he has been largely forgotten. And even those who remember are willing to forget. Charles Posner, the executive director of the Jewish Community Relations Council, a body directing 535 Jewish health and welfare groups in

Los Angeles, commented on the day Artukovic's stay in the United States was extended, "We have no brief for Artukovic. But the man is seventy-five and maybe it's time to forget."

DAVID Whitelaw was not allowed to forget. Artukovic had fled from Croatia ten years before David Whitelaw was born, but still Whitelaw could not forget.

His mother, Judith, came to California the same year as Artukovic, 1948. She also came from Europe and entered New York as a displaced person. But she came alone: Seventy-six of her relatives had died in concentration camps.

David grew up in a Spanish-style house in Los Angeles. As a child he hoped to become a baseball player and then, when older, he decided he wanted to become a neurosurgeon. But much of his youth was spent in the past; his future, in turn, became blurred, almost unimportant. The past was his preoccupation and, eventually, his ambition. His mother raised him on stories from the past. Over and over she told the young boy about the seventy-six dead, the seventy-six who were his grandparents, his aunts, his cousins. The number was repeated so many times to the small boy that it seemed to take on an almost mystical or sacred significance.

Judith Whitelaw is proud that her son has not forgotten the past. She says with obvious satisfaction, "David grew up and asked me where were all his relatives. He asked, so I told him. Tell me more, he kept on asking. Tell me how the seventy-six died. And so I told him everything. I told him all I knew about the Nazis and about the camps. You don't lie to a child. If he asks, you tell him. And David would always ask."

Judith Whitelaw also showed David her collection of

pictures. She had collected pictures of all the German synagogues. She had a shoebox full of pictures: the large, baroque, domed Berlin Synagogue on the Oranienburger Strasse; the moorish Hauptsynagogue in Frankfurt; the romantic, arcaded synagogue in Mainz. She collected pictures because she could never see the actual buildings; these synagogues had been destroyed by the Nazis.

When Judith Whitelaw was a child, she watched as the Nazis burned the Breslau Synagogue. Forty years later she would write the story of the fire, a story she had told her son over and over: "We could see the fire from our kitchen window and it looked like the flames were touching the edge of heaven and the blowing winds made it sound like screams for mercy, but there was none. . . . They called it the 'Crystal Night.' Everything was shining and glittering for them. As for us, the world collapsed. . . . How can I forget to remember?"

Her son, too, was forced to remember. While a student at Los Angeles Valley College, he became active in the Jewish Defense League. The slogan of the Jewish Defense League is "Never Again." It was a slogan and a cause David adopted with excitement. There was a toughness and a defiance surrounding the JDL which appealed to David: Here was a group and a cause which promised action and even vengeance. After all the years of stories about his seventy-six relatives, after all the afternoons spent sorting through the shoebox filled with pictures of razed synagogues, David wanted vengeance very much.

The strange affair of Andrija Artukovic seemed a natural cause for the JDL and David Whitelaw. "It was my opportunity to be involved in something . . . something dramatic," Whitelaw explains. "It was as if I had discovered they were still fighting World War II and they still needed soldiers."

David, at nineteen, awkward and pimply, was quickly recruited into the battle against Artukovic. He wrote letters to INS officials in Los Angeles, New York, and Washington. The answers he received were all the same: The Artukovic case, after twenty-five years, still remained "under active investigation." When letters proved ineffective, David and the JDL tried picketing Artukovic's house. This, too, failed. Surfside was now a private community protected by a gatehouse and guards. The pickets were quickly dispersed.

The realization that "no one in government would respond with anything but an evasive answer about Artukovic" infuriated Whitelaw. "It seemed just like World War II again, when they were murdering Jews in Germany and no one listened or cared. Seventy-six of my relatives were killed by the Nazis and it just didn't seem right that Artukovic, another Nazi, should get away scot free."

Whitelaw becomes enraged just talking about Artukovic. The words spill out in quick spurts and his voice rushes to a higher pitch. "After thirty years they say he was acquitted of all crimes, and there's documented proof that he killed hundreds of thousands of people and yet he's escaped conviction for any crime whatsoever because of his wealth. . . . If that's American justice, then I deplore American justice. This is criminal."

Now convinced that no one else would act, David decided "there was only one alternative. It was time for a dramatic publicity stunt."

Just a few days before David conceived his "publicity stunt," he met a new member of the JDL, Michael Todd Schwartz. Irv Rubin, director of the West Coast JDL, remembers that "Schwartz was recruited from a bunch of hippies in the park. You know, he was one of those kids with the long hair and into drugs, a dropout type. But there was something we must have said which touched a spark in him. There must have been something we said that made him remember he was Jewish. He was tripped out and believed in nothing. We gave him something to believe in."

Whatever his attraction to the JDL, Schwartz participated with a reckless, almost desperate dedication. Immediately he became a true believer. All at once he wanted to be more Jewish, more Orthodox, more committed than his new friends. David Whitelaw now gave Michael Schwartz an opportunity to demonstrate his commitment.

At 2:30 in the morning on January 30, 1975, the two boys crept across a lawn fronting a large ranch house in Sherman Oaks. The house belonged to John Artukovic, Andrija's chief supporter, landlord, and brother. David Whitelaw had decided to make John Artukovic the object of his "dramatic publicity stunt."

The boys crept across the grass until they reached the garage. Parked outside was a blue Mustang. This would be their target.

"One," Whitelaw counted. Both boys lit matches.

"Two." In unison, the boys ignited the Molotov cocktails they held in their hands.

"Three!" Two Molotov cocktails crashed against the empty Mustang. The car burst into flames and the youths ran off into the suburban streets.

They did not get very far. A passing patrolman saw the flames and, after firing a warning shot, stopped the two fleeing boys.

Both David Whitelaw and Michael Schwartz were indicted. The charges of possession of explosives and manufacturing explosives carried possible sentences of five years to life. Bail for each youth was set at $10,000.

Judith Whitelaw put up her only possession, the Spanish-style house in Crescent Heights, as a lien against the bail required for both boys. "I didn't know Mike Schwartz and he looked like a good for nothing," she says, "but when another Jewish boy is in jail your heart bleeds and so I bailed him out."

One month after Judith Whitelaw took the lien against her home, Michael Schwartz fled the country. He went to Israel where he worked on a kibbutz and then joined the army.

As soon as the bail bondsman discovered Schwartz had fled the country, Whitelaw's bail was exonerated. He spent two days in jail before his mother could find another bondsman. "The new bondsmen did not even ask for collateral," says David. "They believed in me." His voice now becomes less aggressive, almost a whisper as if he is about to confide a very personal secret. "I find it very revealing that the man who exonerated my bail, thereby causing my temporary imprisonment, was Jewish. The men who got me out were Italians, gentiles."

In September 1975, David Whitelaw pleaded *nolo contendere* to the fire-bombing charges and was sentenced to six months in jail. He also had to pay for the damages done to John Artukovic's car.

Judith Whitelaw's problems are still not resolved. She will probably be forced to sell her house to cover Michael Schwartz's bond. This is only the second house she has ever lived in, and it is the second house she will be forced to leave. Forty years ago the Nazis took over the five-story brick house her parents owned in Breslau. She is still trying to receive restitution. Now, she feels she is losing another house because of the Nazis.

"After losing one house in Germany, I came to the United States and I lose another," she says, trying not to give in to tears. "Life shouldn't be that cruel."

Michael Schwartz remains, like Artukovic, an exile. The United States has petitioned the Israeli government for his extradition. It is a matter of considerable debate in the Israeli Parliament. Schwartz hopes that political forces will prevent his extradition. Like Artukovic, he, too, hopes he has successfully escaped to a new country where he can start a new life. He, too, hopes to remain a free man.

SOMETIMES Ed Sulka likes to ask his wife if she can still remember the old Ford. "Do you think you'll ever be able to forget," he asks with a broad smile, "what it was like when we drove that old wreck down from the mountains in Colorado packed with little Eddie and everything we owned all the way to California?"

Mary Sulka thinks about the old car and the old times and shares a smile with her husband; success has made the hard work and sacrifices of the past a pleasant, even vindicating memory. Today, Ed Sulka has finally found and is enjoying a piece of the good life he had been pursuing thirty years ago, a chase that brought him down from the mountains of Cortez, Colorado, to the beaches of Surfside, California.

Sulka now drives a white Lincoln Continental Mark IV. The car, severely polished so that it gleams like a signal of success in the California sun, is parked each day outside his real estate office just down the road from his first home in Surfside. The license plate on the car reads ECS-2.

Not long after his neighbor Andrew stopped riding to work with him, Sulka also gave up his job at the P & J Artukovic Construction Company in Los Angeles. "I wanted to be more than a truck driver," Sulka says, "and I thought I knew how." He pauses dramatically as if he is about to announce the solution to a centuries-old riddle, and then says, breaking each word into two syllables, "Re-al e-state."

As Surfside grew, so did Ed Sulka's fortunes. He first acted as an agent, renting other people's homes for them, and then investing his commissions in property. In a community where beachfront shacks sold in 1950 for $5,000 and then twenty years later were resold for over $100,000, it is not difficult for a real estate man to make money. But Sulka started truly prospering after his friend John Artukovic received the first zoning variance to build a three-story home in Surfside. Right next to the wooden bungalows like the one Sulka had rented in 1948, people started putting up Spanish-inspired haciendas with white tiled patios, gushing fountains, and greenhouses. The property Sulka had bought years ago for spare change was now money in the bank.

The greatest dream of Sulka's life also came true. His son, Ed, Jr., made it to the majors. But not for long. Ed played in the big leagues as a pitcher for the Angels for fourteen months. After that, his curve just seemed to hang in the air a little too long and he spent the rest of his career—fourteen years—in the minors. His best year was with Phoenix, the Giants' farm club. He was 8–2 and for a while he hoped his curve might sharpen and he would return to the big leagues. But it just didn't work out.

Both Sulkas, though, have no complaints. The father got to see his son play in the majors and Ed, Jr., says his "life couldn't have been better." Now thirty-three, Ed, Jr., refuses to quit baseball and works as a pitching coach for the Phoenix team. In the winters, he returns to his parents' new home in Huntington Harbor, just miles from Surfside. "It's the most beautiful place I know," he says. "Life down here is super. When I settle down it's going to be right here in Surfside or Huntington Harbor, right there next to the ocean."

Like his friend and old neighbor, Andrija Artukovic also came to Surfside to start a new life. He, too, had hopes for the future and of success. Artukovic, though, never started a new career. A lot of his new life was spent in courts. His wife became the one with a career. She still works as a data processor in St. Mary's Hospital in Long Beach. Each day she drives to work in a Toyota.

Artukovic, also like Sulka, had dreams for his son. He wanted Rad to become a lawyer. This, too, was not to be. Rad now works as a stockbroker in Los Angeles. He is very close to his father and insists that his father has been victimized all these years by the Communists.

During the summer, Rad lives in one of the beach houses his uncle owns in Surfside and drives to work. The Freeway has cut the driving time into half of what it used to be when his father drove up to the city with Sulka.

Lately, Rad spends more time than usual around Surfside because he believes his father needs him. Rad believes that his father's life is in danger. He has felt this way since the fire-bombing of his uncle's car.

The bungalow that Sulka used to live in next door to Artukovic's is now rented by two young women. The women seem to like beach life and like to give parties. The stereo is always playing loud rock music, people are often sleeping on the floor, bodies squeeezed into any free space, and a glass jar near the door is kept filled with neatly rolled joints.

These two girls first met Rad because his father was worried. From a rear window, Artukovic saw something lying in his neighbors' yard, so he sent Rad to investigate.

"What do you mean you'd like to look in our yard?" one of the girls asked.

"These guys up in Los Angeles are giving my dad a lot of trouble, you see," Rad explained. "So if I could just go around and check for foreign objects . . ."

"Foreign objects?"

"Yeah, you know, like bombs?"

"Bombs? Who is your father? Is he in the Mafia or something?"

"Oh, no," Rad told them. He didn't grin or try to make a joke of it. He was very serious. "My dad just has to lay low. He doesn't do much but hide. Look, can I check out whatever that is in your yard. I wouldn't want you to pick it up if it's a bomb."

The "foreign object" his father had been worried about was a gray vase.

That afternoon the girls asked their other neighbors about the man next door.

"It's pretty spacy, all right, living next door to a Nazi," says one of the girls, brushing aside strands of long blonde hair which curve like parentheses around one side of her face. "But he's a good neighbor. That's for damn sure. We party all night long and make all the noise we want and we know he's too afraid to come out and complain."

A STRANGER walks down a narrow Surfside street and people wave. He stops to ask directions and before he can refuse, he is handed a bloody mary in a disposable plastic glass. In the summer at the beach, it is always cocktail time, and the doors of most houses are usually open.

But at the Artukovic bungalow the red steel door is always locked. An ominous peephole stares out from the middle of the door like an all-seeing eye. When someone knocks on the door, the lights in the house are immediately turned off. Day or night, one can knock and there will be no response. The lights are always shut off in the same sequence; it is a well-practiced routine.

Sometimes, though, especially at dusk, Andrija Artukovic enjoys going for a walk along the beach. At seventy-six, he is still suntanned and hearty. This evening he walks slowly, dressed in a white tee shirt, bermudas, and sandals, along the edge of the beach, careful to avoid the surf. The stranger follows.

Artukovic stares out at the ocean for a long time as the sky darkens; a half-mile in the distance the lights flash on around an oil platform moored in the Pacific. The beach is quiet and almost empty; just two figures in the sunset. The only sound is the rhythmic lapping of the Pacific against the shore. Behind Artukovic is the row of beachfront houses, a screen against the rest of the world.

Artukovic remains staring at the ocean for minutes before he realizes he is not alone. Down the beach, just fifty yards away, the man who has been watching Artukovic calls, "Hello."

Artukovic stares at the intruder. He acknowledges this

new presence with only a slight nod. It is as if he is afraid of committing himself to a conversation.

Down the beach, though, the observer is not deterred. He walks toward Artukovic. Perhaps he walks too quickly.

Artukovic stares at the approaching figure and then starts to walk in the opposite direction, toward the houses.

But the other man is years younger and faster. He positions himself in the middle of Artukovic's route.

The two men stare at each other. They are ten yards apart. The stranger's back is to the houses. Artukovic's back is to the Pacific. He is in a panic. His hands are rubbing up and down against his thick legs. His face becomes distorted, his eyes and mouth enlarged as if he wants to scream. After all these years, Artukovic decides, he is finally trapped, caught up against the ocean at the very edge of America.

Artukovic looks at the man now only five yards off and shouts, "No." The word comes in a short, hissing breath. The stranger is puzzled. He only wants to ask Artukovic a few questions. He has a notebook and a pencil in his hand.

He doesn't know what Artukovic thinks he is carrying. All he hears is the wheezing, whispered pleas of an old man who thinks he is trapped.

"Don't . . . don't kill me," the old man says to the reporter. "I know you are from the JDL. Don't kill me," he begs.

And, in desperation, Artukovic turns and faces the ocean. He just stands there, staring at the Pacific, realizing he is trapped. After all these years, there is nowhere else for him to run.

TONY DeVito told the Jewish War Veterans gathered in the Holiday Inn all he knew about Andrija Artukovic.

He spoke slowly, in the deliberate, controlled manner of a person quite aware that he was speaking in public. He took time to tell each detail of Artukovic's court fights, treating the verdicts as if they were ironic morals, punchlines to mean, unfunny jokes.

When he was nearly finished he told the crowd, "I guess all you can do is write your congressman. Ask him why the State Department and the Immigration Service don't think twice about shipping back some Yugoslav seaman who jumped ship to come to America, but refuse to deport Artukovic who killed thousands. Ask him to answer that one.

"But," said DeVito, turning away from the platform to face the audience directly, "you won't get an answer. You won't get an answer because there is no honest answer. The whole affair stinks. Artukovic will stay in this country until he dies."

DeVito then sat down. As the room filled with applause, he sat there tightly clutching his black attaché case, his eyes fixed on the floor.

He remained looking absently about the room for the rest of the hour, uninterested in the speakers who followed him. He acted this way because he knew his words were futile; no matter what he told these people, Artukovic would remain a free man.

DeVito only became interested and alert after catching a few words from the speech of a woman with a thick European accent. He looked up and saw a woman with a blue dress pinched in tightly at the waist and hair piled into a high bouffant.

"I'm a law-and-order person," she told the crowd. "I believe in justice. But let me tell you all a story. There was a man in Poland in 1941. He burned two thousand people alive. When the war was over, he had disappeared.

"This man went to South America. He thought he had escaped. But some people from Israel went looking for him. They found him and they shot him. They shot him dead and then they stuffed his body in a trunk."

Applause interrupted her story. The well-dressed husbands and wives of the Jewish War Veterans clapped with enthusiasm.

After a minute she continued. The applause worked on her as it had, an hour before, on DeVito. Emboldened, she turned aggressive. "They found the body of this bastard in a suitcase. Now I ask you, what's wrong with that? I would like to see some vengeance. If the government won't go after Artukovic, maybe some Jews should."

Again applause interrupted her. DeVito did not clap. He just sat in his wooden chair, staring at the speaker.

When the meeting was over, DeVito left with a friend. He was in a hurry to catch the train back to Long Island. As the two men walked up the Manhattan street, DeVito told his friend, "You know, I've worked for the government all my life. I've never broken a single law. But when that lady spoke, I tell you somewhere in my heart I had to agree with her. When the Immigration Service is rotten, when files vanish, when killers with influential, big-time friends get off scot free, when Nazis can live in this country without anyone being upset, then something has got to give."

The two friends separated at 57th Street. DeVito continued downtown to catch his train, all the time thinking about what to do next, what to do next with his list with 59 names. About what to do next if no one in the government cared.

4

The Pendulum

AFTER playing poker in the back of the restaurant until nearly dawn with the SS man who talked about children's toys, Kurt Wassermann took the subway home and found the letter from Israel.

Wassermann had spent the bumpy subway ride from 86th Street to the Bronx making plans; though exhausted, he had been too excited to sleep. For months on Wednesday nights after he had finished waiting on tables in the Rhein Cafe—one in the string of German restaurants which line 86th Street in Manhattan's Yorkville section—Wassermann had played cards in the back room with a couple of friends and his best customer, the toy salesman.

He was never truly certain why he had first suspected the toy salesman. Wassermann had perceived no undeniable clue. There was nothing specific about the toy salesman to awaken suspicion. He was just a short, baldheaded man with a worried look, deep lines running across his forehead. After a stein or two of beer, a lewd satyr's laugh would ripple through his conversations. Then there

were his eyes, small, hard-blue irises of liquid mercury.
Eyes just like Maywald's. Yes, Wassermann decided, that
must have been the first hint, the push that sent his
mechanism of suspicion rolling forward. Of course, all the
externals also fell into place: The salesman was the correct age, in his early sixties; he was born in Stuttgart; and
he had come to America in 1949. Wassermann had argued with himself that the salesman might have spent the
war in the Luftwaffe or as a soldier freezing on the Russian front or in a million other detestable, yet excusable,
ways. But the salesman's eyes—Maywald's eyes—insisted
his past had been much worse. From the moment he first
took the salesman's order, Kurt Wassermann suspected
he was waiting on an SS officer. Within a week, Wassermann invited him to join the Wednesday night game.

The salesman had been playing for over a month before
Wassermann made his first, tentative probe.

It was Wassermann's turn to buy a round. Usually a
stein of beer was sufficient. But this evening, with an
exaggerated friendliness and a wide, harmless grin, Wassermann turned to the salesman and suggested, *"Ein Glas
Schnapps, mein Kamerad?"*

"Zu Befehl," answered the salesman automatically.

It was a quick, chance response and Wassermann allowed it to escape anonymously into the banter of lively,
half-drunk conversation. But here was a clue that fitted
like a missing key into an unpickable lock. Wassermann
was certain only a true *Kamerad,* an SS man, would
immediately reply with the conditioned and, according to
Himmler, only acceptable response: *zu Befehl.* From that
moment on Wassermann started making plans, plans for
revenge.

But early that same morning after reading the letter from
Israel, Wassermann quickly forgot about those plans. His
concern remained revenge. Except now he had a different,
more personal target.

Wassermann was still sitting in the bright yellow dining
alcove of his Bronx apartment, when his wife awoke to
make breakfast for their daughter.

"Kurt, what's a matter with you? Don't you sleep anymore? I just don't know what's . . ." Her voice trailed off as she noticed his opened briefcase and the piles of paper once again arranged in a familiar pattern on the Formica dining table.

"What is it now, Kurt? More news in that letter about your Nazis? I thought you were done with Maywald."

"It's not Maywald," Kurt answered. "Read this." He handed his wife the letter from Israel and sat silently while she read:

Dear Kurt,

It looks like we are in business again. I thought that Maywald would be the end of it, but I guess I was wrong. Maywald was just one beat of the pendulum. He just shipped the Jews out of Riga. We always wondered what happened to the other end of the pendulum, the men who did the killings.

Now we have part of the answer. In 1965 the Russians had a trial in Latvia where they convicted three men in absentia for war crimes. One of these men was Boleslavs Maikovskis. That name sounds familiar, doesn't it?

And, get this, do you know where Maikovskis is now living? In the United States, in a place called Mineola, Long Island. Ever hear of it?

From what I've been told, your Immigration people started an investigation of Maikovskis not long after the Russian trial, but nothing came of it. Perhaps you can find out how come. I'm enclosing two items which were passed on to me by our mutual friends in Israel. I assume they got them from their mutual friends in the Russian government. See what you can do with these two exhibits. I hope it will shake them up in Immigration.

Let me know how you make out.

Shalom,
Ezra

Sarah Wassermann recognized the signature. She had first met Ezra after the war when he had worked with her husband in the Hagganah. He was Kurt's oldest friend:

Forty years ago they had made the trip in the same rail-road car from Vienna to the Riga ghetto.

Excited and a little apprehensive, she turned to the papers attached to the letter. One was a photograph of a thick-lipped, large-eared, pudgy young man in a German captain's uniform. On the back of the photograph was the name "Boleslavs Maikovskis."

The other paper was a photocopy of an official-looking document. It stated: "On the 2nd of January, the village was burned to the ground and the inhabitants all shot, of these thirty were publicly shot in the Rezekne market-place." The report was signed "Boleslavs Maikovskis."

She read the document, glanced again intently at the photograph as if to memorize the features, and then asked, "Kurt, what do we do now? Who do we tell about this? What do we do?"

"Sarah, Sarah, Sarah. There is nothing to worry about. What we do is simple." He spoke and then unconsciously, as was his habit, shrugged his shoulders; it was a gesture of acceptance, a cynic's surrender to events.

"There is no choice about what we have to do," he continued. "We go after the other beat of the pendulum. That's what Ezra called him, right? We go after Maikov-skis. And, I think I have a plan."

Kurt Wassermann's plan was similar to the strategies of others who refused to forget. Like Harold Goldberg and Dr. Kremer, he decided to share his information with the man who had helped bring Hermine Braunsteiner Ryan to trial.

Only Wassermann refused to meet directly with Tony DeVito. Instead, like a masterspy clinging protectively to the shadows of anonymity, Wassermann sent an emissary. He chose not to meet personally with DeVito because he was reluctant to forfeit his role as an outsider. Wassermann did not just see himself as a waiter. His self-image was something more. The waiter still saw himself as a Hag-ganah agent, a relentless, though unofficial, force tracking down the Maywalds, the Maikovskises, and the war crim-inals in salesmen disguises. Pursuing Nazis was a serious occupation for Wassermann. And it was also—simultaneously—a game, an adventure played with a romantic's devotion to mystery and intrigue. A game played by a man trying to relive the excitement of times a generation ago when he was in the Hagganah.

But there was another, equally complicated instinct motivating his reluctance to meet with DeVito. Kurt Wassermann had a loner's resentment and discomfort toward authority. He was a large, thickly built man in his fifties with wavy black hair who looked like he could handle all situations himself. And that was the way he preferred to do things. There was something of the tough guy in his manner, a brusqueness and a confidence. Even if his victimization by the Nazis had not reinforced his distrust for official titles and government agencies, Wassermann's natural cynicism would have still dominated all his relationships. He found logic in suspicion, distrust, and even paranoia. These were characteristics suitable to a self-confident outsider, an angry man content to remain on the periphery as he looked over the rim of events with supercilious indulgence.

The intermediary Wassermann chose was a woman he knew had previously met with DeVito, helping the INS investigator contact witnesses for the Ryan trial. Before, Wassermann had quickly dismissed her as a *yenta,* a loud-voiced, high-pitched, nonstop talker. Her lips, Wassermann had observed, were habitually covered with a thick piercing red lipstick; it was a color which matched the red polish on her tapered fingernails. She was a woman Wassermann had years ago succinctly judged with a shrug of his shoulders and a definite, "I have no use for her." But Kurt Wassermann had been mistaken.

Following Wassermann's instructions she met with Tony DeVito and told him all about Boleslavs Maikovskis: the 1965 Latvian trial, the previous Immigration investigation, and the new evidence.

DeVito's procedure in his Nazi cases was now routine. He listened skeptically until the initial accusation was confirmed. The confirming evidence was hidden in a special file, a file with a list of 59 names. DeVito listened as the red-lipped lady offered spurts of information on a variety of topics; first Riga, now suddenly Kissinger, then back to Maikovskis.

"Look, could you excuse me for a minute," DeVito interrupted. She was still talking when DeVito left the office to check his list. In the middle of page one he found all the confirming evidence he required to activate a preliminary investigation: the name "Maikovskis, Boleslavs."

As he re-entered the office, she once more began talking. Again DeVito interrupted. This was no longer a social call. His voice was official.

"Well," he said, "it looks like we're in business. Would you mind if I keep that photograph and document for the case file?"

She ransomed off the evidence in exchange for DeVito's indulgence of more of her rapid, disconnected monologue. When she had finally left, DeVito prepared to begin a new investigation.

He moved quickly. He first wanted to learn what the previous Immigration investigation had found. And why it had been stopped. Since Maikovskis lived on Long Island, the records concerning the case would be in the New York office. DeVito asked the clerk in charge of the central index to retrieve Maikovskis's file.

Two hours later DeVito got a call. "Tony," the clerk said, "I been all through the central index. I got a negative on Maikovskis. You must be wrong. He can't live in the New York area."

"Are you sure?" DeVito insisted.

"Positive," said the clerk.

DeVito decided to check the address report index. Maikovskis's name, address, and file number would have to be listed:: A noncitizen, he was annually required to report his address. DeVito personally went through the address reports three times and each time he got the same result—there was no report for Maikovskis.

DeVito's mind raced with old doubts, old uncertainties. This was not the first time a file involving a Nazi case had disappeared.

That afternoon DeVito sent a Teletype to the central index unit in Washington asking for information on Boleslav Maikovskis. If Maikovskis were anywhere in the United States, the central index would know.

The next day when DeVito returned from the Ryan hearing, the reply from Washington was waiting on his desk. The Maikovskis file was located in Detroit. Detroit? What the hell was the file doing there, DeVito wondered.

He immediately called the Detroit office. "Do you have a file on a Boleslavs Maikovskis? That's B-O-L . . . "

DeVito waited on the phone for fifteen minutes before the Detroit clerk returned. "Yes, it's here all right," the clerk announced.

"Does he still live in Mineola, Long Island?" DeVito asked.

"Yeah, 232 Grant Avenue."

"Well, who sent the file to Detroit? What does the G-600 say?" DeVito tried not to convey his excitement to the clerk. The mystery of the missing file was now narrowing toward a solution: The G-600 form—a standard document the INS attached to all investigative files— would detail who in Immigration had ordered the file sent to Detroit and why.

"I'm sorry, Mr. DeVito, but there's no G-600. I guess there should be one, but there isn't."

"Then what the hell is the file doing in Detroit," DeVito finally exploded. "The guy lives in the New York district, but his file is kept in Detroit. That's sort of odd, isn't it? See if you can find out from someone else in the office. Maybe someone has an explanation."

DeVito waited, his mind filled with suspicions, until the clerk returned to the phone. "I'm sorry, Mr. DeVito, but no one here has any idea why the file was sent to Detroit. It must have been a mistake or something."

"Sure," said DeVito without conviction, "it must have been a mistake. Look, could you just get the file to me right away."

Two days later the file reached DeVito in New York. DeVito read its first page dated six and a half years ago, in the spring of 1966. It was a memo from Sidney Fass, an investigator DeVito knew in the New York office, reporting that he had started searching for witnesses and evidence to confirm the Soviet claim that Maikovskis had made false statements on entering the United States in 1951. Fass described his leads as "promising."

But it had been decided, DeVito read, that the promising leads should go nowhere. Fass, according to another memo included in the file, was ordered by the INS central office in Washington to close his investigation. The central office did not give any reason for its decision. And Fass obeyed, writing a brief explanatory memo: "Pursuant to telephonic instructions from Wilbur Flagg, no further investigation required."

This brief memo, though, was enough for DeVito. It was further evidence to confirm his agonized suspicions. The meandering trail of culpability for terminating another Nazi investigation could now be documented to lead directly to Washington, to the office of Wilbur Flagg, assistant commissioner for investigations.

DeVito was awed by this knowledge, but also liberated. Since his first involvement in the Ryan investigation, he had been attempting to piece together a solution to the mystery. The evidence of INS inaction and missing files in so many cases—Soobzokov, Trifa, Artukovic—confirmed the initial theory he had announced months ago in a service memo: "The existence and operation of Odessa here in the United States, even to the point of possible infiltration into our own government." And now, with this newest piece of evidence, DeVito felt theory had been proven as fact. Now, without reservation, he could believe and—more importantly—act on the unbelievable. Tony DeVito was now positive the Immigration Service had been infiltrated.

Flagg, DeVito realized, had been—like Sidney Fass—only following orders. What DeVito wanted to know was who in Washington had told Flagg to pass the word to New York to stop investigating a Nazi. And, who had sent the file to Detroit?

DeVito decided to set a trap for Odessa. It was a trap where Tony DeVito was also the bait.

DeVito's plan was simple. He would now personally and very vociferously reactivate the Maikovskis investigation. Someone would have to notice. And this time when they reached out to terminate the investigation, they would have to grab Tony DeVito to succeed. Only then, DeVito would reach out for them, tracing the orders back up the bureaucracy to the men at the top. To the men linked to Odessa.

For the next few weeks DeVito proceeded simultaneously with his duties for the ongoing Ryan trial and his investigation of Maikovskis. His preliminary findings were optimistic: ". . . it must be frankly stated that the evidence against him [Maikovskis] thus far is most persuasive. Given a free hand, I feel confident that an abundance of evidence will be assembled to show a degree of guilt exceeding that of the recently publicized war crimes charges against Hermine Braunsteiner Ryan."

DeVito sent copies of this memo to his superiors in New York and Washington. The trap had been set and baited. Now DeVito could only wait. He placed the Maikovskis file in a locked cabinet in the fourteenth-floor office he shared with Vince Schiano, the same cabinet which held the information on the Ryan case. Then, as had been scheduled months before, DeVito took his vacation. It would be his first time off since he became involved in the Ryan case and he did not want to disappoint his wife by postponing this holiday. Tony DeVito had no other choice but to wait until he returned to see if Odessa would reach out for the bait.

Kurt Wassermann would also have to wait. He remained unannounced in the background, a waiter eagerly reading the papers to learn if he had set in motion the events which would close around Boleslavs Maikovskis. The waiter, though, was accustomed to waiting. He had been waiting for thirty years, waiting for vengeance ever since he first heard Maikovskis's name in the Riga ghetto.

IT was a four-day train trip from Vienna, Austria, to Riga, Latvia. Kurt Wassermann, then just fourteen, remembers that he did not really become afraid until the third day of the forced journey.

For the first three days, Wassermann did not know what to expect. Armed soldiers had crowded him along with more than five thousand other Viennese Jews into a long line of railroad cars. The Jews were curtly told they were being expelled from the Reich, sent to the Ostland. Wassermann imagined that he and his mother would settle in another city, not quite like Vienna, but not much different; life would go on. For three days the trip was uncomfortable, but uneventful. He and his mother sat pressed together in a corner of the train on a narrow wooden bench.

But then on the third day Wassermann learned life would be worse wherever the Nazis were sending him. Much worse. At each of the train stops in the Ostland, Latvians plundered the cars. As the Nazi guards watched, the Latvians grabbed suitcases, clothes, and jewelry from the helpless Jews. Wassermann could only stare as a man lunged for his mother's small brown satchel and then rushed outside. The man ripped it open, sorting through her most valued belongings—a few favorite dresses, books, many photographs—taking what he wanted. What he did not choose just lay there, scattered helter-skelter by the wind. The train pulled away, Wassermann still staring out the window at the discarded remains of another life, a life now permanently abandoned. It was then, for the first time, that Wassermann became terrified.

Wassermann and his mother along with 190,000 other Viennese Jews were victims of Hitler's plan for the "reunification of Austria with the Reich." In 1938, after the absorption of Austria, Jews had been allowed to emigrate. But, by June 1941, Security Service Chief Reinhard Heydrich wrote to Foreign Minister Joachim von Ribbentrop that emigration would no longer solve the Jewish question; the Reich demanded a "territorial" solution. On July 31, 1941, six weeks after the initial invasion of Russia, the official order was issued which doomed Austria's Jews. The order, issued by Hitler's deputy Hermann Goering to Heydrich, was worded in vague bureaucratic sentences. But these sentences would result in millions of Jewish deaths: "Complementing the task that was assigned to you on 24 January 1939, which dealt with carrying out emigration and evacuation, a solution of the Jewish problem as advantageous as possible, I hereby charge you with making all necessary preparations with regard to organizational and financial matters for bringing about a complete solution to the Jewish question in the German sphere of influence."

In November 1941, as part of this "complete solution" twenty-five thousand Jews were sent from throughout the Reich to the Riga ghetto. In Riga, some would be put to work as slave labor; others would be put to death.

Kurt Wassermann arrived in Riga during the last week of January 1942. The selection of who would live and who would die began immediately. "At the Riga train station, the SS announced to us that we were being transported to the ghetto," Wassermann remembers. "They said it was a short walk, less than a mile. There were trucks, though, for those who wanted them. Those who felt strong enough were told to walk. I wanted to ride in a truck. I was tired. But my mother said, 'No, Kurt, we will walk.' I tried to argue with her, but she insisted that we walk. She must have known from the very beginning what to expect. Those who got in the trucks never arrived in Riga. We never saw them again."

In Riga, the Reich Jews—Germans and Austrians, like Wassermann—were kept separate from the Latvian Jews. Wassermann and his mother were assigned a small apartment, the rooms of previous victims: Furniture lay strewn about the rooms, blood spots marked the walls. Both mother and son no longer had hopes for their future. The remainder of their lives, they felt, could be measured in days.

In five days, Anna Wassermann's future was decided. Her son watched, helpless: "On February 5, 1942, we had to line up in the ghetto after we had been driven out of the houses. An SS officer, a man in a leather coat with a fur collar, questioned each of us separately. He asked our name, our age, and our occupation. He said he was selecting workers for a jam factory at Dunamunde. His name was Maywald. I still remember his eyes when he questioned my mother and me. He had such gruesome blue eyes.

"He questioned my mother and told her to join the group on the right. He questioned me, and I was told to go to the left. She went one way, and I went the other. I just stood there and watched how she was squeezed and pushed into a truck with the others. It was done with such roughness. I knew right away it wasn't right. I just stood there as the truck drove off. From that day on I never heard or saw my mother again.

"Later, the next day, we were told by the Latvian SS that the trucks had been driven to the forest. There the victims had to undress and were shot by the Latvian SS with machine guns. They were buried in graves dug by prisoners of war. A day or so later the clothes of the people sent off in the trucks were returned to Riga. One of the Jews assigned to sorting clothing, Gabriel Hoffer, noticed a name on the order sending the clothes back to Riga. The order was signed by a Latvian police captain named Boleslavs Maikovskis. This name spread throughout the ghetto and that is how I first heard it. It was a name which became synonymous with death."

Those sent to the left, like Kurt Wassermann, were spared until another day. Maywald assigned him to a group which worked on the railroad. Now an orphan, he was moved into the home of another Jewish family. Wassermann still remembers the father in this new apartment protesting to the Latvian SS guards, "But he can't live here. It is not proper. I have two young daughters." Two days later the father was selected by Maywald to go to the right. The father, just days ago concerned with propriety, was pushed into a truck. He never returned.

Day after day the pendulum of death continued to swing in Riga. It beat back and forth at half-hour intervals, swinging between Maywald and Maikovskis, the ghetto and the forest. Maywald selected and Maikovskis executed. Back and forth the trucks moved between Riga and the forest, back and forth they traveled filled with Jewish victims.

"I will never forget that day in February 1942, when my mother was ordered into a truck," says Wassermann. "I stood there and watched her being sent to her death. There was nothing I could do. She left without a word. That day would be a scar I would live with forever, marking me as surely as a man who has lost his arm or leg. I became an orphan whose only inheritance was two names I would never forget—Maywald and Maikovskis. These were two names I would live with for the rest of my life."

WHILE Kurt Wassermann remained a prisoner in the Riga ghetto, Nazi Einsatzgruppen units moved throughout the surrounding countryside killing Jewish inhabitants on the spot. In a report dated just three days before the death of Wassermann's mother, Einsatzkommando group number two announced that in the area outside Riga "the current total of persons shot . . . thus far is 34,193." The report also detailed a specific massacre included in the 34,193 deaths, a massacre which thirty years later would become evidence in the case against a Latvian police chief.

"It was ascertained," the Einsatzkommando unit re-

ported, "that in the community of Vakascheini, area Audrini . . . two Red Army members were hidden. . . .
Their hiding place was a cellar which had been dug before
the onset of the frost. The inhabitants of the village helped
in the construction of this cellar. . . . It took a whole
week. It is therefore impossible that the inhabitants of the
village should not have seen it . . . produce was brought
. . . by the inhabitants of the area Audrini and they gave
it . . . to the Red Army soldiers.

"It can be assumed that during the summer many escaped prisoners of war found a hiding place in this
township. A note was found with one escapee: 'township
Audrini, 12 kilometers distance from Rezekne.' Proof, that
the inhabitants of Audrini were in contact with the prisoner of war camp. . . .

"On orders of the commander of police and the Sicher-
heitsdienst [security police comprised of SS units and
local Latvian police units], all the inhabitants of the village of Audrini, namely sixty-one men, eighty-eight
women, and fifty-one children were arrested. . . .

"In agreement with the commander of police and the
Sd Ostland, the commander of Einsatzkommando number
two ordered

1. That the village of Audrini be burned down, and
2. That all involved villagers be shot to death.

"This order was carried out and the village was set to
flame. . . .

"On January 3, 1942, a number of the inhabitants were
shot, but not in public. On January 4, 1942, at 11 o'clock
in the market square of Rezekne thirty male villagers were
publicly shot. For this, a large part of the citizenry was
assembled. All actions went without interference. The revenge measures were publicized in the Latvian dailies by
an editorial signed by the commander of police . . . and
by the hanging of six thousand placards with the same text
in all the villages. . . ."

In 1965, twenty-three years after the murders, a Latvian court convicted in absentia Boleslavs Maikovskis for

his role as "organizer, inspirer and leader of the massacre of the defenseless inhabitants of Audrini."

At the time of the Audrini murders, Maikovskis was chief of the second police precinct in Rezekne. Born in that town on January 21, 1904, Maikovskis had spent his first thirty years in rough, menial jobs. He did not prosper until he joined the Nazis. After high school, he enlisted in the Latvian army for two years, attaining the rank of sergeant. Maikovskis, though, did not plan to make the army his career. At least not the Latvian army. Following his marriage to Janina Ritins, also of Rezekne, he found work as a foreman for the Highway Construction Department of Latvia. When the Russians occupied Latvia in 1940, Maikovskis worked as a farm hand. But in 1941, the Russians retreated and the Nazis gained control of Latvia. There was a new government and new opportunities. Maikovskis, obviously, had hopes to be something more than a farm laborer.

Announcements in Latvian papers proclaimed, "Young men of the ages twenty to twenty-two! The Reich is engaging volunteers. Service in the Reich is honorable work! You, too, may have the honor of serving in the ranks and in the uniform of the Reich." And, the Nazis did need the help of Latvians who were eager to serve. Each of the Einsatzgruppen units in Latvia was, according to official documents, supplemented with local auxiliary police. These men were recruited by the SS for one pragmatic reason—efficiency. Killing units including local inhabitants who spoke the native language resulted in higher percentages of Jewish dead; columns of statistics were even kept in Berlin to prove this point.

Maikovskis was one of many Latvians who volunteered for the "honor" of serving the Reich. He was, however, more successful than most. He so impressed his superiors at the German Police Officers School in Riga that he was chosen as part of a select group of Latvians sent to the Baltic University in Pinnenberg, Germany, in 1941. Years later, a U.S. federal official would be quoted as saying that Maikovskis received SS training at Pinnenberg. But, according to other sources, there is another explanation for the months Maikovskis spent at the Baltic University, an explanation which helps to explain Maikovskis's quick acceptance by INS authorities when he entered the United States.

In 1941, in his role as head of the Foreign Armies East, General Reinhard Gehlen, the Nazi masterspy, was recruiting agents from the Ostland for his Group III unit: "Baltic natives," he wrote in his memoirs, ". . . who knew the terrain and to them Russian was a second mother tongue." Those chosen were sent to Germany for further training. It is possible that members of the select unit at Pinnenberg were actually Group III agents recruited by Gehlen. And, it is possible that after the war when Gehlen handed his entire spy organization to the OSS (operating, as he explained, "an Eastern intelligence service on German soil using the same management as before, but with American backing"), that these Pinnenberg graduates were among the "anti-Communist" agents welcomed and protected by the U.S. government.

On his return to Latvia from Germany, Maikovskis was appointed a captain in the auxiliary police which assisted the Einsatzkommandos. He also, simultaneously, served as chief of the Second Police Precinct in Rezekne. It was Maikovskis's name the Jews in the Riga ghetto saw attached to the bundles of clothes returned from the forests; it was the responsibility of the head of the killing units to collect and sign for all valuables taken from the Jewish victims. And eyewitnesses survived to document Maikovskis's role at Audrini:

"Suddenly, at midnight, German soldiers and Latvian police stormed into the village. They ordered everyone out of his house on the double. I could hardly persuade them to let me pick up my baby. Soon, everybody in the village was standing out in the street, half-dressed, shivering with cold and fear. Women were screaming. Children were crying. The women were separated from the men. The men were taken to a barn and then transferred to a jail in Rezekne.

"On January 4, all the people in Rezekne were forced to go to the marketplace, even those who were attending a church service. This was to be a public execution. The men from Audrini were taken there ten at a time in two rows. The first row knelt down; the second row remained standing. This formation meant that the bullets shot into the heads of those kneeling would pass on into the stomachs of those men standing. . . ."

This eyewitness, testifying at the 1965 trial in Latvia, identified Boleslavs Maikovskis as the police chief directing and participating in the killings.

On December 17, 1943, Maikovskis was awarded the German Order of Merit and the German Cross, second grade, for his actions at Audrini.

But, on the night of the massacre he helped himself to a more immediate and tangible reward. A surviving eyewitness remembers Police Chief Maikovskis riding from Audrini on a Latgalian thoroughbred, a trotting horse taken from a farmer who would be executed. The eyewitness remembers Maikovskis riding erect at the head of a long line of captured men, women, and children, the village around him in flames.

BY the summer of 1943, the pendulum of death no longer swung back and forth between Riga and the surrounding forests. The time for selections was over; the Nazis were now committed to the total destruction of the Jews. On June 21, 1943, Himmler ordered the liquidation of all the ghettos in the Ostland. The surviving Jews from Riga were sent to Buchenwald for the final solution.

It was on this trip to Buchenwald that Wassermann escaped. He tells the story of his flight in a flat, resigned voice. His manner reveals no pride in his courage or resourcefulness. Elbows on the table, his large hands tucked firmly under his chin as though helping to support a heavy weight, Kurt Wassermann speaks of the past as an observer, not a participant. It is as if thirty years ago he lived another life, played another role: a youthful identity he still does not comprehend. Perhaps he is trying to transcend those events. Or, repress them. Yet, there is a strong, unconscious cadence to his monotone. The rhythm is insistent, like memory.

"From Riga, they sent those of us who were big and strong," Wassermann begins, "to work on a German railroad detail. We were to work our way to Buchenwald. By March 1944, I was seventeen. We were in Madibuk in Germany and day and night we could see the smoke in the distance rising six, seven feet in the air. We all knew this was the smoke from the crematoriums.

"I realized that my only chance of survival was to escape. I thought I could risk it in Germany because there was a hope someone would hide me. In Latvia, I knew there had been no hope—a native farmer would shoot just as quickly as a Nazi.

"I kept waiting for a chance and when none came, I just decided to run. It was a spur-of-the-moment thing. I was on the way back to camp from digging trenches when I suddenly decided to run. I ran without looking back for as long as I could and then I stopped for a minute and took off my blue-striped prisoner's jacket. I threw it on the ground and then just kept on running.

"That night I slept in a haystack. I remember German soldiers came by and stuck their bayonets into the hay. I don't think they were even looking for me. They were just playing. But they almost caught me. A bayonet came this close to my arm.

"After I crossed the Elbe River bridge, I was stopped by two policemen. It was near the end of the war and one shouted, 'There goes an American parachutist.' A shot was fired and I stopped. I spoke perfect German and I tried to get them to believe I worked in a munitions factory. But they didn't believe me. They thought I was a deserter, so they let me go. They never suspected I was a Jew.

"Before long I began to see soldiers from Russian units. I remember going into a German farm town and finding it deserted. All the Germans had fled to the woods to escape the Russians. I went into house after abandoned house and found so much food it was unbelievable. I could not believe there was that much food in the whole world.

"Then I was caught by the Russians. They arrested me because I had no papers. It was 1946 before I got back to Vienna. I was now nineteen. And, I was an orphan." Wassermann pauses, interrupting his monotone for the first time. In a moment he continues, but his voice sounds crushed, "Yes, I was an orphan. All the time I was running I kept thinking about the men who killed my mother. I had to survive, I kept on telling myself, to avenge her death."

A year later, Wassermann was yodeling from the balcony of a former Hitler Youth hostel overlooking the Brenner Pass when he met the woman he would marry. He was yodeling because he was celebrating his success at smuggling another shipment from Innsbruck to Italy. Wassermann was smuggling Jews.

It was not long after the war that Wassermann and his friend Ezra, another survivor of Riga, joined the European arm of the Hagganah. Their job was to guide groups of Jewish refugees from Cracow, Poland, along a route of "safe houses," to Budapest, then Vienna, and finally Innsbruck. From Innsbruck, Wassermann led the refugees across the Brenner Pass where another Hagganah member took over and led them through Italy to a boat which would take them to Palestine. The passengers on the *Exodus* arrived on board after a similar clandestine journey across Europe.

At each stop on the Hagganah route through the continent, Wassermann would question other survivors, "Did any of you ever come across an SS officer Maywald near

the end of the war? Do you know what happened to him?"
Some had heard the name, but no one knew for certain if
he were dead or alive. Most just wanted to forget.

The last "safe house" on Wassermann's route was the
former Hitler Youth hostel in Innsbruck. He was on the
balcony, above the Brenner Pass, yodeling when the
nineteen-year-old manager came to investigate the noise.

"What's going on here?" Sarah shouted. "You sound
like a Nazi."

Embarrassed, Wassermann tried to charm her. Within
three months they were married. It was a time for quick
courtships; old lives had been permanently destroyed,
even memories were painful. Both orphans, they were
eager to form a new family, to create a new life.

Four months later when Sarah became pregnant, she
convinced her husband that they should not immigrate
to Israel. "It was a rough pregnancy," explains Wassermann, "and she worried that the medical facilities were
primitive in Israel. It was very important to us that a new
generation, a generation who never had seen the Nazis, be
born. Anyway, Sarah had an aunt in New York and she
wrote that the best doctors were in America. I had planned
to go to Israel, but Sarah convinced me to go to New
York. I never thought of staying in Austria. Do you know
what it would be like to walk the streets and rub shoulders
with those Nazis, the men who killed my mother?

"When I came to America, I got a job in the garment
center for $16 a week. We moved to a small apartment
in the Bronx and we furnished it with two orange crates
and a $5 crib for my son.

"While I was working in the garment center, I met another survivor from the camps. He talked me into becoming a butcher's helper in New Jersey. I wound up slaughtering hogs from twelve at night to twelve noon.

"It was a rotten job, but with my *mazel* I got a worse
one. I wound up at the Rhein Cafe. For fifteen years I've
been working there. There I am every day in the middle
of Yorkville. I know I'm surrounded by former Nazis. I

know half my customers are war criminals who escaped to this country. Do you know what it is like to live with that? I have never forgotten. I live with the war so deep it becomes impossible sometimes. I have never forgotten Maywald. And I never will.

"Life has not been easy in America, but I guess coming here was the right decision. Look at all my friends who went to Israel. After all the years, only two are still alive. Some died right away, in the '48 war. Others were killed in '67. And then there was the Yom Kippur War. Your luck has to run out sometimes. I mean, how many wars do you think you can survive?"

KURT Wassermann was not the only survivor to join an underground organization at the end of World War II. Boleslavs Maikovskis, who, accompanied by his wife, had escaped with the retreating Nazi forces to Germany in 1944, also joined an organization to assist refugees— Latvian SS refugees.

When the war was over, the members of the Latvian SS realized they could not return to a native land now controlled by the Russians. War criminals and exiles, these Latvian Nazis could only turn to each other for support. In 1945, a Latvian SS regiment stationed at the Zedelgheim prisoner of war camp formed a group called Daugavas Vanagi, "the hawks of the Daugavas," a river which runs through Latvia. The hawks would be a brotherhood of exiles bound by their complicity in common crimes. They would protect each other, hoping to survive until the day Latvia was again a fascist, anti-Jewish, anti-Communist state. And then, in triumph, they would return.

During the next decade, the hawks flew to thirteen

countries, each cell coordinated and, if necessary, financed by a central office in Muenster, Germany. The head of the hawks was Vilis Janauns, former chief of the Personnel Department of the General Committee for Home Affairs in the Nazi-run Latvian government. In Britain, Leon Rumba, a former member of the Fifteenth Latvian SS Division, directed the hawks. Under Rumba, the British hawks boasted they spent over $11,000 annually on "invalids, tuberculous patients, cripples, children . . . and to deserving causes." And in the United States one of the chief hawks was a Mineola, Long Island, carpenter, Boleslavs Maikovskis.

On December 22, 1951, after arriving from Germany, Maikovskis and his wife were admitted for permanent residence in the United States. According to Immigration records, their residency was granted under Section 2c of the 1948 Displaced Persons Act which declared eligible "a person who . . . was a victim of persecution by the Nazi government. . . ." At the time of entry, Maikovskis also signed a standard INS character document: "I . . . solemnly swear and affirm that I have never advocated or assisted in the persecution of any person because of race, religion, or national origin."

Maikovskis and his wife first settled on Ocean Avenue in Brooklyn. He found odd jobs as a carpenter and quickly became active in Latvian and anti-Communist groups. It was not long after his arrival in this country that the obscure Brooklyn carpenter suddenly became vice chairman of the mysteriously well-financed Washington-based American Latvian Association. And, he was appointed a delegate to the European Assembly of Captive Nations. Maikovskis was not the only veteran of the Latvian SS in the Assembly; a former Latvian colonel who worked closely with the commandant of the German secret police in Latvia and the chief Latvian aide to a Nazi SS colonel were also members. But these three Latvians were not strangers: They were all graduates of the Nazi Baltic University in Pinnenberg, Germany.

It was a coincidence which prompted other questions. Were these three Pinnenberg graduates also agents in the anti-Soviet Gehlen organization delivered to the OSS at the end of the war? Did Maikovskis spend his postwar years in Germany still working for Gehlen? Was the INS pressured to overlook Maikovskis's Nazi past because of his value as a potential CIA-controlled anti-Soviet agent? The answer to these questions is buried in files in New York and Washington, files that, unexplainably, vanish after being opened or are sent to Detroit. But in 1975, former CIA agent Philip Agee revealed another clue that darkens the shadows of suspicion surrounding the Maikovskis affair. The European Assembly of Captive Nations, he maintained, was a CIA front organization, a group funded and controlled by the Agency. Could Maikovskis have become a delegate without the CIA's approval and endorsement? And, could the CIA not have known about his past?

Also, was the CIA using the European Assembly of Captive Nations as a banker, a legitimate conduit for paying Maikovskis and other hawks for their information about Communist Latvia? It is an interesting question because just four years after coming to America, Maikovskis, the odd-job carpenter, had saved enough money to buy a home. In 1955, he moved from his Brooklyn apartment to a tree-lined suburban street in Mineola, Long Island.

A TRAVEL brochure written two generations ago described Mineola as "an important junction and the center of transportation of farming products. Many of the wealthiest farmers on Long Island live in this district, the surrounding country leaving evidence of high cultivation." And even back then the town attracted residents who were also foreign agents. In April 1918, a U.S. marshal arrested two "German enemy alien spies" living in Mineola. August Berlich, a construction worker, and Theodor Martens, a local bartender, were convicted of relaying information to Berlin about the departure of American troops for France.

But by the time Maikovskis moved to Mineola, few residents remembered either the farms or the foreign agents. The Long Island Railroad had turned Mineola into another commuting stop on the way to New York City. The farms had been subdivided into pieces of suburbia. For $5,000 cash and a $9,000 mortgage, Maikovskis bought a Florida-bound widow's old Victorian house on Grant Avenue, a relic from Mineola's grander days. There was a spacious porch out front where one could sit and feel the breeze and a vine-covered arbor in the narrow yard in the back. Up and down the block, middle-class neighbors lived in rows of comfortable but newer homes. It was the sort of small-town street where children ride their bicycles to school and wave to all the neighbors they pass on the way. It was also a stable family block, newly-weds moving in not long after their marriages and selling off only when a spouse died.

Maikovskis was fifty-one when he moved to this house and twenty years later it would still be his home. In those years he had become known as a good neighbor, a man with a smile and a friendly hello to everyone on the block. He was always the first on the block to rake his leaves or cut his grass. Maikovskis was friendly but aloof. He made acquaintances in Mineola, but not friends. His life remained very private. No one was sure what he did for a living. Every now and then he had a few freelance carpentry jobs, but mostly he stayed home and worked on his own house. Every Sunday the neighbors would see Maikovskis and his wife walking down the block to the red-brick Catholic church on the corner. When he became older, in his seventies, he would go more often. As he approached death, he told a neighbor, he felt it was important to thank God each day.

LOUISE Ortlepp came to America from Germany in 1925, and now, half a century later, a thin, white-haired woman in her seventies, she still speaks with a heavy, guttural German accent. And, she still remembers the first time she met Boleslavs Maikovskis.

In 1959, Louise Ortlepp was working as a housekeeper for a prosperous Queens, New York, businessman, William Zumstine. Part of Zumstine's wealth came from buying and selling real estate, finding discarded houses in the Long Island communities adjoining New York City and transforming them with a few coats of paint and a new kitchen into attractive suburban homes. In 1955, a house Zumstine had improved and on which he still held the mortgage was sold to a Boleslavs Maikovskis of Ocean Avenue, Brooklyn.

"I remember when Maikovskis came to see Mr. Zumstine to pay off the mortgage," says Louise Ortlepp, sitting in a tufted leather chair in the Floral Park, Queens, house Zumstine bequeathed to her on his death. "I talk *mit* this Maikovskis for five minutes and right away I know something not right. I ask him, 'Oh, you are the new one in the Mineola house?' He tells me like a smart aleck that he not so new and that he has lived there for a few years. Then he tells me he is a lawyer, but he works as a carpenter. He tells me he is able to pay off the whole mortgage in five years. I listen but I'm not impressed. *Aber,* I wonder, why is he telling me all this. I don't ask nothing.

"Then Mr. Zumstine comes down and I have to talk *mit* him about something in the kitchen. I remember I had left $2 on the hall table on a doily to pay for a delivery. *Aber,* when Mr. Zumstine and I come back, the money is gone. Mr. Zumstine and that Maikovskis go off to the study to discuss business.

"Later, after Maikovskis leaves, Mr. Zumstine asks me what happened to the $2. I tell him, 'Your friend the lawyer took it.' Mr. Zumstine starts to laugh and says, '*Ja,* some lawyer.' I will never forget that Maikovskis coming into our home and just stealing $2. I have even kept the card he left that day."

The card is a plain white calling card, the words written in capital letters. On the front is the name "Boleslavs Maikovskis" and the address "232 Grant Avenue, Mineola, New York." A telephone number is also listed: "PI6–2753." On the back, written and initialed by Maikovskis in a flowing script, is "Mortgage for May, 1959."

Louise Ortlepp, however, was not the only one who would not forget. There were those who did not need to keep calling cards as reminders. There were those who remembered larger crimes, murders. There were those who remembered Riga and Audrini.

HE hated being a salesman. There was something, he felt, demeaning about the work. A good salesman, he had been told, sells himself. But he refused. He would not beg customers throughout Germany to buy his brushes and brooms. Instead he mocked the instant friendliness and fraternal intimacy demanded by his work. And, perhaps because of his attitude, he was not very successful. Each month his sales steadily declined.

He had no alternative but to find another job. This time, he decided not to compromise. He would take a job suited to a man of his background and former position. Of course, he knew all along what sort of job he wanted. Perhaps his failure as a salesman had been purposeful, a failure which left him no alternative but to seek the position he had occupied years ago, before the war.

He did worry, though, if he had waited long enough. Hitler had been dead for more than a decade, he reassured himself. Most Germans must have forgotten. Or, perhaps did not even care. The time for false identities and trivial jobs was over. He had been on the run since his escape from a British POW camp in 1946, and now, he told himself, it was finally time to stop. He would now continue his life as if it had never been interrupted by the war. He would apply for his old job, a job that challenged his intellect, a position which people respected.

So in 1958, Gerhardt Maywald applied for the position of detective with the Hamburg police. He might have gotten the job and kept his secret if he had not given himself away on the application. It was not what SS Obersturmbannfuehrer Maywald wrote, but what he did not write.

A year after filling out the application for the detective's position, Maywald was questioned about this omission by the Hamburg state prosecutor:

Prosecutor: Why did you neglect to mention your posting to the Eastern front in your curriculum vitae . . . ?

Maywald: I was of the opinion that it dealt merely with a list of my places of work, and those I listed.

Prosecutor: At least a mention of more than a year–long tour of duty in the East should have been in the curriculum vitae.

Maywald: It only dealt with my educational history.

Prosecutor: I have to contradict. . . . Don't you think you kept silent about your Eastern tour of duty because of obvious reasons . . . ?

The Hamburg state prosecutor was not the first to consider the "obvious reasons" for Maywald's neglecting to mention his war record on the detective application. This omission also made the police officer who was processing Maywald's résumé suspicious. On a hunch, the officer checked the Wanted Book of missing war criminals.

There he found the name of Gerhardt Maywald, accused of crimes against humanity while serving in the Riga ghetto. Maywald did not get the detective's job. Instead, he was placed in jail.

But he did not stay in jail very long. The prosecutor could not assemble enough evidence. The eyewitness testimony against Maywald was fierce but lacking in details of actual crimes. For example, Harry Kahn testified: "I can still today remember Maywald. He came frequently to visit us in the camp. . . . One was warned to hide when it was heard that he was coming for inspection. I still see in my mind's eye how he stood in the yard in a leather coat with a fur collar during the transport of those chosen for Dunamunde. The way I remember it, the transport for Dunamunde was in April 1942. But it also could have been the end of March."

And Maywald would respond: "This testimony tells me everything. It is enough because I see the complete hatred of these witnesses, because it is not true that one had to be warned about me. I did everything to ease the lot of the Jews. Why should these people be afraid of me? They were absolutely comfortable. That is relative . . . of course it was no rest house, but a wooden camp under construction. But nobody had to complain about me, and I had a friendly word for everyone."

The Hamburg prosecutor decided he could not indict Maywald on such evidence and he was soon released. But he was not forgotten. The prosecutor sent an appeal to Jewish organizations throughout the world for witnesses to activities involving SS Obersturmbannfuehrer Gerhardt Maywald.

Two years later, in 1960, Kurt Wassermann was waiting on tables in the Rhein Cafe when he was called to the phone.

"Hello, Mr. Wassermann, this is Dr. Robinson. Remember, from the American Jewish Congress? *Wie gehts?*"

"Fine, just fine, Dr. Robinson, only I'm working. Can I call you back?"

"Well, I think I have something here that might interest

you. Something about that man you're always asking me about."

"What man?" Wassermann knew immediately; he was simply reluctant to be too optimistic.

"Maywald."

"I'll be right over."

Wassermann left the restaurant without even giving his boss an excuse. Within half an hour he was in Dr. Robinson's office reading the request from the state prosecutor in Hamburg. Wassermann read the notice and started shaking.

"I saw Maywald's name and it went through me like an electric shock," remembers Wassermann. "During all those years I never knew if he was alive or dead. And now I had the answer. I had been living with this man for so long and now it seemed I finally had him. I couldn't believe it."

That afternoon Wassermann went to the German Consulate in midtown Manhattan. He sat in a small, windowless room above Park Avenue and remembered Riga. While he spoke, a stenographer took down his words: ". . . on February 5, 1942, I became an eyewitness to a selection by Maywald. On this day we had to line up in the ghetto . . . Maywald asked us our name and age, and we had to separately stand in front of him. The transport was divided into two groups by Maywald. One group had to march to the right in the direction of headquarters . . . my mother Anna . . . who was then forty-two years old, among others . . . was then squeezed into open and closed trucks and driven off. From that day on, I never heard from my mother again. . . ."

Two weeks later Kurt Wassermann received a letter from the prosecutor in Hamburg. On the basis of his testimony, the letter stated, Maywald had been indicted and was being held without bail. The trial of SS Obersturmbannfuehrer Maywald for murder would soon be scheduled.

"After all those years, I finally felt I could relax," recalls Wassermann. "I finally felt I had avenged my mother's death."

FIVE years after Wassermann's testimony, it seemed likely that the men at the other beat of the Riga pendulum of death would also be brought to justice.

On October 30, 1965, the Latvian Supreme Court in Riga convicted six war criminals who while "serving in Hitler Germany's punitive detachments, took part in the extermination of more than 15,000 peaceable citizens (including 2,045 children) in the Rezekne district of Latvia." Three of these six war criminals were further cited as "the organizers, inspirers and leaders of the massacres of 15,000 civilians and had also themselves directly participated in the execution of these mass murders"; they "personally shot defenseless men and women" and, "implementing the Hitlerite racial policy, had murdered all the Jews of Rezekne district—5,128 people." They were also convicted for their roles in "the complete destruction of the village of Audrini, burning its 46 houses and executing 196 people."

More than two hundred witnesses testified against these three "organizers and leaders." They were sentenced to death by firing squad. But all three escaped punishment. One, Albert Eichelis, was now in Germany. The whereabouts of another, Haralds Puntulis, were unknown. And the third, Boleslavs Maikovskis, lived at 232 Grant Avenue, Mineola, Long Island.

On June 9, 1965, the Soviet Ministry of Foreign Affairs delivered a note to the American Embassy in Moscow requesting Maikovskis's extradition from the United States. It seemed to be a legal demand; the United States and Russia were both signators of a 1947 United Nations resolution that "governments . . . on demand of one of the United Nations members . . . extradite the individual who was accused of such [war] crimes to the United Nations member who made such a demand. . . ." The State Department, however, denied the Soviet request.

There were, according to State Department officials, other questions of international law involved in the extradition. The Soviet Ministry, the United States contended, could not justifiably request extradition because Maikovskis was a Latvian—not Russian—national. It was a point the Russians were willing to concede. The Soviet Republic of Latvia would submit its own request. But again the State Department found international complications which twisted the simple request for extradition of a Nazi into an unsolvable legal circle. The Soviet Republic of Latvia's request could not be granted because the United States does not recognize the Soviet Latvian regime. If a country that does not exist because the State Department says it should not exist makes a request, then—by diplomatic logic—it is also impossible to acknowledge the request: Unreal countries speak only silent, unreal words.

The Immigration and Naturalization Service would, instead of pursuing extradition, conduct its own investigation. If Maikovskis had lied about his background when he entered the United States, then he could be deported.

On January 25, 1966, INS investigator Sidney Fass started his investigation of Maikovskis. He had, he would tell DeVito, "sixty leads, things looked very promising." But less than four months later after receiving instructions from Washington, Fass terminated his investigation of Maikovskis.

Six and a half years later the Maikovskis file was found in Detroit. No one in the INS was certain why it had been sent there.

And Maikovskis, now sixty-eight, still lived in Mineola.

ON the Saturday preceding the holiday of Purim, a special portion of the Torah is read in synagogues. It is a story about vengeance.

"Thus saith the Lord of hosts: 'I remember that which the Amalekites did to Israel, how they set themselves against him in the way, when he came out of Egypt. Now go and smite the Amalekites, and utterly destroy all that they have and spare them not; but slay both man and woman, infant and suckling, ox and sheep, camel and ass. . . .'

"But Saul and the people spared Agag [king of the Amalekites] and the best of the sheep. . . ."

This failure to "destroy utterly" the Amalekites so angered the Lord, the book of Samuel warns, that Saul was stripped of his sovereignty. The Lord chose a new king, Samuel, who would obey totally His call for vengeance:

"Then said Samuel: 'Bring ye hither to me Agag the king of the Amalekites.' And Agag came unto him in chains. And Agag said: 'Surely the bitterness of death is at hand.' And Samuel said:

" 'As thy sword hath made women childless,

"So shall thy mother be childless among women.'

"And Samuel hewed Agag in pieces before the Lord."

Jewish tradition insists that Haman, the enemy of the Jews in the Purim story, was a descendant of Agag, the Amalekite king. Centuries later, another descendant was added—Hitler.

It was deliberate, then, that the first day of Purim, a holiday filled with Biblical memories of enemies and vengeance, was chosen by the Survivors of the Riga Ghetto as the occasion for their demonstration. Ten members of this group—including Kurt Wassermann—marched in a single column in front of Boleslavs Maikovskis' house. They walked slowly, some feeling exposed and vulnerable by this public display. A woman held a cardboard sign which simply said "Nazi." She had planned to draw a swastika under the word, but she could not bring herself to; it was that painful. Another woman would occasionally try to coax the others to chant. "Murderers must go. Murderers must go," she said in a firm, but restrained voice. She did not want to shout. Each time she began the chant, a marcher or two would join her. In minutes, though, hers would be a solitary voice.

Wassermann marched because he did not know what else to do. He had been waiting for DeVito, for the Immigration Service to do something. But so far nothing had been done. Another descendant of the Amalekite king—Maikovskis—had been spared. Spared, Wassermann was certain, by a disinterested U.S. government. The moral, Wassermann decided, was identical to that of the Purim story: Unfulfilled vengeance was a sin. The only hope, Wassermann realized, lay in new kings, avenging Samuels to replace complacent Sauls.

But this was a large and unlikely hope. No one in the government appeared to care. On the train to Mineola, Wassermann worked himself up, complaining to his friends, "The government wants to forget about Nazis. It's up to the Jews or no one else. The authorities found out about Maikovskis in 1965. Have they tried to interview any of us? Did they notify any of the survivors in Europe or Israel? They didn't even make one phone call or write one letter. Hell, they never tried to interview anyone. The State Department won't even ask the Russians to help gather witnesses. I guess detente doesn't apply to Nazi cases. I know I'm getting all steamed up, but it's driving me crazy. I'd forget it if I could. America is treating Maikovskis the same way the Germans treated Maywald. All the Nazis everywhere will die happy, old men."

Seven years ago Wassermann thought he had finally caught up with Maywald, but the man he describes as "the beast who killed my mother" escaped once more. The immediate trial the Hamburg prosecutor had promised did not take place. Maywald had been kept in investigative detention for only a few months before he was released on bail. It is a rare event in German courts when an investigative detainee is released on bail and his release is even rarer if he has been indicted for murder. Yet Maywald was freed. It seems, Wassermann learned, that the German minister for scientific research, Hans Lenz, and members of his family had personally posted bail. On the intervention of the minister, the murder suspect, SS Obersturmbannfuehrer Maywald, was released. Years after Wassermann's testimony, the case has still not come to trial.

There is little Wassermann can do but march, a large man wedged into a single thin line. With every step a sentence in his mind is underlined: Maywald and Maikovskis are free. Maywald and Maikovskis are free. He could endure this for only an hour. Perhaps it was not even that long. He was not certain. He just knew he could not continue. The futility of the demonstration was oppressive. He told the others he had to leave.

Wassermann, considering his desperate thoughts, was oddly calm when he left. To the others, he fell into his public role, protecting himself with his tough-guy cynicism. It was his only alternative to despair. He realized he had to control himself or things would become impossible.

When he told one of the women he was leaving, she objected. He tried hard to explain without giving too much of his real self away. He had known her for thirty years, but this afternoon it was difficult to talk to her—or anyone—about his fears and his painful resignation to events. In Riga, after his mother had been killed, he had moved in with this woman's family. It was her father who had objected to a young boy's presence in his house.

"Kurt, go if you want. I understand," she finally lied.

"Do you want to leave?" Wassermann asked.

She considered for a minute and then decided, "No, it wouldn't be right. How can I do nothing while the man who killed my father walks the same streets as I do?"

Wassermann left without telling her that there really was nothing she could do.

She and the others stayed for hours, marching slowly and silently in the blue-white light of late afternoon. It turned dark, not quite night, and it became difficult to read the one sign which said "Nazi." While they marched, inside the house just yards away, Maikovskis remained safe, beyond their reach.

It was dark, past dinner time, when they decided to leave. They were walking down the block, away from

Maikovskis's house, when a neighbor came out. He studied them and, without saying a word, spit loudly on the sidewalk directly in their path. Then he rushed away.

There was something frightening in that sudden act of contempt. The nine demonstrators wanted to return to their homes as quickly as possible. But, instead, they returned to Maikovskis's house and once more began to march. This time when the woman chanted, "Murderers must go. Murderers must go," many voices joined hers. Together, they shouted the words.

They marched longer than they had planned, hours longer. There just did not seem to be any choice.

THE old Victorian on Grant Avenue has been transformed by the carpenter into something awkward and, as must have been his original intention, more modern. After twenty years of shaping and reshaping the house's lines, Maikovskis has succeeded in disguising its elegant architectural past. A roof has been abruptly lowered to give the entrance a low-slung ranch look. A veranda has been enclosed and lavishly Thermopaned. An old, carved door has been replaced by a solid, brutal-looking slab of stained wood. And the original happy white paint has been scraped and a less common suburban color has been substituted—a deep, dark forest green.

His own past has been equally well-disguised. Maikovskis, in his seventies, has succeeded in blending into his new Long Island life. He does not go out much, only in the mornings to attend mass. He and his wife are a secretive, childless couple, their days spent inside the big, old house. He avoids all reporters, never answering his door and when once trapped on the way to church all he would offer was a stiff recital of, "Lies, lies, lies." He spoke in one quick, angry burst. A small, baldheaded man, one's first impression of Maikovskis is that he is not well; there is a fragility and a deliberateness to his movements. He stares directly at people as if trying to focus, his eyes bursting from a thin, sallow face. It is a face which has been stripped so brutally by age that it now resembles a skull.

Most of his neighbors do not believe or are not bothered by the charges against Maikovskis. Some seem only annoyed by the commotion his presence has caused, as if Maikovskis's past has rudely intruded into the quiet, private life they had moved to Mineola to find; Maikovskis has become, like the headlines in the morning paper, a reminder of large and troublesome issues. These people would prefer to forget all that. Nazis or, for example, nuclear nonproliferation are not their problems. The attitude of Bob Herran, Maikovskis's mailman for ten years, is not uncommon: "What he did years ago, he did then. People change. He's just a nice old guy, always tipping his hat and asking about your health. Shoot, he can't be no Nazi. Why he even keeps an American flag on his door."

In the corner of an opaque yellow window cut into the front door of the house at 232 Grant Avenue, a small American flag has been taped. The flag is Boleslavs Maikovskis's tribute to the country which has protected him all these years.

THERE is also an American flag in Kurt Wassermann's house. It is much larger than Maikovskis's, almost a yard long, and his wife keeps it near the bed. She keeps it there so when Kurt starts screaming in the middle of the night, she can awaken him and quickly remind him he's safe; he is in his bed in America. His screams are about another life, a life thirty years in the past, but a life he relives each night in his dreams.

Wassermann has moved to a bigger apartment in the Bronx, but he is once more thinking about moving. "The neighborhood has changed," he complains. "It's no longer safe." Also, the children have grown up and the apartment now seems too large, almost empty.

His son, after graduating from City University, was not accepted by an American medical school. Instead, he had to study in Vienna. This upsets Wassermann. It is further proof, evidence in his growing indictment of America. "I've always felt at home in this country," he says, "but things are changing. It's just not right that bright Jewish boys can't get into medical schools and they let in all those minority students. I think about this a lot—my son had to go back to Vienna for medical school after I moved to America to give him a new life. It's ironic, all right. Who would have believed that something like that was possible?"

With his son away for the past five years, Wassermann has centered both his affection and personality on his daughter. She, in turn, is attentive and even doting. She has grown to share his preoccupation with Nazis, closely following the progress of the Maywald and Maikovskis cases. On Wednesday nights she waits up for him to learn if the toy salesman has revealed more of his true identity in the course of the poker game. Theirs is a very loving and close relationship, the daughter reinforcing and sharing her father's obsessions.

In her senior year in high school, she wrote a term paper about Boleslavs Maikovskis. She is eager, however, to explain, "My father really did all the work. He got all the information. I just wrote it up, that's all." In the paper she wrote, "Should a man like Boleslavs Maikovskis live out his days in peaceful serenity? . . . Should justice fall asleep after twenty years or should justice be carried out?" Her teacher liked the paper, giving her an A–, but noted her contention that the government knows all the details of the Maikovskis case, yet still refuses to deport him, is unlikely. "This sounds way out," the teacher cautioned in red ink along the margin.

The daughter, now a college freshman, also has dreams. She has been having these dreams ever since her father became involved with Maikovskis. She dreams that she is "in a European town and people all around her are carrying bags. Everybody is hurrying, running, trying to get away from the Nazis."

Her father's nights are worse. "I have such dreams," says Wassermann, "that I wake up in a sweat. I see my wife, my children, and myself being thrown into a railroad car and taken to a camp. Each night it is the same. We arrive at the camp and the guard orders, 'You go to the left. You go to the right.' I am sent to the right. My family is sent to the left. Do you know what it is each night to see your wife and children taken away from you and sent to their deaths? This is when I wake up screaming and kicking. My wife shows me the flag and I stop. I realize it is not Riga, but only a dream.

"But lately I look at the flag and cannot go back to sleep. I think that this is the country which has allowed Maikovskis to remain free. I think about that and stay awake. After all these years, night and day I still live with this so deep. After all the years of running through Europe and then trying to start a new life in America, I still cannot escape the Nazis."

IT had not been much of a vacation for Tony DeVito. The events of the past year had totally undermined his life and the tension in his mood was not calmed by weeks away from the office. Even during his vacation it had been difficult to sleep; his anger was complete. He stayed up nights reading a manuscript written by a witness at the Ryan trial, memories of the horrors of Majdanek con-

centration camp. He stayed up nights tense with the aware-
ness of his own solitude and strangeness: He, alone, an
Immigration Service investigator sitting in the living room
of a Long Island tract house, was the only member of the
U.S. government actively committed to the pursuit of 59
Nazis in America.

It was in this mood that he returned from vacation to
learn that the trap he had set for Odessa had sprung in
his absence. Only, the culprits had escaped.

His first day back at the office, DeVito twirled the
combination lock on his filing cabinet and made a discovery—the Maikovskis file was gone.

The cabinet had clearly not been broken into and only
three other men knew the combination: Vince Schiano,
the trial attorney for the Ryan case, Junior Simmons, the
chief clerk, and the security officer on the floor.

It did not take much of an investigation for DeVito
to learn who had taken the file. Junior Simmons readily
admitted the act. But, he told DeVito, he had removed
the file when both Schiano and DeVito were out of the
office under instructions from Ben Lambert, chief of investigators for the New York office.

Once more the trail had come to an abrupt dead end.
DeVito's trap had snared only more suspicions. Lambert
—like Simmons, DeVito realized—had surely been following orders. Both men simply obeyed their superiors.
The questions now were: Who in Washington had ordered
the chief investigators to remove the Maikovskis file? And
why?

Lambert, as was his right as DeVito's boss, refused
to explain his actions. But DeVito refused to leave the
mystery alone. He poked at it until he came up with a
new idea. Perhaps Lambert, like Sid Fass, the original
investigator assigned to the case, had included a memo
in the file identifying the specific source of his instructions.
This proof, DeVito realized, could only be found in one
place—the Maikovskis file.

It took DeVito two and a half months to get possession
of the file from a reluctant Lambert. And he only suc-

ceeded because of the press. In desperation, DeVito had leaked the story of an INS coverup on the Maikovskis case to a *New York Times* reporter covering the Ryan trial. The reporter cornered Sol Marks, regional director of the Service, and demanded to know if progress were being made in the Maikovskis investigation.

The next day, February 28, 1973, DeVito learned in that morning's *Times* that "Sol Marks . . . disclosed . . . that he had appointed Anthony J. DeVito, an investigator normally assigned to the chief trial counsel, Vincent A. Schiano, to carry out the new [Maikovskis] investigation."

Now Lambert had no choice but to return the file to DeVito. Except it was too late. Not only was there no memo detailing who had ordered Lambert to remove the file, but also something else was missing. The memo Sidney Fass had written nearly seven years ago explaining that he had terminated the original investigation "pursuant to telephonic instructions from Wilbur Flagg" had vanished. Odessa, DeVito was certain, had once more moved quickly to cover its tracks through the INS bureaucracy.

His trap, though, had caught something. He was now officially assigned to the Maikovskis case. He could now begin to close in on the carpenter, gathering evidence and witnesses, methodically building his case for deportation.

DeVito, however, now proceeded with apprehension: He was certain his every movement was being watched by Odessa.

Part III

ANOTHER VICTIM

"GOD damn it, Vince, we did it! We made history,"
Tony DeVito yelled above the dense, excited noise in the
courtroom. He jumped up, about to hug his partner, INS
chief trial attorney Vince Schiano. But, abruptly, he
stopped; the spontaneity of the moment was short-lived.
DeVito managed to control himself, once more falling into
his public role as a government investigator in a federal
courtroom. Tentatively, he extended a stiff, professional
hand.

Schiano just laughed. He ignored the outstretched hand
and, instead, enthusiastically embraced his friend. For
only a moment the two men were locked together, celebrating their victory: Chief Judge Jacob Mishler of the
United States District Court in Brooklyn had just ordered
the extradition of Mrs. Hermine Braunsteiner Ryan to
face charges of murder of Nazi concentration camp inmates. In three days, on May 4, 1973, she would be
surrendered to officials of the Federal Republic of Germany.

"We did what they said we could never do," exclaimed
DeVito, breaking into a wide grin as he continually
slapped his taller partner on the back. "They tried to
stop us, Vince, but they couldn't. They just couldn't."

By that afternoon, though, the morning's courtroom
elation had dwindled. DeVito returned to the fourteenth
floor office he had been sharing for the past fourteen
months with Schiano and sat chain-smoking Raleighs, his
thoughts hurried and confused. Rapidly, his mood reversed. The turn had started when he had first returned

to the office. He had expected at least one congratulatory remark or gesture, but he was greeted with silence. "I felt like I was in an enemy camp," he later recalled. And with that feeling came another mood, a depressed, exhaustive melancholy: a day-after feeling. DeVito sat there suddenly headachey, his face drained by the recognition of impending calamity. Now that the Ryan case was over, it struck him, so might be his special role. He had beaten them once. But could he continue to beat them 59 more times? And would they let him?

The Ryan victory, he decided candidly, had been a fluke. They (in his mind, he used "they" or "the opposition" or "Odessa" interchangeably, all euphemisms for an unseen and unknown enemy) had tried to influence the trial, but had lost because of a legal error. Mrs. Ryan's lawyers had agreed to concede citizenship perhaps because they expected a deal. But the case had quickly become too public an issue to allow the INS to make deals. Yet, if Mrs. Ryan had not willingly relinquished her citizenship, she could have fought extradition for at least ten more years.

The Ryan case had changed nothing. No, that was wrong. Its headlines and success had undermined his future. Tony DeVito saw Odessa's next inevitable move with agonizing clarity: They would have to get rid of him. His end would not come by a surreptitious single bullet, or by a deliberate push under the wheels of a wild truck. The opposition was too shrewd. There were simpler, less obvious ways. He sat in his office chain-smoking just hours after his triumph and objectively saw the future: He would become a victim of the INS bureaucracy, disposed of like another annoying file, shuffled off to Detroit or its departmental equivalent, for years of dormancy. And this, to DeVito, was the worst fate.

He had helped build the Ryan case and the Ryan case had helped build him. It had lifted him above an Immigration Service crowded with apathetic and corrupt investigators and made him a man with a mission, an investigator charged by a cause. His remarks to Schiano earlier that morning had been spontaneous, but they were also revelatory. He was a man who needed to be part of a cause making history, a man who was energized by pursuing what others insisted was impossible. The Ryan case had been such a calling and he had anticipated that the list with 59 names would become a life-long mission. It was a mission, however, he feared ruined by initial success. The more he thought, the more he became certain they would not allow him to continue. For over a year he had been living totally with the excitement of this mission. It had dominated his life. He could not allow the INS to shove him into the background, another ignored victim calling for vengeance.

And yet he realized the pursuit of Nazis in America required two simultaneous investigations. The first centered on 59 names, faces, and file numbers which could be identified and tracked down. This strategy could be planned and orderly followed. He thought of his attack and for a moment enjoyed a pensive half-smile. First he would build his case against Maikovskis. Then he would move on to Soobzokov, and Trifa, and Artukovic, and so on down the list.

But he knew he would only be able to proceed if he succeeded in his other investigation. Here the enemy was unseen, its name and face only suspicions. It was an enemy which managed to steal files, lose department memos, and influence Congress. It was an enemy which would be closing in on Tony DeVito unless, somehow, he had the cunning to get it first.

It was in this mood that two hours later Tony DeVito went looking for an ally. That afternoon he met with U.S. Attorney Robert Morse. DeVito had first spoken with Morse during the Ryan trial. The two men shared a similar tense, aggressive, even compulsive commitment to the case and they quickly became friends. Morse's interest was also personal. He saw the case as a proper memorial to the recent death of his brother Arthur Morse, author of *While Six Million Died,* a book charging that President Roosevelt and his advisers had made no move to save

European Jews from Nazi Germany until 1944. Morse's
pudgy face would turn a deep, angry red when he spoke
about the injustice which allowed a Nazi SS guard to
live safely in Queens. He promised DeVito that the case
would be vigorously prosecuted. And DeVito, in turn,
spoke of Morse with his highest words of praise, "This
man is not a quitter. I tell you he is one man who refuses
to give up."

That afternoon DeVito sat in Morse's office and, a little
embarrassed by the implications of his theory, began
cautiously, as if prepared to be interrupted at any moment.
"Mr. Morse," he said, "you might think what I'm gonna
tell you is crazy. But just let me get through the whole
story. Then, if you still think I'm loony, I know where the
door is." So DeVito told him about Odessa and then he
counted off on his short, yellow-stained fingers his strange
discoveries in the past year. He counted each one off very
deliberately, trying to keep a neutral tone. He was simply
reciting facts. First there was the Ryan case—the reluctance to prosecute, the unknown source of defense funds,
the stolen files, the mistreatment of government witnesses,
the threats, the strange call to his wife. Then there was
the Soobzokov case—again stolen files, Congressional influence, CIA employment. The same with Trifa—the
routine of unexplained delays, unusual INS procedures.
And Artukovic—refusal to prosecute, stolen court records, State Department inaction, Congressional influence.
And the same suspicious elements were present in the
Maikovskis case—INS inaction, transferred files, missing
memos. It was all, concluded DeVito, a large mystery.
But it was a mystery, he told Morse, which would allow
59 Nazis in America to escape punishment.

Morse sat silently as DeVito enumerated his evidence.
The U.S. Attorney was a man with a quick temper, but
he controlled himself. As DeVito spoke, Morse just rocked
back and forth in his leather desk chair, each rhythmic
movement tightening his anger another notch.

When DeVito finished Morse considered all he had
heard and then rose from his chair. He moved from be-

hind his desk and stood face to face with DeVito. "Tony," he said with the definitive emphasis trial attorneys save for their final argument, "the only way they're going to stop you is over my dead body."

THREE days later, on the day Mrs. Ryan was surrendered to the West German authorities, Tony DeVito wrote a memo to his INS superiors. The memo specifically referred to the Maikovskis investigation, but DeVito hoped it would set a precedent for fifty-eight other Nazi cases. He wrote: "To insure a performance in a professional-like manner and accomplish a mission in minimum time, it is felt that a course be authorized deviating from the usual norm. An independent arrangement, free of periodic supervisory control from those not directly involved in this investigation, should expedite progress somewhat and urge its acceptance."

The cumbersome, professional bureaucratic language was intended to mask a subtler strategy. "I wrote that memo hoping to get Odessa off my back," DeVito explains. "You see, the Service has this form, an O.I.103.1g form, which has to be filled out for cases when the central office in Washington wants to be notified of how an investigation is proceeding. Now in these Nazi cases, that's just what I wanted to avoid. I didn't want the central office to have any idea what I was doing because if they did I knew they would block me. I knew if Washington received any periodic reports on Nazis that would be tantamount to suicide. They would sabotage each case."

DeVito had no hope for the memo's approval, but he also decided he had no choice but to submit it. He was at the Service's mercy.

Five days later he received an answer. On May 9, 1973,

Tony DeVito was removed from the special attorney's office and reassigned to the subversive section. It was the sort of bureaucratic shuffle DeVito had been anticipating. Only he had not expected it so soon after the announcement in the press of his assignment to the Maikovskis case. And he had not expected this oblique memo to have such an immediate effect. "It must have frightened the hell out of them in Washington. They must have known what I was really up to," he decided.

From his fourteenth-floor office DeVito was moved to an open floor filled with two hundred desks. "It was an impossible way to work," remembers DeVito. "There I was still assigned to a Nazi case. I was supposed to investigate Maikovskis and at the same time my superiors expected to me carry a case load of work for the subversive section. They should have created a special team just for those 59 Nazi cases. Instead, they gave them to me and then also assigned me additional work. It's obvious what they were up to. My superiors in the Immigration Service tried to discourage prosecution in the Ryan case, but in the Maikovskis affair there was outright blockage.

"Look what I was up against. Ben Lambert tells my new supervisor, a desk guy by the name of Graziano, that I'm to maintain a normal case load of subversive assignments. Hell, there were only four investigators in a department that once had sixty. I was given twenty cases to process right away. Each case had a call-up date. It had to be completed by a certain date or else they would be on my back wanting to know why. That's the way they hoped to keep me going. Finish one, get one. Finish one, get one. Only one of my cases didn't have a call-up date. They didn't care when that one was finished. You know which one that was—Maikovskis."

For two months DeVito sat at a gray steel desk in the middle of a floor-long row of identical desks. To his right and left were other rows of desks. Yet, DeVito attempted to remain isolated. He tried to detach himself from the workers and the daily routine which surrounded him. For twenty years before the Ryan case, Tony DeVito had passed his days frustrated by this routine, a nine-to-five day of filing memos and typing forgotten reports. For twenty years he had been enraged by a system propelled by special favors and political deals. The Ryan case had seemed to liberate him from these daily, tedious, meaningless affairs. But, he was now back where he had started. This was the most painful part of his victimization. His fears of Odessa, the sleepless nights, even the phone call to his wife, were not as tormenting. They were part of a high drama filled with Nazis and promising great deeds. But this return to a career filled with corruption and insignificance was only degrading. DeVito went to work each day humiliated and defeated. The excitement of apprehension faded, only to be replaced with despair.

Long before his involvement in the Ryan case, DeVito had come to the conclusion that the Immigration Service was corrupt. Long ago he had decided that he worked in the company of thieves. It was an opinion commonly held by others in law enforcement. In 1972, the Justice Department conducted its own investigation of the INS called Operation Cleansweep. The result was a series of indictments against INS investigators on charges including selling border crossing cards, smuggling heroin, and accepting bribes to remove files of aliens facing deportation. If Odessa wanted to spend money for special favors, DeVito had little doubt there would be takers in the INS.

And if funds were offered to congressmen, DeVito knew politicians could be found who were willing to influence the INS. The word "Nazi" need never be mentioned; the favors, DeVito was certain, would be asked for Yugoslavs or Latvians, political victims and anti-Communists. "The entire business of the Immigration Service is catering to the wants of congressmen. You walk down the row of desks and all you see is letters from certain congressmen requesting favors," says DeVito. The findings of Operation Cleansweep back up this charge: Congressmen intervene in 5 percent of the immigration cases handled in the New York office.

"For twenty years I saw it all happening. Bums getting

appointed supervisors because of letters from congress-men. We all heard the rumors about the investigations of big-time Mafia guys that were killed by orders from the top [rumors Cleansweep confirmed in a case involving a heroin dealer tied to the Gambino family]. I never took a dime, but it was happening all around me. It was a cor-rupt atmosphere, all right."

And for those twenty years DeVito remained an out-sider, officially part of the system, but—curiously—de-tached. He watched as the power in the Immigration Ser-vice gravitated to a few select hands. The men who controlled the Service were known as the '41 Club; that was the year they had joined the INS. It was these mem-bers of the '41 Club who made the decisions, not the immigration commissioner. The commissioner was only a political appointee. These men were professional bureau-crats, trained by the system and able, in turn, to make the system work for them.

The futility of his present position and, at the same time, the exasperating possibilities for success if he were ever given a free hand grated at DeVito constantly. He mulled his inefficacy over day and night until he raced toward a new theory, a theory that made an outsider comfortable: It was the '41 Club which was the source of DeVito's predicament. They had passed the word to tie his hands.

With this realization, his hatred intensified. Odessa had been an anonymous foe. These men were constantly, infuriatingly visible. They became the faces against which he armed his armory of hate. They became his new Judenrat, the moral descendants of the *kapo* he had seen thirty years ago being stoned in Dachau. These men were the new collaborators, the new enemy.

It was these men, DeVito was convinced, who held the answers to why Nazi war criminals in America were allowed to escape justice. These men, either knowingly or unknowingly, were the lackeys of Odessa. These were the men who issued orders.

Any chart of the flow of power in the Service, DeVito

realized, had to start with Ed Loughran, deputy director, and his assistant, Sid Rawitz. They would most probably have had to approve orders which went to Wilbur Flagg to terminate the original Maikovskis investigation, to Ben Lambert to remove the Maikovskis file, to Sol Marks to reassign DeVito to the subversive section, and to Carl Burrows to discourage the Ryan investigation. These orders, DeVito imagined, were passed like whispered secrets, passwords to the boys in the fraternity: Each of these men was a member of the '41 Club.

DeVito realized there was only one last hope for success in the Nazi cases. He had to break away from this system. He needed the freedom to conduct an independent investigation supported, but not directed, by the INS. On June 5, 1973, he wrote another memo asking that "the writer be relieved from other subversive investigation case load and be authorized to concentrate on this matter on a full-time basis and thereby do proper justice to all concerned."

DeVito wrote this memo in frustration. It was the act of a man simultaneously assigned to twenty subversive and 59 Nazi cases. But it was a request he could realistically hope might be granted. For now, for the first time, he thought the opposition might be frightened. It seemed DeVito's ally had joined him in the battle.

Just a week earlier, U.S. Attorney Robert Morse wrote a letter to DeVito with copies sent to the INS District Director Sol Marks, Assistant District Director Ben Lambert, and U.S. Attorney Whitney North Seymour, Jr. The letter said: "It is apparent to me that you have raised some serious questions concerning the administration of the Immigration and Naturalization Service with respect to the situation concerning people whom you believe to be suspected Nazi war criminals. . . . Accordingly, it is my intention to call this matter to the immediate personal attention of the Deputy Attorney General and request that he commence an immediate in-house investigation to determine the facts."

"I read that letter and thought this was it," remembers

Tony DeVito. "I thought Odessa was going to have to go on the run. Here was the U.S. Attorney backing me up, promising an investigation. I thought it wouldn't be long before I was back full-time in the Nazi business. For the first time since the Ryan trial I was beginning to feel alive again. You know, after reading that letter I felt I could go to work without being ashamed. I said to myself, 'Tony, by Christmas you'll have Maikovskis in the courtroom.'"

CHRISTMAS came and Christmas went, but Boleslavs Maikovskis remained a free man, still living in his house in Mineola. There had, however, been some changes in the Immigration and Naturalization Service.

The "immediate in-house investigation" Morse had requested never took place. No one pushed for it and perhaps it was no longer necessary. Most of the officials DeVito had hoped would be questioned simply left the Service not long after the letter was circulated.

Each of these men of the '41 Club insists his leaving and the timing of the letter were "coincidental." Ben Lambert, assistant district director, says he "retired for no reason at all. After thirty-seven years I just felt I had done enough." Wilbur Flagg, assistant commissioner for investigations, explains he is "very sick and will not make any further comment." Sol Marks, district director, and Carl Burrows, the assistant commissioner, also refuse to divulge any specific reason for leaving.

Ed Loughran, the deputy director, and Sid Rawitz, his assistant, also left the Service not long after Morse's call for an investigation. These two men left the Service for the same employer—Senator James Eastland and the Senate Subcommittee on Immigration. They left important and powerful posts where they directed hundreds of men for an eight-man subcommittee which has not held a formal meeting in a decade. Only Rawitz will comment for the record. "The Morse letter," he says, "was not warranted. It had nothing to do with our leaving. It was sheer coincidence."

U.S. Attorney Robert Morse could never press for the in-house investigation. His pledge to Tony DeVito had become grim prophecy: The pursuit of Nazis in America was stopped "over his dead body." Six months after he wrote the letter calling for an investigation, Morse was found dead, his body crushed and broken on a sidewalk in Brooklyn. According to the police Morse had been a suicide, jumping out of his fifth-floor apartment window. Investigators said "there was no indication that Mr. Morse's death had been prompted by anything other than personal problems." The authorities explained that Morse had been "tense" and "depressed."

Tony DeVito was also depressed. His subversive case load kept him prisoner. Each day he sat at his desk and typed papers. Each night he lay awake and pursued Nazis. His frustration was unbearable.

When there no longer was any hope for an internal INS investigation, Tony DeVito felt only one alternative remained. After twenty-two and a half years, Tony DeVito resigned from the INS.

"I decided to remove myself from a corrupt atmosphere," DeVito explains. His resignation was not so much an act of withdrawal as it was a rebellion. He was not giving up his pursuit of Nazis; rather, his leaving confirmed his commitment to the cause. It was an emotional, idealized gesture, the act of a man concerned with his dignity and reputation. Tony DeVito refused to yield to the Service, so he resigned. DeVito left with the hope that if anything more were to be done about 59 Nazi war criminals living in America, he would still be the avenger. He left, retired at fifty-two, with one vision dominating his mind: Tony DeVito, a lone, exiled investigator reaching out and, one by one, delivering 59 Nazis to justice. He left certain that his exile was only temporary. There would be triumphs and a return. He left excited by the future.

NOT much has been accomplished by the Immigration and Naturalization Service in the four years since Tony DeVito's resignation.

In fact, not much has been accomplished since 1943, when the United States proclaimed that "most assuredly the three Allied powers will pursue them [war criminals] to the uttermost ends of the earth and will deliver them to their accusers in order that justice may be done." Fifty-nine Nazis did not have to flee to the "ends of the earth"; it was only necessary to come to America. The enthusiasm of 1943 quickly disappeared, constrained by a muddle of procedural questions.

"Legally, the problem is quite complex," says Verne Jervis, an Immigration official and the Service's chief spokesman. "If we have accusations that somebody is a Nazi war criminal, we must carry out an investigation to determine, first, exactly what the accused said when applying for entry into the United States. Now, if the person is found to have hid something—such as concealment of membership in an illegal organization—we can ask the U.S. Attorney for denaturalization proceedings, which is a trial subject to the laws of evidence and such. That's just to take away citizenship. If we want to deport the accused, there is another legal proceeding that must be followed, a deportation process, subject to the U.S. Supreme Court. And this assumes that the U.S. Attorney agrees with us that the case is worth prosecuting."

The legal problem of evidence is further complicated, according to other INS officials, "by the reluctance of the State Department to cooperate in locating overseas witnesses." The State Department, in spite of detente, has been reluctant to meet with Soviet or any Iron Curtain officials concerning the testimony of eyewitnesses to Nazi atrocities.

Six years after receiving the list with 59 names, the INS has still not worked out these evidentiary and legal problems. It does not seem to be in much of a hurry.

Still, the new commissioner, former Marine Corps Commandant L. F. Chapman, Jr., is "optimistic for success in the Nazi cases." He sits in his office in Washington, a meticulous, pink-cheeked, incredibly smooth-skinned man. Despite his business suit, he still looks more like a Marine than a bureaucrat. It is a look he is proud of. On one side of his desk stands an American flag. On the other is the flag of the Marine Corps. "Every effort," he says, "is being made to complete these investigations expeditiously and they are being handled on a high priority basis." He dismisses DeVito's charges of INS irregularities as "vague allegations, certainly not the sort of thing I think should be honored with an investigation. The record will show that I am going for broke in these cases."

The record, though, is less convincing. Commissioner Chapman cites what he describes as the "box score" in the Nazi cases: Of the original list of 59 names the Service received in 1971, seventeen have died natural deaths. Most of the others on the list are already old men. Forty-one of the investigations remain active. In the forty-second case, that of Bishop Valerian Trifa, a denaturalization hearing is planned. The date, however, has already been twice postponed.

The Commissioner's "box score" omits certain other participants in the Nazi cases.

Harold Goldberg, the former cop who gathered the evidence against Soobzokov, is "sorry I ever went to Paterson. My boss at Social Security keeps getting letters from all kinds of big shots asking what is going on and I got to bear the brunt of it. I wouldn't be surprised if this investigation costs me my job."

Dr. Kremer is upset that the Trifa trial has been delayed. Twice he has had to postpone his trip to Detroit and twice he has had to delay his seeing Trifa for the first time. "How long are they going to wait," he complains. "I'm seventy-nine and I'm not prepared to wait forever."

David Whitelaw, the youth who fire-bombed Artukovic's brother's car, has been released from jail. He is worried that the forfeited bail will force his mother to sell her home. "If she had to lose her home because of me, I don't know how I would live with that," he says.

And Kurt Wassermann still cannot sleep. He is certain Maikovskis will die a free man. His doctor has prescribed a stronger sleeping pill, but even this does not help.

The commissioner sits at his desk and reviews his box score. "It is likely, I imagine, that many of these Nazis will die a natural death before we can prosecute." He says this with a shrug, as if even he is powerless to prevent the inevitable. "These investigations are very complicated," he explains.

But, he is challenged. The Service first received this list with 59 names in 1971. Would an investigation in the Marine Corps have lasted six years without results?

"No," the commissioner answers quickly. "We wouldn't have let something like this drag on for so long in the Marines."

He pauses for a moment, realizing what he has said. The commissioner tries to recover. "Well," he says, "you have to give us credit for something. We did extradite Hermine Braunsteiner Ryan."

DURING the four years since Tony DeVito left the Immigration Service, most of his hopes for success have been drained. "The Nazi cases," he explains, "have made me sick." His exile has become complete: There is no hope of justice; there is no hope of return.

He spends his days reading about Nazis. He sits on the

green couch in his living room, the shades purposely drawn so as to make the room dark, almost secretive. He reads and he incorporates each new fact to fit his past experiences. A new clue to the mystery, he is now convinced, involves the 750 foreign companies Martin Bormann ordered established in 1944. "It all fits," he says, obviously pleased with his deduction. "This was the source of funds for Odessa. This is where the opposition got the money to buy protection after the war in America."

At night, while his wife sleeps, he stays awake and writes. He sits at a small desk in the living room and works on a manuscript which "will set out everything in a factual presentation about the Nazis in America." The manuscript is all that he has left. It is his last act of vengeance.

His wife often tells him that she wished he had never gotten involved in the Ryan case. "It's driving you crazy, Tony," she finally screamed. DeVito is also concerned that others, especially those who have taken his place in the Immigration Service, might think him crazy or obsessed. "Should the opposition use such terms," he wrote in a note to a reporter, "it is merely an indication of their frustration to deal adequately with their dilemma."

Lately, he has been especially preoccupied with thoughts of the opposition. He has taken to calling acquaintances and trying to explain about "the Judenrat which runs the Immigration Service." "It is very important that you know about this Judenrat," he tells them. "The Nazis had the future all worked out. The first move is to assemble all the Jews into the ghettos. So they said, 'Let's organize a Judenrat to help us. We'll give them privileges and they'll do our dirty work.' When the war was over, some of those Jews were murdered. Some committed suicide. In this particular case of the Immigration Service, we have another Judenrat helping out."

Lately, his mind focuses frequently on the Jewish collaborator he had seen in Dachau thirty years ago, a man crawling on his knees, dodging rocks and sticks. It is an image that comes to him in the middle of a sentence while he is reading or at night while he is writing. He thinks of it, he has decided, because it is a scene of vengeance. And that is what he now wants more than anything else.

His only hope, he is convinced, is his manuscript. It is the focus of all his efforts. He refuses to take another job until the manuscript is completed. In the manuscript, he will tell all. And yet, he often doubts anyone will care. He wonders if it is another futile hope.

He works on it each night, though, chain-smoking while he writes. Between thoughts, he holds the cigarette with two fingers at its very end, clouds of smoke twirling above his head, trapped like spent emotions in the small, dark room.

For months his wife has been warning that the smoke will choke her plants. And for months the spider plants have been slowly dying. The plants have turned yellow at the edges and then a rotten dirt brown. One by one, she has been forced to throw them out. At first she bought fresh green replacements. But they did not last long. They, too, died and were discarded. There no longer seems, she finally has decided, any reason to buy new ones.

Acknowledgments

MANY people across the country were helpful in the research and writing of this book. Their time and efforts are appreciated. I particularly would like to thank: Joan Raines, my agent and friend, whose wise advice, supportive words, and unlimited energy were my constant, valued companions; Jon Segal, my editor, who was expansive in his enthusiasm and incisive in his criticism; Congressman Ed Koch, who helped me cut through the Washington bureaucracy; Verne Jervis, of the Immigration and Naturalization Service; Ralph Blumenthal of *The New York Times,* Paul Meskil of *The New York Daily News,* and Bob Jones of *The Los Angeles Times,* three fine journalists who did original reporting on this topic and who generously offered information and advice; David Horowitz of the *United Israel Bulletin,* Jeff Martin of *Coast Magazine,* Peggy Mann of *Present Tense,* and Charles Allen of *Jewish Currents,* whose published work in those magazines were valuable research sources; the staffs of the Library of Congress and the YIVO Institute; Jeff Brown of *Esquire,* who made perceptive comments on a draft of the manuscript; David Schneiderman of *The New York Times* for his *Weltanschauung;* Dan Wolf and Ed Fancher, who over many lunches encouraged me to explore the psychology of the actors in this story; and, Annette.

A Note about the Author

Howard Blum was the co-recipient in 1976 of the Meyer Berger Award for distinguished reporting. A former staff writer for *The Village Voice,* he has also written front-page investigative stories for *The New York Times* and his work has appeared in national magazines. Mr. Blum lives in New York City.

BESTSELLERS